PARENTING
Toward the
KINGDOM

ORTHODOX PRINCIPLES
OF CHILD-REARING

PHILIP MAMALAKIS, PhD

ANCIENT FAITH PUBLISHING

CHESTERTON, INDIANA

Parenting Toward the Kingdom:
Orthodox Principles of Child-Rearing
Copyright © 2016 by Philip Mamalakis, PhD

Published by:
   Ancient Faith Publishing
   A Division of Ancient Faith Ministries
   P.O. Box 748
   Chesterton, IN 46304

ISBN: 978-1-944967-02-4

Printed in the United States of America

20 19   15 14 13 12 11 10 9 8 7 6 5 4

I cannot dedicate this book to Georgia, my wife,
because it is her book as much as it is mine.
Together we journey to raise our kids,
and together we "wrote" this book.
Together we dedicate this book to:

Our parents, Markos and Angelica Mamalakis
and George and Dorothea Lambros
You gave us the best thing any child could want: your whole selves.
Your sacrifice and love have shaped who we are and how we parent.

And to our children,
Kyranna, Alexandra, Kassiani, Nikolia,
Markos, George, and Alexios,
who gave us, beyond the material to write this book, a full life.

Contents

Acknowledgments

THIS BOOK WAS MADE POSSIBLE BY THE LOVE of my seven children—Kyranna, Alexandra, Kassiani, Nikolia, Markos, George, and Alexios. Without them, Georgia and I would never have experienced the deep joy that comes through the struggles of raising children. I delight in my children's company and feel blessed to be close and to observe them growing into beautiful adults. They are a delight to be around. They are not my "experiments," although I have experimented on them with parenting strategies as I have learned how to be their dad.

I write this with both deep joy and sadness, knowing that my days with my children in my home are numbered. They are going to leave to journey on their own, and we look forward to accompanying them and supporting them throughout their lives and with their children. That is the joy of parenting. They may not read this book, but that's okay because they have lived this book.

This book was also made possible through the efforts of Christina Andresen, a devoted mother of two (for now) who not only helped to put the text together, but contributed to the outline and organization, offering her clear review, analysis, and editing. Her belief in me as well as her deep understanding of Orthodox parenting has made it possible for me to cross the finish line with this book.

Special thanks to Sally Farhat Kassab, a great mother, wife, daughter, and person, whose encouragement and enthusiasm were unmatched. Thank you to Anna Higgins for her assistance on earlier drafts, and to all the friends, mothers, and parents who reviewed some of the earlier versions of this text.

I would like to acknowledge John Sommers-Flanagan and Diana Reetz-Stacey, my "father" and "mother" in parent education, and all the staff at Families First in Missoula, Montana, who sparked my interest and enthusiasm for parent education and showed me, among other things, the importance of parent education and how to run a successful parent education organization. Those days were beautiful.

And, of course, this book would not be possible without the support of Georgia, my wife. She lives her life in the midst of our children and has devoted herself completely to their well-being and upbringing. She is an example to me of how we offer our whole selves to loving our children. Most of her efforts as a mother go unnoticed and unappreciated. She is, in many ways, the heartbeat of our family, but we never really pay attention to the consistent, tireless beating of our heart that sustains us. This book is our offering, together, because who I am becoming as a man, a husband, a father, a therapist, and a professor has come out of our union, and it is only through her efforts that I have been able to take the time away to put this work together.

Introduction

Upbringing is the cause of everything, both good and evil.
—St. Theophan the Recluse, *Raising Them Right*

ONE SATURDAY, AS I WAS PREPARING a parenting talk at my desk, I was interrupted by my daughters, Alexandra, who was six at the time, and Kassiani, five, fighting about something. They were playing on the couch, or more specifically, with the couch, building a couch fort with pillows and blankets. Apparently one of them was not doing it the right way or something. As their disagreement escalated, so did their voices. They were yelling at each other, pulling on an innocent blanket.

My first instinct as a parent was, predictably, to holler at them. "Quit fighting," I yelled, with all the conviction of a parent who did not want to stop what I was doing. I guess I was hoping, against all historical evidence to the contrary, that they would stop what they were doing, look over to me, and say something like, "Okay, Dad, we'll figure this out on our own so you can keep working."

They responded far more appropriately for their ages. They stopped momentarily, looked at me, and then resumed their fight. I wanted to keep working, so I prepared to do what most parents are tempted to do when children don't listen the first time: we tell them *again* to quit fighting, maybe louder this time. As I warmed up for another vain attempt at what I call remote parenting—giving commands from a distance in the hope of not having to stop what I am doing and go over to them—I noticed my computer screen, filled with parenting ideas and strategies. Looking at the screen, I could see I had a lot of choices.

I could tell them a few more times to quit fighting or be quiet. I could ignore them. I could kick them out of my office or send them to their mother. I could just be "patient" and let them keep playing and fighting. I could threaten them with a consequence I had no intention of acting on, such as "If you don't quit fighting, you'll never be able to play down here again." I could get up and figure out who was right and wrong, or even go teach them the proper way to build a couch fort. Or I could intervene in a way that would help them figure out how to solve their own problems by giving them parameters for working it out and allowing them to stay only if they could work together peacefully.

In every parenting situation, we can intervene in many different ways. Do we know what our choices are, and how do we know which one is best? This book is about learning how to make the best choices as parents as we intervene and interact with our children.

This book comes out of my deep conviction that there is no greater vocation than that of a parent, because nothing shapes the soul and the life of a person more than how he interacts with his parents or primary care providers. The choices we make as parents, often instinctively more than intentionally, have a lasting effect on the lives of our children. However, when I as a dad pause to think about how to respond to my child's misbehavior, the situation is often confusing and complicated, and I have no idea what to do or say.

Most parents want to raise healthy, happy, successful children. Christian parents want to raise children who love God. Unfortunately, few of us are taught how to do this. Children don't come with an instruction manual, and most of us spend more time learning how to work a remote control than learning how to parent our children. Yet raising happy and healthy children is what we worry about the most and desire more than anything.

What This Book Has to Offer

This book is the instruction manual I wish someone had given to me and Georgia, my wife, when Kyranna, our first child, was born twenty-one years ago. I write this book knowing that bookstores are filled with parenting books, both Christian and secular, and many are very good. I list some of the best resources at the end of this book. Many have good ideas, but often they have conflicting approaches and different points of emphasis. What's missing is a parenting book that connects the daily struggles of family life and parenting to the timeless truths of the Orthodox Christian Church.

This book might be called *Biblical Principles for Parenting*. However, there are many different ways to understand and interpret the Bible. This book approaches these biblical principles for parenting from the Orthodox Christian tradition informed by contemporary research on child development. From St. Paul in the New Testament times, to St. John Chrysostom in the fourth century, all the way to St. Theophan the Recluse and St. Porphyrios in the nineteenth and twentieth centuries, the Orthodox Christian tradition is filled with wisdom and guidance about the biblical path of salvation that is consistent with the best research of our time and relevant to how we respond, for example, when our children talk back to us. Yet this guidance remains largely inaccessible to parents and often disconnected from the parenting challenges we face in our homes.

This book will help you make the connections between the spiritual life as we understand it in the Orthodox Church and the ongoing challenges of raising children, between what God has revealed to the saints throughout history and what He is revealing to your toddler, another saint, as he is drawing with markers on the wall. We want to connect what happens at church on Sunday morning with what is happening in our homes each morning as we struggle to get everyone up and out the door without a crisis. We need to make these connections for ourselves, not just for our children, and learn how family life is about our journey together in love more than a series of tasks to be accomplished. This book takes the best child development research and connects it with the timeless truths of our Christian faith to offer you real strategies for navigating the challenges of daily life.

I am a father of seven children, and what is in this book is informed as much by what happens in my home when my two-year-old drops his toy in the toilet and clogs it as it is by what I have learned in my career—in seminary, in my PhD program in child development, as an Orthodox marriage and family therapist, and in working with hundreds of parents. I'm always wary of parenting books that are written without a firsthand understanding of how tough it is to raise children.

If you are suspicious of parenting techniques, that is a good thing. Parenting cannot be reduced to a series of steps, techniques, or strategies. The goal of this book is to help parents understand how the daily challenges of parenting relate to our journey in Christ and our child's journey in Christ, intimately connected to the life of the Church, and how that connection can inform our responses. Understanding this, we can put all the techniques and strategies in this book in their proper context. Using this book requires that you take a genuine interest in your child and reflect on your own personal spiritual journey. Understanding this, we can put this book in its proper place.

Throughout this book, I use examples from the past twenty-one years of my own life as a dad trying, together with Georgia, to raise our seven children: Kyranna (now twenty-one), Alexandra (twenty), Kassiani (eighteen), Nikolia (fifteen), Markos (thirteen), George (eleven), and Alexios (eight). In my examples, I indicate the ages of our children at the time of the story. Other stories and examples come from parents and friends who've shared their own struggles and experiences with me.

This book will not solve your child's problems or the challenges of parenting. I wish I could say there is a way to get children to stop fighting, listen to what we tell them to do, stop talking back, and just clean their rooms. I can't do that because children are not problems to be solved but persons to be loved and guided. This book is a guide to understanding what is happening and to responding effectively in all the struggles we face as parents. Parenting is about loving and guiding our children through those very challenges more than controlling their behavior. The challenges we face daily with our children are exactly what God gives us as we seek to raise our children to understand the path of salvation. The better we understand this, the more effective we'll be as parents and the more in control we will feel. Of course, it is easy to lose sight of this in the midst of the hectic demands of daily life.

It is not uncommon for parents to feel the pressure of needing to have perfectly behaved children. This is particularly true when we go to church and even more so if you write a parenting book. I have no expectation that my children are perfect or behave perfectly. I do expect them to behave like children. This book is not about how to stop our kids from acting like children, but how we, as parents, can guide them as they become adults.

If you see my children, you are likely to see them misbehave. They are still children. And you are likely to see me make mistakes as a parent. I am still a struggling parent. Too often we believe that good parents, especially Christian parents, do not make mistakes. This is a denial of the very nature of the Christian life, spiritual growth, and parenting. We are all still learning and still make mistakes. This book is not about how to be a perfect parent but how to be perfected in Christ as a parent.

Finally, this book is not just for Orthodox Christian parents. In a society that allows for a huge variety of Christian traditions, this book is for any parent interested in learning about the ancient Christian faith and how this faith can transform the way we raise up our children in the Lord. This book is suitable for any parent interested in learning how to be intentional in his or her parenting. It seeks to clear up some of the mystery of parenting to allow parents to choose how to intervene in the daily struggles of family life.

Oh, by the way, how did I respond to the girls fighting over the couch pillows? The answers to that question and many more parenting dilemmas can be found in this book. Once you read the book, I bet you'll have an even better response than I did. I hope you enjoy the learning.

❦ PRINCIPLE 1 ❧

Always Parent with the End in Mind

CHAPTER 1

Think Long-Term

If from the beginning we teach them to love true wisdom, they will have greater wealth and glory than riches can provide.
—St. John Chrysostom, *On Marriage and Family Life*

THE BEST PLACE TO BEGIN A CONVERSATION on parenting is at the end. We need to know what we're working toward so we can talk about how to accomplish our goals. Parenting is a long-term commitment and a long-term process. The best parenting response to a child's misbehavior depends on what our long-term goals are as parents.

One evening, as we were finishing dinner, Markos, seven years old at the time, returned to his seat at the dinner table with a toy car.

"That's my car!" said George (five years old).

"You weren't using it," Markos said as he continued to play. George had just gotten the car as a gift, and it was the new toy of choice for both of them.

"Give me it!" said George. "It's mine!"

The fragile mealtime peace was unraveling, and I knew I had to intervene. I could respond in several ways. I could play judge, determining who was right, and say, "It's George's toy, Markos, give it to him," or the equally valid, "You're not using it, George, let him play with it." I could take the toy away, reminding them, "No playing with toys at the table." I could also excuse them from the table just to hang onto the last remnants of a peaceful dinner. I could make sure that we have two of every toy to try to avoid these fights, or take the toy away to avoid getting caught in the middle of a sibling squabble. Doing nothing is always an option, but I suspected that if I left them unattended the situation would escalate. I was not optimistic that I could find an easy intervention that would allow me to sit a bit longer and enjoy my dessert. What was the best thing to do?

Our Long-Term Goals as Parents

If my goal is to sit longer and enjoy some quiet time with my wife, sending the boys out of the room makes the most sense. If my goal is to make sure my sons don't fight with each other, I should just buy two of every toy. If my goal is to teach my children how to work together to resolve their own disputes and live together in peace, I should intervene in a way that helps them develop those skills.

In the short term, I just wanted a quiet dinner and children who behaved. Some other tempting short-term goals are having children who listen and do what we ask, children who don't fight or misbehave, or a quiet house with everyone getting along. Sometimes our short-term goals can distract us from our long-term goals. Parents are tempted to intervene to stop misbehaviors in the short term in a way that undermines our long-term goals. That is like giving your child the answer to his math homework. In the short term, he finishes his work more quickly and without struggle, but in the long term, he doesn't learn math. Getting a child to stop misbehaving can solve the short-term problem of misbehavior, but it does not necessarily teach him, long-term, how to control his own behavior. Sometimes we need to give up our short-term desires to work toward our long-term goals.

To figure out the most effective response, we need to be clear about our long-term goals. Consider your long-term goals for your children. Thinking long-term means thinking about how you want your children to conduct themselves when they are on their own, away at college, or married with children of their own. What type of adults do you want them to become? Here are some common responses I hear from parents:

» Competent
» Able to have healthy relationships
» Happily married
» Independent, personally and financially
» Kind
» Generous
» Moral
» Hard-working
» Disciplined
» Self-controlled
» Compassionate
» Caring

As parents, essentially, we want our children to be successful in life. As Christian parents, we need to be clear about what we mean by *successful*. That's where God's perspective on success becomes important.

God's Goals for Our Children

God reveals His ideas about success and His goals for our children in the Scriptures and Church Tradition.

In 1 Timothy 2:2–4, we read that God desires "that we may lead a quiet and peaceable life in all godliness and reverence. For this *is* good and acceptable in the sight of God our Savior, who desires all men to be saved and come to the knowledge of the truth."

——◆——

The primary lesson for life must be implanted in the soul from the earliest age. The primary lesson for children is to know the eternal God, the one who gives everlasting life.

—St. Clement of Alexandria,
"Who Is the Rich Man That Shall Be Saved?"

——◆——

God's desire is for us to raise children who know Him, who live in His love, and who walk in His ways. God wants our children to know who He is and grow up near Him, to become saints. That is success. He desires that our children live righteous lives in this world as they prepare to live eternally with Him. He desires this because this will make us and our children truly happy, truly successful. He tells us if we seek Him first, everything else will be taken care of.

——◆——

*"But seek first the kingdom of God and His righteousness, and all these things shall be added to you."
(Matthew 6:33)*

——◆——

The Values and Virtues of the Kingdom of Heaven

Parenting is not about getting children to behave, although that's a tempting short-term goal. Our long-term goal is to raise up children who understand themselves as children of God, who live their whole lives according to His commandments. We should think less in terms of stopping bad behavior and more in terms of disciplining—nurturing disciples, raising children who understand that they are citizens of heaven. "For our citizenship is in heaven, from which we also eagerly wait for the Savior, the Lord Jesus Christ" (Phil. 3:20).

Citizens of heaven are those who live in the world according to God's ways, God's values, and God's virtues. We learn about the values and virtues of the Kingdom of God from the Bible, from Church Tradition, from the writings of the Fathers and Mothers of the Church, and from the lives of the saints.

Blessed are *the poor in spirit,*
For theirs is the kingdom of heaven.
Blessed are *those who mourn,*
For they shall be comforted.
Blessed are *the meek,*
For they shall inherit the earth.
Blessed are *those who hunger and thirst for*
righteousness,
For they shall be filled.
Blessed are *the merciful,*
For they shall obtain mercy.
Blessed are *the pure in heart,*
For they shall see God.
Blessed are *the peacemakers,*
For they shall be called sons of God.

Blessed are *those who are persecuted for righteousness'
   sake,
For theirs is the kingdom of heaven.
Blessed are you when they revile and persecute you,
   and say all kinds of evil against you falsely for My
   sake. Rejoice and be exceedingly glad, for great is
   your reward in heaven, for so they persecuted the
   prophets who were before you.
(Matthew 5:3–12)*

Love suffers long and *is kind [to a sibling]; love does
not envy [your brother's Christmas gifts, or your sister's new cell phone]; love does not parade itself [with
a new birthday gift], is not puffed up; does not behave
rudely [toward a friend], does not seek its own [at
the dinner table], is not provoked [when your brother
calls you names], thinks no evil [about your parents
or your siblings]; does not rejoice in iniquity [when
your sister gets in trouble], but rejoices in the truth;
bears all things [such as a little brother or sister],
believes all things, hopes all things, endures all things
[such as sharing a toy]. Love never fails. (1 Corinthians 13:4–8)*

*Raise my children to be wise as serpents and as
   innocent as doves.
Raise my children to have knowledge of good but not
   of sin.
Raise my children to be wise against the snares of the
   devil.
Raise my children to order their lives wisely, following
   the example of the saints.
Raise my children, nourishing them with the milk of*

*hidden wisdom of God that they may seek it all of
their lives.*
*Raise my children, O Lady, to be made worthy of
the Kingdom of Heaven and make them heirs of
eternal blessings.*
—Akathist to the Mother of God, Nurturer of Children

The Goal of Parenting

Successful children are those who internalize the values and
virtues of the Kingdom of God, so that when they go away to
college or get married they live according to these values—not
because we are watching or because we say so, but because they
believe these things deeply in their hearts.

*But the fruit of the Spirit is love, joy, peace, longsuf-
fering, kindness, goodness, faithfulness, gentleness,
self-control. Against such there is no law. And those
who are Christ's have crucified the flesh with its passions and desires. (Galatians 5:22–24)*

Beyond just having compliant children, we want our children
to acquire patience, kindness, gentleness, self-control, and
all the virtues that will help them thrive as adults. We want
them to learn how to seek true wisdom and acquire a selfless
love toward others. We want our children to grow up hunger-
ing for righteousness so that they may be filled. We want our
children to know, deep within their souls, that the true path
of success is to struggle to become holy, to become saints.

Our goal is to enable our children to see themselves and
others as children of God, icons of Christ, as holy images

23

of God Himself (Gen. 1:26). Successful children know, deep within their hearts, that they are loved by God and by us, and they desire to return that love freely. This is real self-esteem. This is a tall order for us as parents, but it is our vocation, our role. The rest of this book is aimed at learning how we can do this.

Parenting is not about stopping misbehaviors or getting children to listen to us. It is the process of shaping and guiding our children's souls in and toward God's love through the tasks that need to be accomplished and the struggles of daily life. We are teaching them about the spiritual life and the path of holiness as we break up sibling fights or get them to clean their rooms. We are walking with them on that path, on that journey, of growing closer to God in daily life.

"Markos, no toys at the table," I said to him. He was defiantly quiet. "Please pass the toy to me," I directed him. "I will keep the toy here, and after dinner, when the two of you have made a plan for how you will share the toy, you may have it." He struggled and protested. After a few moments, Markos and George were excused from the table and did not return. I ended up, this time, with the toy. We'll have plenty more dinner-table opportunities in the future for them to learn what they need to learn.

❧ Children acquire virtues not overnight but over time.

Thinking long-term means also that we need to allow our children the time to acquire these skills and virtues by staying attentive to our long-term goals as we create the best environment for them to learn and grow. Parenting is a long-term commitment, not a short-term solution.

A mother came to me because her two-year-old was biting

other children. One of my own daughters struggled with this when she was two. (If this is your child right now, know that it's more common than you think.) We followed the steps presented in this book and figured out that her son would bite when he was angry, excited, or overwhelmed. We discussed a plan for removing him from situations, redirecting him, and setting firm but gentle limits around his behavior.

Two weeks later, she called me to tell me that our plan was not working. He was still biting. I suggested to her that just because her son had not learned impulse control in two weeks, that did not mean her plan was not working. Good parenting is about implementing a good plan consistently, patiently, every single time, over time. I reminded her that her son was learning more than simply not biting. He was learning how to control himself when he got angry or overwhelmed, and he needed time to learn these things. There is no strategy to stop him from wanting to bite, but our strategy would teach him to do something different in life whenever he felt overwhelmed or angry. I promised her that her son would learn to cope in ways other than biting. My daughter has.

Parenting requires patience—not the patience that puts up with inappropriate behavior, but the patience that intervenes effectively, repeatedly, as long as our child struggles. This allows our children the opportunity to struggle to grow, to learn, to love, and to acquire the values and virtues they will need as adults. Patience means we respond consistently and appropriately every time they struggle, because we have our long-term goals in mind.

———◦•◦———

The chief end of our life is to live in communion with God.
—St. Theophan the Recluse, *Letters to Various People*

Beware of These Tempting Short-Term Goals

Many short-term temptations can cause parents to lose sight of the long-term goals of parenting.

Tasks to Complete

Parents can easily fall into the temptation that parenting is about getting our children dressed, fed, up in the morning, and then in bed at night. On top of that, we have work to do, money to earn, homes to clean, meals to make, laundry to clean, and bills to pay. The list is endless. It's easy to slip into the temptation that children are "another thing we have to do," or that they get in the way of getting things done, particularly when they misbehave.

While things do need to get done, children are not tasks to complete but persons to love, and we love them by attending to them as we get things done. Love is not a series of tasks to complete. We were not created just to get things done, but for love, to learn to love and to be in relationships of love. This means that sometimes we don't get as many things done as we want, and we pay attention to our children in the midst of all the demands on our time.

A Peaceful Home

Having a peaceful home is an admirable goal. However, it becomes a short-term temptation when we expect our children to keep the peace, and we become frustrated when they ruin that dream by being kids. Our children are not here to make our lives peaceful. Full, yes, but peaceful, not so much. The peace of Christ is an internal peace in the face of outward chaos. We need to seek Christ in order to acquire inward peace rather than expecting peace to come from our children's behaviors. We are on pretty shaky ground if our peace is built on the decisions of four- or six-year-olds. Peace will come, but not a peace that avoids or reacts to struggle—rather, one that comes through struggle. We need to give up peace in the short-term for our long-term goal of raising healthy children. External peace may not come till they're off and raising their own kids.

Protecting Our Pride as Parents

We can be embarrassed or ashamed when our children fight, misbehave, talk back, or refuse to listen to us, if we imagine that normal or happy families don't have these struggles. It's easy to think we have good kids and to feel proud when our children are kind or generous. These reactions are judgments on our children, both ways. We need to recognize how the Holy Spirit is working in our homes in the midst of these struggles and successes. Our children are good, all the time, and they make good and bad decisions, all the time. Life and parenting (as well as marriage) are about growth, and growth means making mistakes and learning. It is through the struggles and misbehaviors that they are working toward our long-term goals. We should not judge our children when they misbehave. They are not here to make us proud. We are here to help them grow, no matter how they behave.

Protecting Our Children from Struggles

Our goal is not to make our children's lives struggle-free, either. If you remove the struggles or solve their problems, they cannot grow. We'll talk about this in Chapters 5 and 6, but for now, it's important to mention that children need to struggle in order to thrive. Good parents do not make their children's lives easy but stay connected to them as they navigate the struggles. Protecting your kids from struggles, like solving their problems or doing their homework, is a short-term strategy that undermines our long-term goals. Removing or solving our kids' struggles disables them by removing the very steps they need to grow. If we love our children, we walk with them through the struggles; we don't remove the struggles.

Being the Perfect Parent

Our goal is not to have the perfect parent response every time. We'll talk more about this in Chapter 17, but for now, we have to remember that our goal is not to be perfect, because that's not possible. Parenting itself is a struggle we cannot escape. One of the dangers of talking to "experts" and reading parenting books is that we may become preoccupied with having the right response every time. It is great to strive for the best response, but no amount of learning and reading can protect you from being human and making mistakes. That's okay. Children need human parents who struggle to learn with them.

If you've taken a moment to consider your long-term goals for your children, or God's long-term goals for them, you've already taken the first step toward helping your children. We should expect children to act like children. The best we can do as parents is to act like adults in the way we respond, and choose the response that moves us toward our long-term goals.

If parenting is the process of guiding our children to internalize the values and the virtues of the Kingdom of God, or a long-term process of helping our children acquire the skills necessary for a successful life, we have to take a moment to consider how children learn.

CHAPTER 2

How Children Learn

Instruct your son, and he shall love you; and he shall give honor to your soul, lest he follow a lawless people.

—Proverbs 28:19 (LXX)

I CAME HOME ONE EVENING TO QUITE A SCENE. Kassiani, age eight at the time, was standing on the dining-room table. Her two sisters (ten and eleven) were shouting at her. Markos (three) and George (one) seemed to be grazing under the table. Predictable chaos reigned as everyone got ready for dinner.

"Just ignore Kassiani," Alexandra (ten) said. "She just wants attention." We'll get to what she wanted in Chapter 4. For now, it's important to understand what and how we teach our children in moments like this.

We can all agree that it is not appropriate to stand on tables. And parents need to take control of situations like this. Taking control does not mean reacting but stepping into the situation prepared to work toward my long-term goals for my children. It seems obvious that I should be strict, tell her to get down, and give her some sort of consequence. Resisting my strong urge to freak out at what I saw, and ignoring the thoughts that came to my mind about how my parents might have reacted if I had stood on a table, I took a deep breath, said a brief prayer, reminded myself this was an opportunity for teaching, and said, "Kassiani, would you like a hug?"

She froze, surprised at not getting a negative reaction from me. "Yes," she said.

She got down, came over, and hugged me. After a moment, I asked her what she should be doing.

"Setting the table," she replied.

Before I let her go, I asked her, "What's a good thing to do if we want a hug?"

"Ask for one," she answered knowingly.

Just for the record, I asked, "Do we ever stand on tables?"

"No," she replied remorsefully as she began to set the table.

Naturally, not standing on the table is a strict rule in our home. Maybe a consequence would have been appropriate if she'd kept doing this, but I doubted this was a serious problem of hers. We'll talk more about what I chose to do in later chapters, but for right now, it's important to recognize that teaching Kassiani not to stand on tables was secondary to teaching her one of our long-term goals about herself—something we want to teach our children by *the way we are strict* about not standing on the table.

When do we teach our children the values and the virtues of the Kingdom of God? Do we give them a lecture when they turn eighteen, as they are headed off to college, about how they are to conduct themselves in the world? First of all, they don't listen to our lecturing, and second, even if they did, it would not work. Children don't learn through lectures.

Children Learn in the Struggles of Daily Life

We are called to teach our children through the hundreds of parent-child interactions that occur every day over the years. Children are shaped in and through each interaction we have with them, from the moment of conception to the moment we depart this life. God gives us each interaction with our children as a means of communicating His truths.

More specifically, children learn most by how we respond when they misbehave. Children learn that we love them no matter what when we respond respectfully and effectively when they fight, talk back, disobey, or stand on tables. Children internalize our reactions to them at these difficult times more than when they behave. It is specifically in the midst of the daily struggles that we teach most effectively and shape our children's hearts, minds, and souls. It is when we finally do sit down to eat, and then someone knocks over the milk or our toddler dumps his food on the floor because he's finished, that our children will learn whether patience really is a virtue and whether we really do respect them.

Children don't learn the virtue of patience when everyone is getting along or getting what they want. Children do not learn self-control or generosity if each child has his own toys and never needs to share. Kids can only acquire the values and the virtues of the Kingdom of God by struggling with everyday life. There's no shortcut to learning patience, discipline, and self-control. Children learn most when they struggle to share with each other, struggle to do what we ask them, or struggle to live within the limits we set for them.

In the incident I mentioned in Chapter 1 about Markos and George arguing over the car, they were not just fighting over a toy at the dinner table but learning patience, kindness, and generosity. Naturally, it will take more than one fight or one toy for them to learn. But there will be plenty of opportunities daily to learn these things. It's our role to recognize this and figure out how to support that kind of learning.

The constant challenges and struggles of parenting are not only meaningful but are in fact the most meaningful moments in which to teach our children how to live and love in the world. The teaching opportunities occur when our children misbehave, when they struggle. Far from being something we should avoid, our kids' misbehaviors are the opportunities we have to do our most effective teaching. We want to learn to use our parenting tools wisely to take advantage of these opportunities.

The three most important tools we have as parents are:

» the way we live our own lives,
» the way we relate to our children, and
» what we say to them.

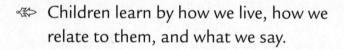 Children learn by how we live, how we relate to them, and what we say.

Modeling: Be the Person You Want Your Children to Become

> What saves and makes for good children is the life of the parents in the home. . . . The behavior of the children is directly related to the state of the parents.
>
> —St. Porphyrios, *Wounded by Love*

The single most effective parenting strategy we have is the way we conduct ourselves. Consider what kind of adults we want our children to become: helpful, caring, respectful, patient, self-controlled, strong in faith, peaceful, responsible. How are we as parents doing in these areas?

The remainder of this parenting book is about how to live out, in all our parenting interactions, the very virtues we want our children to acquire. Parenting cannot be reduced to strategies and techniques, because it is our behavior that teaches our kids the most. And that's why taking time out to read and learn about parenting is so important—because your behavior toward your child on a daily basis shapes your child.

The Fathers and Mothers of the Church teach us that if we want to teach our children how to live according to the values and virtues of the Kingdom of God, then, first and foremost, we need to live that way as parents.

The sanctity of the parents is the best way of bringing up children in the Lord.

—St. Porphyrios, *Wounded by Love*

The best parenting interventions or responses will model the very virtues we want our children to acquire. Children learn the value of patience when they see their mom or dad model patience and respond effectively with patience when Markos and George are fighting for the tenth time over the same toy. But patience does not mean enduring suffering as a parent. It means responding clearly and consistently no matter how many times our children fight.

If we want to teach self-control, we have to use self-control in our interactions with our children. If we want to teach our kids to think before they act, we have to think before we interact with them. If we want to teach our children how to treat people with respect, they need to see us treating others with respect in the home. If we want to see our children growing closer to God, they need to see us growing closer to God. If we want children to know that God is present in each moment of life, they need to see us living our daily life in His presence.

Children will learn what is true by how they see us behave more than by what they hear us say. If they see us behave one way outside the home or in church, and another way in the home, they will believe the way we act in the home is true and real, and they will learn how to pretend in public. If my children see me model the Christian virtues in public, but then see me gossip, criticize, or get angry with family members at home, they will learn that the gospel is something you pretend to believe, but not something that is real.

Don't worry that children never listen to you; worry that they are always watching you.

—Robert Fulghum,
All I Really Need to Know I Learned in Kindergarten

Much has been written on the value of self-esteem in children. Some experts have suggested we should praise our children, and others have pointed out that praising kids is bad for them. Self-esteem can be a confusing concept for Christian parents because it sounds a lot like pride, which we know is bad. However, it is clear that we want to teach our children respect for themselves, others, God, and His Church. Children do best in life when they've acquired a deep sense of self-respect and respect for others.

Children who are neglected, dismissed, criticized, attacked, or abused by parents internalize negative and destructive ideas about themselves and carry these ideas into adulthood.

They internalize ideas, feelings, and beliefs about themselves such as "I'm bad, unlovable, nobody cares, I am a burden." These lies are destructive and contrary to the gospel.

The truth is that God loves us deeply and cherishes each and every one of us, no matter how we behave. Each of our children is uniquely loved and adored by God—so much so that He gave His only Son for each one. Our children are incredibly valuable and special to God, not because they are perfect and no matter what they say or how they act. God simply loves them. The decisions we make in life can draw us closer to God and fullness of life or push us further away from Him, but our decisions never change the depth of God's love for us. We want our children to internalize this truth in their hearts.

Children will internalize this truth about themselves and God if we treat them with love and respect—all the time, but particularly when they misbehave. Children can only learn unconditional love when they experience their parents' love and respect when they misbehave.

Our Children as Icons of Christ

Although Christians have used icons since the time of the apostles, this practice was at the center of a controversy around the eighth century. Was it appropriate to depict Christ in a painting? The debate raged for over a hundred years. On one side of the debate were the iconoclasts, who rejected icons as idolatry condemned by God in Exodus 32. On the other side of the debate were the iconodoules, who loved icons and understood that we don't worship icons, but venerate them. When we kiss an icon, this expression of love is directed toward the person depicted in the icon, not the wood and paint of which it is made.

At stake in this debate was much more than church art, but a fundamental understanding of the material world we live in and the way God reveals Himself to us. Does God reveal Himself to us through physical matter, such as wood and paint, water, oil, bread and wine? The Holy Spirit guided the Christian community toward the answer. Because the Second Person of the Trinity revealed Himself to us physically in the person of Jesus Christ, we can paint a picture of Him and venerate that picture. God, who is unseen, truly became a man and reveals Himself through physical matter. Icons are an affirmation of the Incarnation of Christ. The Christians understood that icons are to be venerated, not worshipped or defaced.

Each one of us is created in the image and likeness of God (Gen. 1:26). We are, essentially, icons of Christ. As icons of Christ, we are called to venerate each other, and that veneration is ultimately directed toward Christ. When we help a person or act respectfully to someone, we are showing respect to Christ. When we insult or criticize someone, we are insulting and criticizing Christ. We see evidence of this in the New Testament, when Christ teaches that whatever we do to the least of these, our brothers, we do to Christ (Matt. 25:40).

Parenting is about raising children who understand themselves and others as icons of Christ. This is true self-esteem. Kassiani will internalize this self-identity if I venerate her as an icon of Christ as she's standing on the dinner table. I venerate Kassiani by showing respect for her and what she is learning as I am strict about our rule of not standing on the table. She already knew we don't stand on tables, so telling her what she already knows insults her intelligence. There was obviously something else going on, which we will talk about in Chapter 4, but in the moment it was important that I, as the parent, work toward my long-term goal: teaching my daughter that she is an icon of Christ by treating her as an icon, even as she is standing on the dining-room table.

We would never deface an icon, yet when we get angry, attack, criticize, insult, or mock our children, we vandalize the icon of Christ. We don't worship icons, either, yet when we are lenient or indulge our children's desires, giving in to their demands, we are worshipping our kids, not Christ—which is equally destructive. We'll talk more in Chapters 8–13 about limits and consequences, but for now let me say that it would have been worshipping the icon of Kassiani if I had let her stand on the table just because she wanted to do that. We worship the icon rather than the Creator when we give in to our children's demands in ways that are bad for them. The Church reveals that we must venerate icons, which in terms of parenting means respecting our children as we set firm limits for them.

☞ **We venerate our children as icons of Christ by respecting them as persons as we set limits with them.**

I've had "icons of Christ" talk back to me, roll their eyes at me, challenge my authority, draw on the walls, and throw tantrums. None of that is okay, but it doesn't change the fact (a fact we want our children to know) that they are images of Christ—icons of Christ. There's only one way to teach that fact: by relating to them as icons and venerating them when they misbehave as much as when they behave. The remainder of this book will detail what it means to venerate our children as icons of Christ.

If we want to teach our children respect, they need to feel respected by us, even when they talk back. If we want them to learn how to listen, they need to feel heard, even when they don't listen to us. If we want them to know the nature of God's love for them, they need to experience God's love from us, particularly when they are unloving toward us. Children really do learn what they live—most deeply when they struggle and misbehave.

Learning how to parent is not about learning how to control our kids' misbehaviors, but about learning how to respond effectively and consistently to whatever misbehaviors they present. We must remind ourselves that it is in these moments particularly that we are teaching our children something powerful about themselves.

What We Say to Our Children

We'll talk a lot in Chapter 5 about how to talk to our children, but I want to mention here that what we say and how we talk to our children has a lasting effect on them. Notice, however, that talking is third on the list of the ways we can influence our children. Parents are tempted to think we are only teaching when we're talking. Actually, talking is the least effective tool we have, but it is still one of the tools, and we want to use it wisely. Yes, it is important what we say to our children, but far more important is how we live and how we relate to our kids. More on that in the chapters that follow.

Talk more to God about your children, than to your children about God.

—Sister Magdalen, *Conversations with Children*

Naturally, these three tools—(1) how we live, (2) how we relate to our children, and (3) what we say—are all interrelated. What's important is that we are aware of the fact that, for good or for bad, our children are always learning, and we are always teaching. Specifically, they are learning the most when they are struggling, and we are teaching the most by how we respond to the challenges and misbehaviors. That is why we want to be intentional about how we use these tools in the daily challenges and misbehaviors of family life.

In each parenting interaction, we are either working toward our long-term goals or actively, though unintentionally, undermining them. To be intentional about our parenting, we need to learn how to respond to our children's misbehaviors rather than reacting.

⫷ PRINCIPLE II ⫸

Respond, Don't React

CHAPTER 3

Responding to
Our Children

So then, my beloved children, let every man be swift to hear,
slow to speak, slow to wrath.

—James 1:19

WHEN MY DAUGHTER ALEXANDRA WAS FOUR, she often
would hit her younger sister, Kassiani (two). When Kassiani annoyed her, Alexandra would become frustrated and
hit. Kassiani would cry, and we'd intervene. One day, after the
seventh time Alexandra hit, I got fed up. I pointed at her and
shouted, "Quit getting angry at your sister!"

Alexandra froze and stared at me. I stopped, looked at my
outstretched finger, and realized that I was getting angry—
even as I told her not to do the same. The hypocrisy was too
striking for me to miss. I thought about what I was teaching
Alexandra. Maybe I was modeling how to react when you're
angry, while telling her not to react when she gets angry. Maybe

I was showing her that adults say one thing but act another way. Maybe I was teaching that when you're young you can't get mad, but adults can. I certainly wasn't teaching her anything good. And, of course, I likely hurt her by scaring her.

The Temptation to React

Reactions are those knee-jerk, instinctive things we say and do to our children without much thought or reflection. All parents react, for a variety of reasons and in a variety of ways. Parents feel an impulse to react with corrections, directions, anger, criticism, judgmental statements, accusations, punishments, or simply giving in. Our child's misbehavior can be frustrating, embarrassing, overwhelming, or shocking. We might feel out of control or as if our authority is being undermined. Some parents feel a need to constantly correct any "mistakes" a child makes. Christian parents can have reactions when they see their children acting in "selfish" or "non-Christian" ways.

Maggie came home from seventh grade and told her mom, "I hate my teacher!"

"We don't talk like that in this house, dear," her mom reacted. Maggie stayed angry and learned that she should not talk about it anymore.

In another house, another parent reacted.

"I hope Eliana has a horrible day at school!" four-year-old Lukas said at the breakfast table.

"That's a very mean thing to say, Lukas," his dad retorted. Eliana was going to her first day of kindergarten. The conversation ended. Lukas remained upset and learned his dad did not care about what was really happening.

> ≪≫ Reacting is a short-term temptation, not a long-term solution.

44

Reacting is usually about stopping behavior we don't want to see in the short term rather than teaching skills, behaviors, or virtues we do want to see in the long term. Reacting to our children's misbehaviors short-circuits or co-opts their good learning process. They will still learn; they just won't learn anything good.

Reactions are all about us as parents: our mood, our expectations, our impulses, our fears, or our judgments of our children. If we're in a good mood, we tolerate misbehavior, but if we are upset, tired, or in a bad mood, we react. Sometimes we tolerate, tolerate, tolerate, and then react. Reacting to children shifts the focus from the child's choices to the parent's mood or emotional state. When we react, we hurt our children and damage our relationship with them.

Reactions are about our feelings and are rarely well thought out. They tend to be arbitrary, inconsistent, and extreme. We typically say things that hurt our children and are impossible to follow up on.

» "You're grounded for a month!"
» "I'll take that toy away for good!"
» or, a personal favorite, "I'll leave without you if you don't come now!"

These are reactive statements parents make in the heat of the moment. When parents calm down, they realize they cannot follow up on these statements, so they change their minds. This teaches children to ignore what their parents say, and that if they wait for things to calm down, they'll get what they want. Reacting models poor self-control and disrespect. We all do this, I know, and we all need to learn how to stop doing it.

The most damaging thing about reacting to misbehaviors is that it communicates to a child that he is bad and that we do not love him because of a choice he made. That teaches a child that there is something wrong with him and our love is conditional, that he needs to earn our love by behaving well. Children learn to comply so they can receive our "love," but they can grow up confused about their real worth and identity and become really good at pretending to act a certain way so they will be loved by others.

As I write this chapter, I'm looking out at my backyard. In the midst of the grass and the garden are weeds. I don't like weeds, and I'm not that fond of getting rid of them. So I'm tempted to do the quick and easy thing of just mowing over the weeds or weed-whacking them. In the short term, it works great. I get a nice-looking lawn—for a few days. But the weeds come back, bigger and more plentiful. If I'm serious about getting rid of them in the long term, it takes a little more time and effort to pull the weeds and fertilize the lawn.

Weeds are like our kids' misbehaviors. Of course misbehaviors are bad, and we have to get rid of them. However, reacting is like mowing over weeds. In the short term, the weeds seem to disappear. Responding is the more time-intensive process of pulling weeds from their roots and fertilizing the lawn. It is more difficult, but the results are beautiful and long-lasting. There's no shortcut to a beautiful garden or to successful children. Don't mow over or weed-whack your kids!

If we are teaching our children the values and the virtues of the Kingdom of God in each moment, we must learn how to respond to our children rather than reacting to them.

The Call to Respond

Responding is an intentional, thought-out parenting intervention designed to allow a child to learn our long-term goals. Responding focuses on the person of the child and considers the reasons behind the misbehavior. Only by responding to misbehaviors can we communicate to our children that we are interested more in loving them as persons than in controlling their behaviors. Reacting isn't that nuanced. Reacting to children ignores the reasons for the misbehaviors and, as a result, communicates a lack of respect for the person of the child.

⋘ Responding takes into account the person of the child and the reasons behind the misbehavior.

Looking back on Maggie and Lukas, we can see what a response might look like and what happens when we choose to respond.

Maggie came home from seventh grade and told her mom, "I hate my teacher!"

"What makes you say that?" her mom responded. "What's wrong?"

"She gave me a *D* on the test and wrote that she didn't think I was trying as hard as I could. I did try hard!"

This led to a discussion on Maggie's struggles with studying. Her mom ended the conversation by saying, "We don't talk like that about someone, Maggie."

Maggie replied, "I'm sorry."

In the other home we visited: "I hope Eliana has a horrible day at school!" four-year-old Lukas said at the breakfast table.

"Why would you say that?" his dad responded curiously.

"If she goes to school, then I'll be all alone at home," Lukas said with a sad voice.

"Are you going to miss her?" Dad asked, and they talked about Lukas having to say goodbye to his favorite playmate.

Responding does not mean we should excuse inappropriate talk. It means focusing on our child as a person as we teach appropriate talk.

Parenting is about guiding the souls of our children rather

than just correcting behavior. To teach proper behavior, we must respond to our children rather than reacting to their behavior.

The Icon and the Lawnmower

When Markos was four, he got a toy lawnmower as a gift. He loved this mower. The next day, Markos asked to take his lawnmower with him on a family walk. As we started on our walk, Markos headed for the street.

"Markos, the lawnmower needs to stay on the sidewalk," I said and continued walking. That would have been enough instruction for his sisters, but not for him. A moment later, he headed into the street again.

If I repeat myself, "Markos, I said no lawnmowers in the street," I will teach him to ignore me the first time I say things, because I'll just repeat myself. I could be patient, as we might think Christian parents should be, and keep telling him to walk on the sidewalk every time he goes into the street. That would teach him that he could ignore what I say, and he would likely just keep going into the street because that would be a fun game to play. If I repeat myself a lot and then get angry and take action, I will teach him that he only really needs to listen to me when I get upset. Then I will complain that my child only listens to me when I get upset.

If you want to teach your child to listen to you the first time, say something once, say it a second time with a consequence, and then act on the consequence.

"Markos, it's hard to stay on the sidewalk, isn't it?" I asked him.

"Yes," he replied with a mischievous smile.

"What might happen if you go into the street?" I asked.

"A car will hit me," he said.

"Lawnmowers stay on the sidewalk. If you push the lawnmower in the street, I will take it away," I stated, calmly and matter-of-factly, and continued walking.

He's a four-year-old boy. He really wants to push his mower in the street. He is learning to control his desires and to listen to what I say. I knew this would be tough for him. He is also learning that his choices have consequences. We should not expect compliance. We should expect learning. I expected an opportunity to teach Markos how much I respect him and how his choices have consequences—in life. Patience means setting up a framework for him to learn and letting him learn to live within that framework.

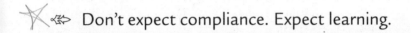 Don't expect compliance. Expect learning.

As we walked, Markos edged closer and closer to the street while still, technically, being on the sidewalk. He was struggling. But alas, the temptation was too great. A few more steps and his mower was in the street.

He disobeyed me. He was defying my authority. (We'll talk about what he was doing in the next chapter.) I could get mad—and wishy-washy—and tell him again, louder, "I said, 'No going in the street.'" This would be vandalizing the icon of Christ and would hurt him personally. Plus, it's confusing because I just gave him a choice, and now I'm getting mad that he made a choice.

I could be patient—and wishy-washy—and say, "Markos, I'll let it go this time, but next time, I'll have to take it away." I don't want him to lose his lawnmower. I want to go on a walk and not carry a lawnmower or take it back home. I don't want the struggle that will follow if I take it away. I want him to be happy and to like me. All these temptations are about me, not about what's best for him. These types of reactions would teach Markos that he doesn't need to worry about his choices and that I do not mean what I say when I speak. That is disrespectful to him.

Or I could venerate that little icon, respect his choice, and respond.

"So sorry," I said as I picked up the lawnmower and carried it back home. Thankfully, we had not gone too far. He cried. "I want to walk with my lawnmower!"

The third temptation for parents is to give in or be lenient when we face the pushback, the pleading, or the anger when we set a limit. I might be tempted to react with, "Okay, okay, just stop screaming and promise me you won't go in the street again." This teaches a child that if he throws a fit he can get what he wants, and he'll get really good at throwing fits. If we give in to the pushback, he will never learn how to control his impulsive desires. What type of husband will he be if that is what he learns? Why would I want to teach that to my child? If I am lenient, Markos and our home will end up being controlled by his desires.

Parents who give in to their children's tantrums end up being terrorized by and resentful of their children. This is the destructive effect of worshipping our children by indulging their desires.

≈> **Children learn best when we are firm and gentle, not lenient or angry.**

I sympathized with his grief. "I'm sorry you lost your lawnmower," I said, and reiterated, "I said, 'If the lawnmower goes in the street, I take it away.'" He was sad for a while and happy when he got his lawnmower back after the walk. When he got it back, I repeated, "Lawnmowers stay on the sidewalk. If you push it in the street, I take it . . ."

"Away," he concluded and went to play.

It's appropriate for a four-year-old boy to be learning self-control and how to listen to his parents. It's not okay to push his lawnmower in the street. He will learn how to make good decisions as he becomes clear that his choices have consequences. He will learn that my love for him is unconditional by the way I respond—not react—as his parent when he takes his lawnmower into the street. He will take the lawnmower into the street again, I know, and I will patiently respond in the same way, firmly and gently, each time. At least I'll try. I am focused on my long-term goals for him: learning good judgment in the face of temptations and desires.

∻ Responding does not stop children from misbehaving. It stops parents from misbehaving.

Markos is still a child and still learning. Responding gives children the freedom to learn free of criticism, shame, judgment, anger, and blame. Responding does not mean being lenient. It means being calm when we are strict. Responding communicates to our children the truth about the gospel that they are deeply loved in the midst of their failures and struggles. It communicates our respect for our children as persons in the midst of their learning and mistakes. In this way, we model God's love, which becomes embedded in their hearts.

Learning how to parent is not about learning how to get our children to behave; it's about learning how to get ourselves to behave. Remember, modeling is the most effective way to teach our children. The goal of this parenting book is to invite parents how to learn to act like adults, no matter what childish behaviors our kids present to us. My kids will always act like kids. The only question is: Will I react like a kid or respond like an adult?

Common Reactions to Avoid

Parents often believe they are being loving to their children when they react instinctively to their misbehavior. Many parents have good intentions but bad patterns and habits of reacting to their children.

Responding to our children requires self-reflection and thoughtfulness. It is Christ and His Church who reveal to us the nature of selfless love, not our instinctive reactions. We need to reflect on our instincts and reactions and the effects they might have on our children. Of course we love our children. The question is: Do our reactions to their misbehaviors reflect Christ's love for them?

> ⋙ You can't love a child too much, but you can express love to a child in the wrong way.

I want to highlight some of the most common reactions parents have. Some reactions happen when parents lose control and stop thinking about what we're saying or doing. Other reactions are misguided expressions of love we've inherited from our own parents or bad patterns we've adopted.

Reacting with Punishment

"I'm not going to tolerate that behavior!" the father of a ten-year-old told me emphatically at a parenting talk. He was clearly upset as we discussed how to respond when a child talks back.

Children will do things that embarrass, alarm, frustrate,

upset, or offend parents. Hitting, swearing, stealing, or lying can shock parents or "make us look bad" as parents. Sometimes even smaller things can create this reaction in parents, like drawing with markers on a wall or throwing a cup across a room.

When parents get frustrated, rather than thinking about a good response and allowing time for children to learn, we are tempted to look for some way to punish the child so he "never does that again." Responding might feel like tolerance or leniency. We live in a culture that does not like to let any good crime go unpunished. However, our record-setting prison population is evidence that punishment is, typically, not the most effective way to address problems or teach new skills.

The temptation is to think that the more frequently and the more severely we punish a child for his mistakes, the sooner he will learn. When he, inevitably, makes the same mistake again, parents look for ways to increase the punishment, as if our goal is to crush the child into submission. It quickly becomes an "us-against-them" parent–child war. We definitely struggle with our children, but beware of war metaphors for parenting. We are on the same side as our child, and our goal is to shape persons, not just stop bad behaviors.

Punishments are, typically, reactions to kids' misbehaviors that undermine our long-term goals. They focus on causing pain in order to stop behavior in the short term and foster fear and resentment in the long term. Punishment does not teach a child how to do things the right way. If your child were struggling to learn math, you would not increase the punishments for mistakes, but increase the amount of time you took to teach them how to solve the problems correctly. Our children are learning about life, which is a lot harder to learn than math.

Parenting is not about punishing your children but about

disciplining them. Discipline is the ongoing response to children's misbehaviors that supports their learning and growth. This includes setting limits and issuing consequences. Children need consequences for their misbehaviors, and we'll talk about that in Chapter 12. What they don't need is punishment, and they react negatively to it. Children need discipline, and they do well with it, even strict discipline. Discipline focuses on teaching children over the long term.

 ## Responding is not leniency but the most effective way to be strict.

I am asked regularly by parents, "But what if my child keeps misbehaving?" What they're really asking is, "Then is it okay for me to punish them?"

Your child will continue to misbehave because he continues to learn. Discipline is about responding patiently and firmly each time our child makes a mistake, each time he stumbles and falls. If a child continues to struggle, then we step back and reflect on what might be going on, consult with others, possibly revise our expectations, and, if needed, consider a different response. Some children need more time to learn than others.

Reacting by Getting Angry

"I just get furious when my daughter looks at me with an attitude," said a mother of a five-year-old girl.

Sometimes our children push our buttons. All you need is a teenage daughter to roll her eyes and say "Whaht—ev—er?!" to learn this. Sometimes even a five-year-old's eye roll can send a parent over the edge.

You can't stay in charge if you can't stay in control.

Getting angry does teach children; it just doesn't teach them anything good. Getting angry teaches a child that you don't like her, that she is bad. Children are typically unaware of their actions and even less aware of how their actions and misbehaviors affect us. What they are very aware of is our emotional reactions to them. It is not okay to talk back or misbehave. However, anger doesn't teach our children what they should do. Anger doesn't help us toward our long-term goals. Our children will internalize our emotional state through the numerous interactions we have around their misbehavior. We want them to internalize the truth, not destructive lies.

Patience means letting our children learn, not letting them misbehave.

Many parents think patience means putting up with inappropriate behavior. So we tolerate inappropriate behavior without setting a limit. That only works for so long until the parent explodes. That's not patience, just ineffective parenting. If you find yourself in this situation, consider setting a firm limit sooner, before you get angry.

 Set limits before you become angry.

Anger happens. However, St. Paul teaches us, "be angry, and do not sin" (Eph. 4:26). Parents get angry when we feel confused, trapped, threatened, or out of control. These reactions are all about us as parents and not about the normal disobedience and misbehaviors of children. If you're getting angry, take a step back, calm yourself down, figure out what's going on, and decide on an effective response to your child that will help her learn what she needs to learn.

If you find yourself getting angry a lot, go talk to someone about that. Most things children do are typical kid stuff. If that's upsetting you, there's probably something you want to look at within yourself. Whatever buttons your child is pushing in you are probably buttons that need to be disconnected and healed. Our children are very effective at revealing where we as parents need to heal. Don't miss this opportunity. We'll talk more about this in Chapters 16 and 17.

Reacting with Leniency

Giving in, being lenient, having low expectations, and being permissive are reactions that undermine our long-term goals. Sometimes parents are worried about being too strict or letting their child struggle. Some parents feel too tired to put up with the struggle if they set a limit or have a hard time seeing their child upset or mad at them. Some parents have low expectations for their children or are so competent they can take care of all their children's needs.

These reactions are not in the best interest of the child. Kids need to struggle to grow. If you rescue a child from this by indulging her or giving in to her demands, she will lose respect for you. If your expectations for your children are too low or you are taking care of them when they can take care of themselves, they can't learn how capable they are. It is hard to be firm and teach children to take care of themselves, but neither is as hard as living with indulged children. We'll talk more in Chapters 9 and 10 about setting and keeping firm limits.

It is hard to know where to draw the line when accommodating our children's requests. It's one thing to make their favorite meal on their birthday or let them wear their favorite clothes to a party. It's another thing if they always get their favorite meal or if you can't leave the home because your two-year-old refuses to go without his favorite pants and they're in the washing machine. You know it's gone too far when you feel trapped or resentful and the entire family is held hostage to the whims of your (often youngest) child.

To be successful in life, children need to learn how to struggle with not getting what they want. If we love our kids, we'll teach this to them sooner rather than later. After reading this book, look for the opportunities life brings to help your children learn to cope with not getting what they want. It's hard, but it's invaluable for them to learn.

Reacting as Criticizing or Micromanaging

Some parents are quick to tell their children what to do, how to think, and how to act. Parents who react this way are typically well meaning. They might be worried their child will make a bad choice and suffer consequences for it, and they think they're helping their kids by telling them what to do and how to think. "This will help them in life." "They can avoid making mistakes and learning things the hard way," the thinking goes.

However, that is like doing your child's homework for him. Children don't learn what they need to learn if we're always telling them what to do or how to think. This is disrespectful to the growing child, who never learns to think for herself. Worse, she learns she cannot think for herself. We'll talk more about giving children instructions and directions in Chapter 9, but beware of this common reaction.

Related to this reaction is the tendency some parents have to point out their kids' faults and mistakes. Well-meaning parents think it will help their child if they point out all his mistakes, or they fear if they don't correct their child constantly, the child will never learn. Often, these same parents avoid commenting on their child's good choices for fear of creating prideful children. Parents who were themselves criticized as children tend to repeat this same pattern with their own children. Notice, modeling is the best way to pass on either good or bad habits and behaviors.

No good learning happens this way. Your child will feel criticized, not loved. Your relationship becomes focused on negative things and will become strained. No child wants to be corrected or criticized all the time, and don't expect them to visit home once they leave. Constantly correcting your children, like telling them what to do all the time, is disrespectful because it focuses on behaviors and not persons. It reflects a lack of respect for the child, and it hurts. Constant correction communicates that the child is not smart enough to think for himself or make good choices.

In order to learn, children need to be allowed to think, feel, and make mistakes free of criticism. There's no other way. It's not that we should never correct our children or tell them what to do. It's just that we should not *always* correct our children or *always* tell them what to do. Children need space and time to figure things out. Before we correct our children or tell them what to do, consider other possible responses, such as those we'll discuss in this book. You will get better results in the long term.

Reacting as Being Proud

The flip-side of reacting when your children misbehave is reacting when they behave well. Thinking children "make us look bad" or "make us look good," along with comments such as, "I'm so proud of you," "You're such a nice boy," are about us and what we're feeling as parents, not about our children. The fact is, our kids are learning. Sometimes they get it right.

58

Other times they get it wrong. Reacting either way makes their decisions about us and our feelings rather than about their learning and growth.

They're not here to make us proud or to embarrass us. They're here to learn, and we're here to help them learn no matter what they do. Our role is to respond in their best interest, accepting each misbehavior and each good decision as part of the journey. Avoid comments such as "I'm so proud of you." Instead, comment on their effort or virtues.

> » "I noticed you shared your toy with your brother."
> » "I noticed you were patient."
> » "You really worked hard."

Commenting on their effort or virtues might feel fake or contrived only because we might not be used to speaking like this. However, if you change the way you speak, your child will feel your support and encouragement when she makes good choices. We'll talk more about this in Chapter 5.

Venerating Our Children by Responding

Reacting to our children does not take much effort from parents. It's quick and easy and requires little thought. Sometimes it's effective in the short term at getting obedience or quieting everything down in the home. Responding to our children, however, is proactive, not reactive, and makes more of a demand on us.

> Parenting is about responding to children, not about getting rid of problems.

I understand that parenting is complicated, and it can be frustrating listening to "experts" who make it seem easy. Responding is not easy. It's just respectful to your children.

❧ **Responding to our children is not a parenting strategy but our vocation as parents.**

Some people think parenting should come naturally to us. While I agree with those who think parents should trust their instincts more than what experts say, beware of your instinct to react. That's destructive. Use your instincts to figure out how to respond. In fact, responding in the appropriate way takes learning. That's good. Learning new and different ways to interact with our children models the very types of things we want them to learn. However, it can feel unnatural, forced, or formulaic. Yup, and that's okay, because what feels natural and unforced might just be reacting to our children. The fact that something "feels natural" does not mean it is good, right, or best for our children. Kids do best when parents take the time to learn to respond to them.

Responding requires us to be intentional, patient, kind, gentle, self-controlled, long-suffering, meek, faithful, wise, and loving when our children misbehave. Responding is the way we model all the virtues we want our children to learn. Responding to our children is the way we venerate them as icons of Christ and requires a certain amount of trust that God is working in our children through the struggles over time. They will become adults naturally as we provide the conditions for them to thrive. Reacting reflects a lack of faith that God is working in our child's soul.

Beware: The Dangers of Reading a Parenting Book

As I have learned about the difference between responding and reacting to my kids' misbehaviors, I feel pretty bad about my own parenting. I realize how much I react to my own kids' misbehaviors. It is so easy to react to my children without thinking. One of the scariest things I've experienced as a dad is the thought that my actions or reactions have hurt my children.

Reflecting on our parenting often includes moments when we realize we've done things wrong. That's painful, but it's good to recognize it. We all make mistakes. Professionals recognize that most parents are not perfect and most children do fine with what is called "good enough" parenting. Most parents love their children, try to do what's best for them, and try to set limits. Our kids will come to understand that we love them, even if they experience our imperfect love.

Having said that, embracing this vocation of parenting and challenging yourself to respond rather than react is an act of love toward your children, and you will watch them respond with love. This book cannot solve the problem of parenting because parenting is not a problem to be solved. This book is intended to take away some of the mystery, the uncertainty, and the confusion that surround parenting and to help you be intentional about how you intervene with your children.

Responding requires us to think through our options and make the choice that allows our children the best opportunity to learn. The best way to teach children how to think before they act is to model thinking before we act as parents. Responding means recognizing every misbehavior as an opportunity to teach.

"But it's impossible to always respond to our children and never react!" "It's unrealistic what you're suggesting we do as parents." These are common responses I receive from parents. It *is* unrealistic to think we'll never react, I agree. We'll talk about that in Chapter 16. However, these same parents expect their children to listen and be patient, kind, gentle, and self-disciplined, and they react when their kids make mistakes. *That* is unrealistic. I'm not suggesting we need to be perfect. I'm suggesting if we want to teach our children how to respond rather than react to all the struggles they face in life, we need to learn how to respond rather than react as often as possible to the struggles we face in parenting them.

We've already discussed in Chapter 1 the first step in learning how to respond to our children: reflecting on our long-term goals. Responding recognizes and respects the fact that our children are learning patience, kindness, gentleness, self-control, discipline, good decision-making—essentially, our long-term goals. If children are always learning, we are always teaching. As we respect our children by responding to their behaviors consistently, we nurture our relationship with them and model for them how to respond. It is within this close parent–child relationship that children follow our lead, model our behavior, adopt our values, and learn what it means to become adults. We don't need to make them adults; that will happen naturally. We just need to learn how to respond to them and their misbehaviors as they learn and grow.

———◦——

*For generally the children acquire the character of
their parents, are formed in the mold of their parents'
temperament, love the same things their parents love,
talk in the same fashion, and work for the same ends.*
St. John Chrysostom, *On Marriage and Family Life*

When I get to this point in my teaching on parenting, I often hear, "Okay, I get that I'm supposed to respond, not react, but what should I do? What is my response?" Stopping yourself from reacting, and considering your long-term goals, will change your parenting right away. But in order to figure out how to respond, we need to consider the reasons behind our children's "misbehavior."

CHAPTER 4

Why Children Misbehave

Our goal as parents is not to transmit faith; that is the work of divine grace, and our task is to foster the work of grace.

—Sister Magdalene, *Children in the Church Today*

Imagine you're tucking your five-year-old into bed, and just as you're bending down to kiss her, she sneezes all over you. What do you do? You might laugh. Would you get mad? What if she sneezes a lot? Then would you get upset? Would you try to stop her from sneezing? She can't control her sneezing. Sneezing for whatever reason—sickness or allergies—is part of childhood. It's not your child's fault that she sneezes, and you'll never be able to stop her from sneezing. Trying to stop your child from sneezing will only lead to frustration and disappointment for you and hurt and confusion for your child.

Few things communicate love to a child more than a gentle smile right when we've been sneezed upon. Rather than becoming upset or trying to stop the sneezing, our role is to teach them how to use a tissue and attend to what's causing the sneeze. Misbehavior is exactly like sneezing. We will get frustrated trying to stop children from misbehaving. We'll have more success and peace in our homes if we focus on figuring out why they're misbehaving and by keeping lots of "tissues" around.

Look Beyond and Beneath the Misbehavior

"My two-year-old keeps hitting his new little sister," a mom of three reported to me. "What can I do to stop him? I can't believe how mean he is. It gets me so mad to see him hurt the newborn."

It's easy and tempting to react, to try to stop a two-year-old from hitting a new baby. If we want to respond, we need to stop ourselves and consider why he might be acting this way.

All instances of a particular misbehavior look the same. Hitting or fighting is always hitting or fighting. And parental reactions are the same no matter what the reason for the misbehavior. However, the best response to hitting or fighting depends on the underlying reasons. It's one thing if your two-year-old is hitting the new baby because he's feeling a loss of connection with his mother and is jealous of the newborn, and quite another if he's mad because the newborn won't play with him. Neither of these reasons makes the hitting okay, but we must respond differently to these two similar behaviors. We can't respond effectively until we understand what exactly our child is struggling with.

> Before you react, ask yourself, "Why is my child behaving this way?"

When I receive calls from parents asking for parenting advice, I ask why they think their child is misbehaving. The typical reply I get is, "I have no idea." Usually, they have not thought about why and would just like to know how to stop the bad behavior.

When I pose this question in my seminars, parents are initially stumped. After a few minutes of reflection, the answers pour out. They say children might be hungry, tired, sick, bored, scared, sad, angry, lonely, learning self-control, modeling behavior they have seen at home, trying out things they have learned from friends . . . you get the idea. There are many reasons.

Our family arrived home from a fifteen-hour road trip. As the sole driver, I went up to my bed and just fell onto it. One minute later, Kyranna, ten, dropped next to me, followed immediately by Alexandra, nine.

"Girls," I muttered after a few minutes, "you need to go to your own beds."

"Okay, Dad," I heard vaguely as they remained motionless.

"Girls, you need to go to your own beds," I repeated. No response.

They were disobeying me, not listening to what I told them to do. Of course they were ignoring me because they were exhausted. And I did not want to get up to take them to their beds because I was exhausted.

Ignoring me is not okay. They need to learn that you still need to listen to your parents even when you're exhausted. What is the best way to teach them that sometimes we just have to do things even when we're exhausted? I picked each of them up and carried her to her bed. That's not lenient. It's just the most effective way to teach.

When children misbehave because they're overtired, we keep the same limits and prepare for more struggles. The best response is patience and getting them to bed earlier the next night.

There is not enough room in this book, let alone in this chapter, to explore all the different reasons for children's misbehaviors. I encourage you to read some of the resources listed at the end of this book for more ideas. Understanding what's going on with our children at certain ages and stages is essential to effective parenting. I will highlight the most common reasons for misbehaviors and suggest some possible responses to them.

"My Child Just Wants Attention!"

I'm devoting a section of this chapter to "attention" because I hear this so often. And, of course, parents mean it negatively. While some children act up because they want everyone to look at them, I'd like to suggest that most often our kids are looking for a *connection* with their parents, not for mere attention.

 ### Children are looking for connection, not attention.

Children desire to connect with us all the time by being physically close, spending time with us, getting to know us, and letting us know them. Connection is central to our human nature, and children are wired to seek it.

Connection is food for our children's souls. We are created as relational beings in the image and likeness of a relational God who is three Persons in one communion of love. It's through our relationships with each other and with God that we experience intimacy and develop as human beings. Children grow as persons in and through the connections they have with those in the home. Parenting is all about connecting with our children as we go through life together and teaching them how to connect in positive ways.

Children will seek out connection in any way they can. "Mommy, look what I drew!" or "Daddy, I can spell a-i-r-p-l-a-n-e," are examples of constructive and positive attempts to connect. When children are excited, they want to share their excitement with us. When they are sad or hurt, they want comfort. Kissing a child's scraped knee or elbow actually makes them feel better. That's the power of connection. When they're feeling lonely or have been away from us for a while, they want to connect. That is not attention seeking; that's a natural human need and desire for intimacy and closeness.

We can connect with our children in all sorts of positive ways, from simple, small gestures such as a smile, eye contact, a gentle touch, or a hug, to deep moments together, listening to them, spending time with them, inquiring into their thoughts and feelings, reading to them, playing with them, or doing things together with them one on one.

Children will figure out the most successful strategies for connecting. They quickly learn that the fastest way to get an older sibling's attention and connection is to poke her or bother her. And the most effective way to get a parent really close is to misbehave.

When we react to misbehaviors, we provide children with an intense, although negative, connection. Parents reinforce this negative way of seeking connection if we don't connect with our children when they are behaving but quickly get in their faces when they act up. Unfortunately, these moments of strong connection are filled with anger and hostility. Yet, for children, negative connection is better than no connection.

Because connection is at the heart of our personhood, connecting with our children and teaching them appropriate ways to connect are at the heart of parenting.

My sons seek connection like little boys. They run into me, jump over me, and climb on me, whether I'm on an important phone call, eating dinner, or shaving. They are still learning *how to ask* if they can run into me or climb over me.

I've learned that during the first thirty minutes when I come home in the evening, each of my children seeks connection with me. The challenge is that they all seek it at the same time. I've learned not to change out of my work clothes until I've connected with each one.

Our youngest, Alexios, when he was under two years old, wanted to be held immediately when I came home and would get upset if I had to put him down. My response was to talk with the other children while I held him. When I did have to put Alexios down to change my clothes, I would smile, keep eye contact, and sing to him as I changed out of my work clothes. I felt like Mister Rogers. If I cut them off or shut down these moments because I wanted some peace and quiet after a long day, the result would always be misbehaviors. I get to relax and unwind after I respect their need to connect.

spoiled

The most effective way to attend to our child's need for connection and teach them positive ways to connect is to connect with them when they are behaving well. Connecting with children is the way we work toward our long-term goals. This connection is at the heart of passing along our values and virtues to our kids. Children will model our behaviors and mannerisms and adopt our values more thoroughly the more connected they feel to us. They will learn how to connect to others and the world around them by how they connect with us. Learning how to parent is about learning how to connect with our children all the time, as we get our tasks done throughout the day.

Children behave better when they feel connected to us. Why is it that our children "demand our attention" just when we are busiest, before company arrives, or when we're in a hurry to leave? It's because in those moments they feel disconnected from us. Deep connection with our children sets the context for setting limits to their behaviors, and the best parenting responses to misbehaviors allow us to connect with our children as we are setting limits or giving consequences.

Remember Kassiani standing on the dining table? Her ten-year-old sister claimed she wanted "attention." I suspected she wanted connection, not attention, so I gave her a hug before I said anything about her behavior. Responding to her desire for connection set the stage for teaching her how to ask for connection as well as keeping her off the table. She has never stood on a table since, although I really wasn't worried about that. However, since that incident, she regularly requests hugs whenever she feels disconnected. While it is not appropriate to stand on tables, it was appropriate that Kassiani was learning what to do when she feels disconnected.

We need to prioritize connecting with our children daily and teaching them how to seek connection in constructive ways by using their words, asking to talk, asking for time or a hug, and learning how to share what might be troubling them. The more attentive we are to connecting with our children throughout the day, particularly when they make good decisions or do the right thing, the more we reinforce good behavior.

> ✺ **You can give your children too much attention, but you can never give them too much connection.**

The opportunities for connection throughout the day are limitless. We simply need to pay attention to this central aspect of parenting. The whole atmosphere of the home changes when parents pay attention to connecting with their children, even in the simplest ways, as they go through their day. Eye contact, a smile, kind words, and gentle touch do not take any more time from us as parents, just a little attentiveness. Our children are not needy, just persons longing for intimacy and closeness with us.

Getting things done around the house does not need to mean disconnecting from our children. It's easy for children to feel disconnected from us when we're busy. While kids can cause destruction in a kitchen, we can connect by having our children nearby, participating in everything from cooking to washing and drying dishes. We need to learn how to connect with our children through eye contact, simple conversation, or setting them up nearby in the midst of all the busyness and chores that fill our day, so that life does not become a series of tasks to be accomplished. When you mow the lawn, rake leaves, or shovel snow, invite your children to follow along with their play mowers, tiny rakes, or little shovels.

⋘ **We don't need to constantly entertain our children. We need to constantly connect with them.**

Why does it seem as though children have radar that tells them when parents are on the phone or checking email? They might be quiet and content, but when we start talking on the phone, they misbehave. We disconnect from them, and they feel it. Responding to their need for connection when we're on the telephone or checking emails is simple: we could smile, hold hands, have them on our laps, or simply keep our conversations short.

"My two-year-old son comes over and turns off the TV when we're watching it," a mom complained to me.

"Why might he be doing that?" I asked.

"I do zone out in front of the TV," she admitted.

Children can feel disconnected from us when we watch television. I suggested holding or playing with her son when she returned from work every day before she turned on the television and then holding him while she watched. After trying these things, she reported to me that he stopped turning off the TV (although I was on his side on this one).

Beware of the bad habit of talking on the cell phone while you drive with children. Although it seems like a great way to multitask, they quickly begin to feel bored and disconnected, which leads to fighting and misbehavior. Take these opportunities to engage them or connect with them in the silence.

Older siblings typically misbehave at the birth of a new child as they feel pushed out and disconnected with everyone focused on the new baby. They might want to play with the newborn and can't understand why the baby is not responding to them. The best response to their misbehavior is to focus on staying connected to them and teach them how to interact with a newborn.

Give the older children one-on-one time with Dad and let them help care for baby:

» "Look how your little sister loves your gentle touch."

» "You are Mommy's best helper."

» "Thanks for bringing the diaper to me."

» "Here, sit right next to me."

We don't want to push our children away when they are seeking closeness. Closely supervise the older siblings around the newborn. Set gentle limits focused on teaching your child how to treat the newborn with phrases like "gentle touch." And, when necessary, keep the newborn out of reach!

If children are misbehaving because they're seeking connection, the best response is to draw close to them, connect with them, and remind them of the behaviors you would like to see.

No matter why they are misbehaving, connecting with our children needs to be central to how we respond to any misbehavior—which we'll talk about for the remainder of this book. Nurturing connection with our children strengthens our relationship with them and empowers them to make good decisions.

Beware: Negative Interpretations Lead to Negative Parenting

Parents often tell me their children misbehave because they're lazy, rude, mean, selfish, or spoiled. These interpretations, which seem so accurate, are in fact judgments and criticisms, and they lead to negative or critical parenting behaviors. Negative interpretations ignore the fact that children are learning. Your child is not supposed to be hardworking, selfless, kind, and patient. He is supposed to be *learning how* to be hardworking, selfless, kind, and patient. If our children are learning, we should expect struggles and mistakes, and we should interpret our kids' misbehaviors in a way that reflects these long-term goals.

~~> Strictness is good. Judgment and criticism are bad.

Misbehavior as Developmentally Appropriate
"It's hard to figure out how to respond," a mother shared with me. "It took me a couple of days to think through how to respond when my daughter would scratch people all the time. She would just scratch people who came close to her. I wanted to shout, 'Stop scratching!'"

"How old is your daughter?" I inquired.

"Five months old," I was surprised to hear. The mother added that, after thinking about it for a few days, she realized her daughter did not even know what she was doing. "Once I realized she is not aware, I figured it is best just to redirect her hands."

"And clip her fingernails," I added.

When the misbehavior is developmentally appropriate, the best response is to help the child learn from life's opportunities with clear limits, gentle reminders, and appropriate consequences.

We must remember that it is developmentally appropriate for children to act like kids, and mistakes are part of learning. If children are always learning, then we are always teaching. The best teachers are clear, calm, firm, and consistent. The more a student struggles to learn something, the more patient the teacher must be. Naturally, their learning is even more difficult when they are hungry, tired, or sick, or when their schedules are upset. Responding with extra patience at those times will teach them more than any reactions.

It's inevitable: every Sunday morning, dressed impeccably in their nice church clothes and shoes, my sons can't resist jumping in puddles. Saying, "Don't jump in the puddle in your church shoes," simply dangles the temptation in front of them.

But if I say, "If we keep our shoes and clothes clean, we can jump in puddles after church," my boys focus on making a good choice. (Yes, we have this same conversation every Sunday morning. Remember—long term.)

Or I can give gentle reminders: "Markos, when can we jump in puddles?" or "Markos, what kind of shoes and pants do we want to have for church?"

"Clean shoes and pants!" he replies enthusiastically.

73

Gentle reminders should focus on the behaviors we want to see rather than on the ones we don't.

Most of our children's misbehaviors *are* developmentally appropriate when we consider that growing up is all about acquiring virtues and learning new skills and behaviors. Children don't need a consequence for being six years old and loving puddles. Responding to our children takes into account that our children are always learning. Reacting to them ignores this fact.

When you're two years old, a marker and a blank wall seem like a match made in heaven. While seeing our daughter scribble all over a newly painted wall is frustrating, we must remember this is normal for her age. Children should not be punished for acting their age. We need to set up her world so she can learn what she needs to learn. Keeping markers out of reach, or saying something like "We use markers on paper" and having her clean the wall are appropriate responses.

What can we expect from a group of three-year-old boys trying to share a slide? They get so excited that they push, cut each other off, and slide into and on top of each other. Although we can expect this, if we don't say anything, this teaches that pushing is okay. Reacting with shock, disgust, or anger communicates that there is something wrong with them. Neither is true.

✺ Don't overreact or under-respond.

Preparing the child beforehand about proper behavior, giving gentle reminders, and indicating different consequences for different choices are the best responses. We can say,

» "Take turns."
» "Hands are for helping, not for hitting."

» "If you push, you'll need to sit off to the side for a turn. If you take turns, you can keep sliding together."

Consistent and gentle enforcement of limits will allow the boys to make choices and learn that choices have consequences. They will not be three years old for very long, but they'll always be males learning to control their impulses and desires.

Backtalk is also developmentally appropriate, although it is not acceptable from our children. The fact that we can expect it does not mean we need to accept it. A good response might be to deescalate the situation by asking, "What's upsetting you? What's wrong?" and letting your child calm down. When she's calm, bring the issue up again and figure out, with your child, what's behind the backtalk. It's necessary to set a limit or give a consequence for backtalk, but you don't need to do that right in the moment. We'll talk more about limits and consequences in Chapters 8–13.

 ❧ Expect poor behavior—don't accept it.

Misbehavior as a Result of Temperament

Some children take longer than others and have a more difficult time learning to listen, doing their chores, treating people with respect, or behaving properly. We have no control over the temperaments of our children, but we have a lot of control over how we respond to them. We set the same limits for all our children. For some of them, saying it once is enough. For others, we can expect them to take longer to learn.

This doesn't mean we have to react, become angry, criticize, or punish our child. It does not mean there is something wrong with our child, and we should never compare a child to his siblings or to other children. We have to respect the unique temperament of each of our children. Some children are more fussy about the clothes they wear or more particular about their food, struggle transitioning between tasks, or are more prone to irritability than other kids. Parents can be tempted to blame children when they have these difficulties or wish for a "better" child. But God gives each child a unique path in life. Often, the children who struggle the most learn the most.

When the misbehavior occurs because of our child's temperament, we should be more intentional and disciplined in the way we parent and let go of the expectation that the child will learn quickly. If it takes a child longer to learn, we simply apply the same strategies consistently, for a longer period of time. Children who struggle to learn are often called "difficult" kids. What they are, actually, is children who need more clarity, consistency, connection, firmness, and time to learn. This does not make *them* more difficult, but it does make *our role* more difficult. This book is for parents to learn how to be deliberate and intentional in their interactions with their "difficult" children.

✎ **The more "difficult" the child, the more deliberate the parenting responses need to be.**

I suggested in Chapter 1 that all children are learning the values and virtues of the Kingdom of God. Some children have cognitive or emotional disabilities that make it difficult for them to learn. Typically, these kids need more intentional parenting that is informed by the child's unique gifts and limitations. Consider talking to a child-development professional or reading a book that will help you learn how to respond to the unique person of your child. I recommend that parents take the time to read some of the resources at the end of this book about parenting these types of children.

❧ We respect our child by taking the time to improve our parenting skills.

Misbehavior as Modeling Poor Behavior

As part of the learning process, children pick up the manner-isms, behaviors, and habits of those whom they observe.

When I told Kassiani, then four, it was time to go to bed, she responded, "Oh, yeah? You can't make me. You're not the boss of me."

I could feel my blood start to boil at her blatant defiance, but I was softened by the little smile that crept across her face, betraying her underlying motive. I realized this was not a real challenge, so I asked, "Kassiani, where did you hear that?"

She replied, "At Sarah's house."

"Do we talk like that in this house?" I asked with a smile.

She smiled, said no, and headed up to bed.

Many of us see our children copying the poor behavior they see on television, in movies, or from their friends. Responding as parents needs to include a discussion of these influences as well as limits on the type and quantity of books, television, movies, music, and friends they are exposed to.

Children typically need a time of transition when they return from playing with friends as they adjust to being in the home and with their parents. This is particularly true when children return from longer periods away, such as camp.

When misbehavior comes from modeling, a good response is to be patient, allow for a period of transition back into the home, explore where the child picked up the behavior, discuss appropriate behaviors, monitor the child's exposure to outside influences, and set clear limits.

What's most obvious, but often the most difficult to con-sider, is if our children are modeling *our* behavior. When mothers ask me why their children don't listen better, I always ask what behaviors the father is modeling. Children will learn whether they need to listen to their mother by watching how well Dad listens to her.

Parents are often unaware of their own language, actions, and behaviors until they see their children modeling these same behaviors. Often parents will react to children when they behave or speak in the same ways parents permit themselves to act. This is confusing and undermines our long-term goals. Children are watching what we do more than listening to what we say.

Misbehavior as Emotional Distress

> *A child's heart is sacred ground where s/he meets God.*
>
> —Sister Magdalen, *Children in the Church Today*

When one of my daughters (who shall remain nameless) gets hurt by her sisters, she comes unglued, freaks out, and melts down. She will scream, cry, fall on the floor, and sometimes lash out in anger. To respond effectively, we have to address her distress first and then her behaviors. I can allow her to calm herself down, give her a hug, and listen to her pain. Then, when she's calm, we can talk about what happened, what she can do when she's hurt, and what the consequences will be for her outbursts.

When the misbehavior results from emotional distress, a good response is to attend to our child's distress first, and then discuss behaviors.

Instead of an attitude of "I don't care what you're feeling; you can't behave like that," we can take the attitude of "I care about how you're feeling, and you can't behave like that."

What helps us when we're feeling hurt? Typically, it is someone who cares more about what we're struggling with than about how we're misbehaving.

"What can you do when your sister hurts you?" I asked after she calmed down.

"Scream and hit her!" she replied.

"That will only get you in trouble," I continued. "What else can you do?"

She paused for a moment and said, "Come and tell you about it."

A child might feel sad, anxious, lonely, uneasy or unsettled, unheard or unloved. Often, the more a child is troubled, the more the child acts out. This requires greater attention to their distress, not greater consequences. Emotional distress can be part of a child's temperament or can come from the environment; it is usually a mix of both. Children respond negatively to anger, hostility, or emotional disconnectedness in their homes, and they throw fits. The research on this is clear. Even an infant cries when parents fight. Responding to our children means taking their hearts seriously, and nurturing a peaceful home. We can't change a child's temperament, but we can do a lot to create a peaceful home environment.

Sometimes, the best response when a child is upset is to allow a child some space to calm herself down, as in going to her room if she's too angry. When she calms down, she can return. This is a powerful way to set a limit on misbehavior while still respecting the emotional distress. We'll talk a lot about this in Chapter 7.

"How Do I Know Why My Child Misbehaves the Way He Does?"

This is one of the questions I'm asked most often. The answer is: Get to know your child. Learn about him, pay attention, listen, and check in with him. Most of us react first and ask questions later. That never works. Although children usually don't know the rationale for their behaviors, asking them communicates care and respect and will help them develop the habit of figuring it out.

Talk to other parents. Talk to professionals. Read about your child's age range and temperament style. Not only will you learn, but you'll realize how "normal" your child is.

Talk to your parents or reflect on your own childhood. Children often struggle in the same way their moms and dads struggled when they were younger. Temperament is genetic. A dad came to me distressed because his twelve-year-old son Peter didn't have any friends and told his dad he didn't like his school. The dad complained to me about the insensitive teachers and mean classmates.

He told me the teachers reported that Peter said inappropriate things out loud throughout class and didn't make any effort to connect with others. I asked the dad what he remembered about his own seventh-grade experience, and he immediately said, "I had no friends. I didn't know how to relate to other kids."

He didn't make the clear connection, so I asked if he noticed Peter struggling with the same issues. When he made that connection, he immediately calmed down and said he'd work with Peter on how to be a good friend.

Notice patterns of misbehavior. The most difficult challenges we face are the things our children do repeatedly. In some ways, perhaps God is allowing the struggle to continue until we figure out how to respond. Taking time to notice and reflect on patterns of misbehavior can shed light on the real problem and allow for an appropriate response.

Questions from Parents

Understanding the reasons for misbehaving sounds like excusing the misbehaviors. What's the difference?

A mom of a fifth grader who had attended my talk and was trying to respond to her son's misbehavior at school asked her son why he did not listen to his teacher. He said he was just so tired. She wondered if he was making an excuse.

"Would a parenting response be to make sure he goes to bed early?" she asked me. "And what about how he talked to his teacher? Just because he did it because he was tired, do I ignore the misbehavior?"

I suggested that it was good of her son to recognize that being tired made it hard to listen. Responding means we should give a consequence for his actions and require him to go to bed earlier. We have to make sure to address the underlying reasons as well as the misbehavior. It is not either/or, but both/and.

Why does it matter why my child misbehaves? What he does is still wrong and it still needs to stop, right?

We must focus on our long-term goals as we address the misbehavior. Rather than focusing only on behaviors, we're focusing on the person of our child, as well. Only when we focus on the person of our child, considering the reasons for her misbehavior, can we determine the right response to the misbehavior and work toward our long-term goals. We teach our children how to pay attention to themselves and others as we model how to respond in this way.

"Dad!" cried six-year-old Kyranna. "Can you get Kassiani (age two)? She's messing up our game!" Alexandra (five) and Kyranna were trying to play a board game, but Kassiani kept walking in the middle of it.

"Kyranna," I asked, "why is Kassiani trying to ruin your game?"

"I don't care," she replied. "Can you just make her stop?"

"Kyranna," I said, "she probably just wants to play with you. If you figure out a way to include her, she won't disrupt your game."

Kyranna and Alexandra reluctantly figured out a way to give some of the pieces to Kassiani and invited her to play next to them. Before she joined them, I asked Kassiani, "Do you want to play with the girls?"

"Yes," she answered.

"What do you do if you want to play with them?"

She was silent for a moment.

"Ask them if you can play. Use your words," I said.

This ritual was played out a few more times before Kassiani learned to ask to play and the older girls respected Kassiani's desire and came up with creative ways to include her. Figuring out how to play together was the way the three of them were going to learn how to respect each other and get along over a lifetime.

Attending to the underlying reasons for misbehavior not only communicates care and respect, it opens up more possibilities for us to respond. If they're hungry, we can give them a snack to eat and then teach them how to ask for a snack or get one themselves. If they're hurt, we can listen. If they just need a hug, we can give a hug and teach them how to ask for one. If they're tired, we can prepare to be more patient and make sure to put them to bed earlier. This does not mean tolerating destructive behaviors. It means paying attention to the underlying reasons for their misbehaviors as we teach them how to behave.

Living according to God's way, His values and virtues, is a real challenge, and it's in the struggles of family life that we are called to acquire these virtues. It is precisely when children misbehave that we are invited to follow Christ and teach them these truths. There are many different ways to interpret our kids' misbehaviors. The way we interpret or understand their misbehaviors needs to be focused on our long-term goals.

Understand Struggles in Terms of the Values and the Virtues of the Kingdom of God

Name Your Child's Struggle

Therefore, as the elect of God, holy and beloved, put on tender mercies, kindness, humility, meekness, longsuffering; bearing with one another, and forgiving one another.

—Colossians 3:12–13

IF PARENTING IS ABOUT HELPING OUR CHILDREN learn the values and the virtues of the Kingdom of God, then this is the context in which we must interpret their misbehaviors.

love this

❧ Frame each struggle in terms of the values and the virtues of the Kingdom of God.

I remember a classic parenting situation. Alexios, when he was four, was crying before dinner. "He wants a cookie," reported his older brother.

"Alexi," I asked, "do you want a cookie?"

"Yeah!" he cried.

"When do we get cookies?" I asked.

"I want a cookie now!" he demanded.

Now that we've talked about the reasons for misbehavior, we can ask, "Why is he misbehaving?"

Negative interpretation: He's spoiled and is throwing a fit because he is not getting what he wants.

Respectful interpretation: He's a normal child. Every kid wants dessert before dinner. We might say he is learning that dessert comes after dinner, not before.

However, if we frame his struggle in terms of our long-term goals of acquiring the values and virtues of the Kingdom of God, we would say he is struggling to learn patience, self-control, and discipline. He is learning to resist the temptation to act on his impulses and desires and to do what is right and good. That's a good thing.

❧ Within each struggle, our children are learning the values and virtues of the Kingdom of God.

Alexios is learning daily, with every meal. If we give in to his desire for a cookie or two, he will lose his appetite, pick at his dinner, and be hungry later. If he can't control his impulses and desires and lives his life acting on his impulses, he might feel pleasure in the short term but will feel empty over time. Healthy relationships, successful marriages, and success in life require that we control our impulses and desires and choose what's right. This is the nature of life. If I love him, I will do whatever I can to help him learn how to succeed in this struggle, rather than giving in to his desires and demands.

Alexi is learning what he needs to learn as he struggles to live within my limits and to wait until after dinner for a cookie. What Alexi needs from me is that I stay close and allow him to learn these things.

"I wish you could have a cookie," I said sympathetically.

"Waaaahhhh!" he exclaimed.

"It's hard to wait until after dinner," I repeated.

He remained upset and kept crying. (Now can I react? No! Now is when the real learning happens.)

I lifted him up and carried him to the time-out chair. "Do you want a cookie?" I asked again. "It's hard to wait until after dinner," I observed. He wailed. "When you calm yourself down, you can come back in the kitchen," I stated matter-of-factly.

Children learn important skills of life as they struggle to wait until after dinner for dessert. God gives us the struggles of dinner before dessert, and all the struggles of childhood, to help us acquire the values and the virtues of the Kingdom of God.

In the home, in the struggles, is where we are learning patience, kindness, gentleness, self-control, sharing, taking turns, helping others, and, essentially, selfless love. It is in the home that we are working out our salvation, being perfected in Christ, and being made holy.

The only way to learn patience and self-control is to live or interact with someone who tries your patience and tempts you to react. The spiritual life is a struggle to learn how to love as Christ loves, with Christ's love. It's about:

» Learning what to do when we don't get what we want or when we have to share

» Learning to do the right thing even when it's hard

» Learning to control our impulses and desires and follow God's commandments

» Learning to say "I'm sorry" when we've hurt someone

» Learning to forgive someone when we've been hurt.

We can't make the spiritual life easy, but we can help our children understand the spiritual struggle and succeed in it.

We should expect our children to lose their patience or self-control as part of the learning process. Learning to love is hard, but it is good. The only thing harder than acquiring patience and love is living a life without patience and love.

We want our children to understand that in the home, in family life, is where we are all learning Christian charity. To do this, we must frame our kids' struggles according to the values and the virtues of the Kingdom of God. Framing our children's struggles in this way keeps our long-term goals in the forefront of every parenting intervention. If they are learning all the time, we are teaching all the time by the way we interpret their struggles and by what we say.

Sibling Rivalry and the Kingdom of God

"That's mine!" yelled George (seven) as he chased Nikolia (ten) around the first floor of our home.

"You weren't playing with it," said Nikolia.

He caught up to her, she hung onto the toy, he grabbed, she grabbed, he hit, she screamed. The cycle of siblings fighting is as familiar to parents as fingerprints on windows and spilled milk at mealtimes. Siblings fight over space and stuff and tend to compare and compete with each other. Parents find themselves measuring out their time and attention like scoops of ice cream, carefully and precisely, to avoid the predictable sibling protests, "He got more than me!"

It's not that siblings fight all the time—only when they're awake! All right, it's not that bad, but it can feel that bad to us as parents. There are few things that exasperate parents more than sibling fighting. It is in these moments that we wonder whose idea it was to have children in the first place.

"Why are you two always fighting?" I said in vain, lost in my own adult world.

"Why can't you two ever get along?" I said. Mistake number two.

What does sibling fighting or a child's misbehavior have to do with the Kingdom of God? It's easy to lose sight of our long-term goals in the face of constant sibling conflict. It is easy to forget that children are icons of Christ when they treat each other rudely or hurt each other. It's hard for us to remember that they're struggling to acquire patience, kindness, gentleness, and love as they wrestle over a toy, or steal ("borrow") each other's clothes, or draw a big white line down the middle of the shared bedroom, daring the other to cross. These struggles catch me off guard all the time. In fact, I never have time for their fights. However, I have to remind myself that this is what my time is really for.

It's hard for us to remember, and impossible for children to see, that through those struggles they're acquiring the timeless virtues that will transform them and lead to a perfect, holy, peaceful, and sinless life. These struggles are the path of learning. We are working for the salvation of our children's souls, and God is forming them as persons through our responses to sibling conflict and rivalry.

✍ Family life is about acquiring the virtues we need to succeed in life.

After taking a deep breath and reminding myself that I was a dad, I separated Nikolia and George and confiscated the toy. "What's going on?" I asked.

"Nikolia took my toy!" "George hit me!" "She grabbed me!" "You weren't playing with it!" they shouted simultaneously.

I am facing two simultaneous stories about how the other

person is to blame. That story is as old as Adam and Eve. Often it's hard to see—and usually a mistake to try to figure out—who's to blame, although when one of them is obviously more at fault, it can be easier. If one child hit or bullied the other, or took something personal without asking, that should be addressed. Usually, there's a lot of blame to go around. When children are tired, bored, stir crazy, or feeling disconnected, sibling fighting increases.

When siblings are fighting a lot, consider separating them until they have worked out a plan to be together peacefully.

After hearing them out, I said, "George, what do you do if Nikolia wants to play with your toy?"

No answer.

"Nikolia, what do you do if George wants his toy back?"

Again, no answer.

These statements imply that I expect them to think and I expect each of them to be responsible for his or her own behavior no matter what the other one does.

"George, how does a caring brother behave?"

George was silent.

"It's hard to share our toys," I said quietly.

"Nikolia, how does a caring sister behave?"

Nikolia was silent. The silence was a nice break.

"We don't take things without asking," I said calmly to Nikolia, who did not seem to care.

"When the two of you can work out a plan to share, you can have the toy back," I said as I took the toy away. Anguish and cries came from both of them.

"It's hard to share," I gently affirmed to both of them. This statement communicates that I hear their pain, I understand it is hard, and they need to learn this. Sharing is hard, but it is not optional. This needs to be said with compassion, not with sarcasm or anger.

All things being equal, they each have a struggle—to share and to care for each other. They are each learning they can't have what they want all the time. They are learning how to work together, to be patient, and to problem-solve. Lecturing them will not help them learn. They can only learn these things in the struggle—if I allow them to struggle. We frame the struggle by what we say.

Does this strategy work? In the short term, no. It will not stop them from fighting and struggling. They may be icons of Christ, but they are not angels! But in the long term, it is the only strategy that works. Because this happens so frequently, we have this same conversation all the time. They have learned several solutions to their dilemma, but in the moment, they don't feel like using them. They know how to share; they just don't want to. If your children are young, it is appropriate to brainstorm solutions with them.

They can take turns, or play together, or one of them can find another toy to play with. There are actually plenty of options they may choose from. The real issue is that this requires each of them to give up something. That is the struggle, and this is when they are going to learn. I help them see it and walk with them through it, time and time again.

Use Your Words to Teach Your Long-Term Goals

⌘ What we say to our children in the struggle is written on their hearts for a lifetime.

I leave them to work it out

Consider what comes out of your mouth when you react to your child's misbehaviors. Most of us end up saying the very things our parents used to say to us, no matter how much we swore we would never do that. It's instinctive. Our parents' statements are written on our souls, and what we say to our children in these moments will be engraved on their souls.

We can choose the messages we want our children to carry with them their whole lives. Choose wisely. It is an act of love toward our children to engrave godly, biblical messages of truth on their souls.

Beware of making negative statements toward your children.

- » "You're just lazy!"
- » "You're selfish!"
- » "You're mean!"
- » "You don't listen to me!"

"But they are lazy!" a dad challenged me at a parenting talk. "My kid plays video games, but right when I tell him to do his homework or clean his room, he can barely move," he explained, defending his negative interpretation and judgment.

- » "My kid can act so selfishly!"
- » "My child throws a fit when another child plays with his toy."
- » "My child doesn't listen to me."
- » "Isn't it laziness that my kids don't pick up their toys after they're finished?"
- » "My kid is so stubborn that she only picks up her toys when she feels like it. I can't get her to pick them up until she feels like it."

These are all common criticisms I receive from parents about their children. If we say these things to our children, they will carry these messages about themselves with them for a lifetime.

"I tell him a hundred times to put his bike away and take off his uniform after soccer. He just comes home and lies around the house!" a mom of a twelve-year-old complained to me.

"Clearly," I answered, "he did choose to disobey and does not want to get up." Then I added, "Or is he learning to listen to instructions even when he's exhausted? He doesn't disobey because he's tired, but it is harder to do the right thing when we're tired. He needs to learn how to do the right thing, even if he is tired."

If that boy was learning math, the teacher would not say that he chose to make a mistake on his test. She would just mark it wrong, give him his grade, and tell him to figure out his mistake and try again. Mistakes are understood to be part of the learning process—at school, at least. Why not at home?

"It's hard to put your stuff away when you're tired after soccer, huh?" might be an appropriate first response. If the child was overtired, I would make a mental note to make sure he goes to bed earlier, and then follow with an empathic statement, give him a choice, and keep the limit firm.

"You can put your stuff away right now, or rest for ten minutes and then put your stuff away." Then, in ten minutes, return and make sure that before your child goes off to do something else, he puts his things away. Remember this boy will have this same struggle every day after soccer. Naturally, sometimes we help our children, but beware of making that the regular pattern.

John does this

If we say, "You don't listen," or "Why do you always lie around?" or "You're mean to your sister!" these messages will end up etched on the souls of our children. We don't want that. We want to engrave things on their hearts that will be useful for them the rest of their lives.

» "Listen to each other's words."

» "First we clean up, then we rest."

» "Be kind to your sister."

❧ Engrave the values and the virtues of the Kingdom of God on the hearts of your children.

Lectures about the spiritual path are ineffective for teaching. However, one word or a short statement spoken with compassion and clarity in the moment can suffice to point to the path, while respecting our child's struggle.

» "Patience," instead of "Stop being so rude!"

» "Share," instead of "You're selfish."

» "Speak kindly," instead of "Don't talk like that!"

» "How does a kind sister respond?" instead of "You're mean to your sister."

» "What does a kind older brother do?" instead of "Stop being a bully."

» "I want to hear respectful talk," instead of "Quit yelling all the time," or "Why do you always yell?"

» "It's hard to do your work when you want to go play," instead of "You're lazy."

» "Use your good judgment," instead of "Don't be stupid!"

These statements are not about trying to "be positive" or learning some parenting formula. It's not about using a trick to manipulate our children. It's about paying attention to the words we use to speak to them, because they will carry these words on their souls the rest of their lives. Words won't make our children patient and kind, but they will teach them that patience and kindness are the path of life.

We want the language of the home to be filled with the virtues of God, even in the midst of the struggles. When children are distressed, they are not able to listen, and short statements go a long way toward communicating what is true. Remember, these struggles will happen all the time, and we have a long time to form our children by what we say. In the struggle is when they learn the most, and what we say in those moments is what they will remember the most.

⋘ How we speak to our children teaches them how to see themselves and the world.

Imagine your child eventually being at college, on a Thursday evening with homework due the next day, and his friends ask him to go out. What do we want him to think instinctively?

» "I'm lazy."
» "All I want to do is lie around."

Or,

» "Before I go out to play, I need to do my work."
» "It's hard to do what I have to do."

What about in his future marriage? What's better to write on our child's heart:

» "Why are you always so mean?"
» "You're selfish."

Or,

» "Be kind. How does a caring person respond?"

They will learn about life by the way we frame their struggles. We teach our children that God is present in our homes and His Word is real and true by framing the struggles in the home according to the values and virtues of the Kingdom of God. We want our children to see the spiritual struggles in their misbehaviors and learn that the right choice will make them happy. They will experience it firsthand and interpret the struggles according to our words. They will come to interpret the behavior of others and the world around them in this way.

I was grocery shopping with Nikolia, age three at the time,

when we noticed a child kicking and screaming in a shopping cart. It was apparent to both of us that he wanted something and his mother was not complying.

"He's having a hard time listening to his mother," Nikolia observed.

"Yup," I concurred, and we went on.

She did not criticize or label the child but had learned to respect the person of the child in a way that was clear. He needed to learn to listen. She knew all about that struggle. We have thousands of opportunities to teach our children how to interpret themselves and the world around them. We need to be intentional about what we say, because we'll be saying it a lot.

Name Your Child's Struggle

"I'm so bored," my daughter whispered to me in church one day.

"It's hard to stand and pay attention," I affirmed.

Children get bored in church. It is hard for them to sit or stand nicely when they're bored. This is a normal struggle. We need to expect this. Adults get bored in church too. But how can we feel bored in church? Is it possible to be bored in the presence of the eternal God? Do we think the saints up in heaven are bored, waiting for eternity to be over? No, there is no boredom in the Kingdom of Heaven, only life, peace, and joy. Boredom is a symptom of our own distance from God. Part of the struggle of the spiritual life is wrestling with this boredom. Children can learn, through struggling with boredom, about the whole of the spiritual life.

"I don't want to go to church today," George (eight years old) said one Sunday morning. Actually, this happens all the time.

"It is hard to get up and go to church sometimes," I replied, naming his struggle.

That is the nature of the spiritual life. Much like getting up and getting exercise, going to church takes effort. However, when we make that effort, we feel better and thrive. The spiritual path is hard. It's easier to lie in bed than to get up and pray or worship God. As we force ourselves to stand before Him in His presence, we experience His grace and healing, and we feel strengthened. If we stay in bed, we turn away from God. When we indulge our desire to sleep in, we hurt ourselves. The paradox of the spiritual life, much like that of exercise, is that the hard path will make us happy and the easy path will make us miserable. That does not make it easy to go to church, but it makes it a necessity. But when you're a child—or an adult—lying in bed, you forget this.

One of the characteristics of the spiritual life is struggle. It is a struggle to live righteously, to seek the Kingdom of God, to resist temptations to indulge our desires or our own will. Yet the alternative is even worse—living a life enslaved to our selfish desires, disconnected from God. We cannot avoid the struggle, only choose which struggle to engage in: the struggle toward salvation, or the struggle of a life enslaved to our passions.

———◆———

And not only that, but we also glory in tribulations,
knowing that tribulation produces perseverance; and
perseverance, character; and character, hope. Now
hope does not disappoint, because the love of God has
been poured out in our hearts by the Holy Spirit who
was given to us. (Romans 5:3–5)

———◆———

It is hard for children to clean their rooms, get dressed, be patient with each other, share, listen to their parents, wait until after dinner to get a cookie, or wait until their room is clean to play. The list is endless. It's hard to be two years old and have to wear your church clothes to church and your pajamas to bed and not the other way around. It is hard letting go of what we want. The path of true life is hard. If we never learn how to struggle to do the hard thing, we end up miserable in life.

This does not excuse bad behavior, but it helps us understand how to use these moments to help children learn about the nature of life and how to thrive. This means that to respond effectively, we need to respect the struggle as we attend to the misbehavior and guide our children. In fact, the long-term goal we're seeking is to have children internalize the spiritual struggle toward holiness as their path of life and success. We want them to know, to experience deep down, that this is a struggle unto life, and the more they learn to struggle toward righteousness, the happier they will be.

Beware: Temptations to Avoid

There are several temptations we need to avoid as parents: ignoring or dismissing children's struggles, indulging their desires, or trying to solve their problems.

The first temptation to avoid is ignoring their struggle when we keep the limits firm.

» "You have to go to bed."
» "You have to come in now."
» "You have to go to church."
» "You don't have a choice."

While these are true statements, if we simply force our children without naming their struggle, we communicate that we don't understand or care that our child is struggling. We miss out on the opportunity to connect with our child and to help our child see the struggle as the nature of life.

Giving them reasons sleep or church is important also misses the point.

"I don't care how important sleep is or what kind of day I'll have tomorrow if I stay up late. I just don't want to go to bed now. You don't get it!" they might reply.

The second temptation to avoid is to change the limits because we listen to their struggle. "Okay, but promise me you'll clean your room after you play." "Okay, you may stay up a little longer, but then you need to go to bed." "Okay, you can sleep in this Sunday, but next Sunday you have to go to church." If we indulge our child by loosening the limits, lowering our expectations, or giving in to their pleadings, we deprive them of an opportunity to grow strong, and they miss out on the joy and peace that come from becoming strong and learning to resist temptations.

"Thank you for letting me indulge my desires. Now I will become increasingly enslaved to my own will and desires and less able to resist temptations as I go through life." They won't say this, but they might as well.

The Art of Parenting: Name their struggle. Keep the limits firm. Brainstorm. Repeat.

Child: "It's hard to go to church."
Parent: "Yup. It's really hard to go when we're tired. What can you do if you have to go to church and you don't want to?"

Child: "It's too hard to clean my room. I can do it later. Why do I have to do it now?"
Parent: "It's hard to clean our rooms before we can play. What's the best way to start?"

Child: "I had that toy first!"
Parent: "It's hard to have to share. What can we do when you both want to play with the same toy?

Child: "Church is boring!"
Parent: "Yup. It's hard to pay attention when we're bored. What can you do when you're bored in church?"

Does this work? Unfortunately, naming the struggle and brainstorming do not solve the problems of boredom, work before play, sharing, or not wanting to go to church. Children still struggle. In fact, my children just want me to rescue them from the struggle. In the long term, naming their struggle, keeping the limits firm, and brainstorming is the only strategy that works, because we can't solve the problem that it is hard to turn away from our desires and do what is good and right. We can only help our children understand the nature of the struggle and join them in it.

Naming their struggles and keeping limits firm draws us close to our children as they learn that this is their struggle and they are perfectly capable of figuring things out. Boredom, cleaning up, sharing, and not wanting to go to church are their problems to solve, not ours. Naming their struggle is the best response because it communicates empathy and caring.

Any attempt you make to solve their problem will likely fail. Giving children "great ideas" when they're bored, like giving them great reasons why sleep is important, is only met with hostility and resistance. "I don't want to do that," they retort. No matter how many great reasons you give them, it does not change the fact that they simply don't want to do something they need to do.

⚜ **Naming the struggle does not solve the problem but invites children into their struggle.**

The real "problem" is that they need to learn how to struggle, and you can't do that for them. What you can do is point the way, model how to walk, stay close to them as they figure it out, and pray for them. They need to figure it out on their own, but not necessarily alone.

Naming their struggle, when done with compassion, communicates empathy and respect and allows us to join our children in their struggle without rescuing them. Parenting is not about getting children to do the right thing or making their life easy, but trying to walk close to them as they learn how to struggle to do the right thing.

⚜ **Naming their struggles connects the life of the Church to our homes.**

As we frame the struggles of life in terms of the spiritual life and the values and virtues of the Kingdom of God, children will recognize in church the things they are learning at home. Children will make the connections between what they hear at home and what they hear in church. They will hear the gospel, the lives of the saints, and the hymns of the Church, which all speak about the spiritual life and the struggle to follow Christ in the face of temptations—just like what they're learning when they fight over a toy or struggle to wait till after dinner for a cookie. The teachings of Christ and His Church will make a lot of sense to our children as they make these connections.

"But I'm afraid my child will become resentful and hate

church because I force him to go." This is a common concern parents share as they are tempted to ease the limits and requirements for their children.

Skipping church should not be an option, just as lying, cheating, and stealing are not options in our homes. Are we afraid our child will become resentful of our prohibitions on stealing or lying and when they leave they will steal? No, we believe our children will eventually adopt the values we uphold in our homes, even if they struggled to accept them. We prohibit bad things and require good things because these things are real and true. As we raise children in a loving home with these values, they will internalize these truths for themselves. Church is mandatory. Lying, cheating, and stealing are wrong.

It is not enough to make church mandatory, though. If church is a strange, foreign place, in a foreign language, where children are forced to visit once a week and stand still, they are likely to walk away from church as soon as they are old enough. If they get the idea that we care more about getting them to church than about who they are, they are likely to reject church as adults. Paying little attention to our children and then forcing them to go to church is almost guaranteed to raise up kids who want nothing to do with church.

We want to communicate to our children that church is real and is the source and center of life because Christ is real and is the source and center of our lives. Connecting our homes to the Church is how we respond to boredom in church. Church is very boring if we are not connected to what is happening. If we do not understand the liturgy, the hymns, the readings, the sights and sounds of church, it is hard to be attentive. The more our children are familiar with what they see, hear, and smell in church, the more easily they engage. We help children engage with the liturgical life of the Church by bringing the practices of the Church into our homes.

There are a number of ways we connect our homes to the Church and numerous resources to help us do this. Read the Gospel reading at home before liturgy on Sunday and watch how your children pay attention when they hear it in church. Pray together as a family before meals, in the evenings, and/or in the mornings. Learn the hymns, get to know the priest and the other church families, even learn the language of the liturgy, and your children will feel at home at church. Allow children to be a part of the liturgy, serving in the altar and the choir, and they will experience liturgy as something they participate in rather than observe.

Naming the struggles of family life in terms of the values and virtues of the Kingdom of God helps children learn to make the connection between liturgy on Sunday and real life during the week. Children learn the spiritual life by spending time in church and by bringing the spiritual life of the Church into the daily struggles of the home. This doesn't solve the problem of struggles, but it helps them see the path of life and develop the skills to succeed.

⟴ Naming their struggles teaches siblings how to view each other.

As we understand that each of our children will struggle, but in different ways, we set the stage for how we want siblings to be together. Some of my children struggle with patience more than others. Some kids take longer to learn self-control than others. Some have greater struggles with keeping their rooms clean, or listening, than others. Siblings learn about the spiritual path by seeing their siblings struggle in their own unique ways. Everyone is learning something.

As parents, we're tempted to compare siblings to each other or to compare our children to others. That is disrespectful to everyone and fosters animosity and resentment among siblings. Children remember these comments for a long time, because they are deep criticisms and they hurt. It's rare to talk to adults about their childhood without hearing about which child Mom or Dad liked best.

Comparing your children to their friends or others is destructive. The fact is, different children struggle with different things, and everyone struggles with something. That's the way the world is. Comparing them communicates that there is something wrong with them because they struggle, and their sibling is better because he doesn't struggle that way. That's a destructive lie. We want to teach our children that God loves them completely, no matter what they struggle with or how long they struggle. We don't want our children to learn that we have to earn God's love by being good or that we lose God's love by misbehaving.

Comparing your children to other children discourages them in their struggle. It makes it harder for them to succeed in their struggle if they think there is something wrong with them. What's even more confusing is that we have no idea what their friends or other kids actually struggle with in their homes or at school. But your kids do. Our children behave better at the neighbor's home, just as their children behave in front of us. And all kids return home to misbehave. When you compare your children to others, you lose credibility and communicate disrespect to your child.

⋘ Never compare your children to other children.

The children who struggle the most often learn the most and become the most adept at navigating the path of salvation, because the learning happens in the struggle.

"How come Kyranna never gets in trouble?" Alexandra (age six at the time) exclaimed as she was sent up to her room. I resisted the temptation to compare her to her sister and framed Alexandra's struggle, and by extension Kyranna's struggles, as the path we are all on.

"It's hard to listen to Mom. When you're ready to listen, you can join us for dinner."

One time five years later, when Kyranna, age thirteen at the time, was sent to her room, she nearly collapsed in sadness. Alexandra looked at her with compassion and concern and said, "Kyranna, just say you're sorry, and it will be okay." Sage advice from a younger sibling who's been down that same road many times.

Allow each child to struggle in his or her unique way and delight in them, even though they struggle. One of the most powerful messages we can communicate to our children is that we are glad that we get to be their parents—and the best time to teach that is when they make a mistake or misbehave. We communicate that love and respect as we respond by naming their struggle, keeping limits firm, and giving consequences. Help everyone in the home recognize that we are all on the same journey, each of us struggles with different things along the way, and we're glad we get to struggle with them.

Notice Effort as Much as Outcome

For children who struggle the most, let's say with boredom in church, cleaning their room, or being patient, it is unfair to compare their behavior with others who don't struggle in those areas. If our goal is to have children learn the struggle, then we must recognize their efforts as much as their outcome.

> » "I noticed how hard you tried to pay attention in church," I said to a daughter who really struggled to pay attention.

She did not behave as well as her siblings, but she had a greater struggle.

» "I noticed you tried to be patient with your younger sibling."

» "Look at how your sister responded because you included her in your game."

» "I can see you're trying to listen to Mom," I said to my ten-year-old daughter, even though she was muttering as she walked away.

Noticing effort respects the child in the face of the struggle. This affirms the path—you still need to go to church, be patient, clean your room, treat each other respectfully, and listen to Mom—and it affirms the person of your child as s/he navigates. They don't need to be perfect, but they do need to struggle. This communicates that we are on their side as they do so.

Name their struggle when they make good decisions.

Parenting is more than just responding to misbehavior; it also involves learning how to respond with our long-term goals in mind when our children behave well. Although most parents read parenting books to figure out how to handle misbehavior, parenting is also about responding to good behavior in a way that teaches our long-term goals. We can name our children's struggle when they do the right thing.

Noticing your children making good choices or doing the right thing is another powerful way we can teach them about the path of salvation as we name their success in terms of the values we want to teach.

» "You were very patient with your sister."

» "You shared your toy with your brother."

» "You tried very hard not to talk back to your mother."

In these moments, we draw attention to their good choices, which connects us with our child. These are powerful ways to communicate to our children that we are noticing that they have good judgment, they are maturing, and they are capable of making good decisions. We have to become capable of noticing these instances and pointing them out to our children. In this sense, I support those parenting experts who recommend "catching your child when they're good." Although they are always good children, we want to "catch them making good choices" and let them know that we are seeing them living according to the virtues that God reveals will bring them fullness of life.

Children don't need to be praised or told they are great, because those are empty words. What they do need is to have their efforts and good decisions recognized. This keeps the focus on the path we want them to keep walking on.

Most parents only think about their kids' behaviors in the midst of a struggle and miss the great teaching opportunity to revisit the difficulties later. Although we might be worried about bringing up something negative, one of the best times to teach children how to make sense of what they struggle with is when we follow up on their misbehaviors later, when they are calm. Your goal, when things are calm, is not to stop them from misbehaving (that should never have been your goal anyway) but to help them think through what happened.

We'll talk more about following up on kids' misbehaviors in Chapter 11. For now, it's important to note that life provides us with many opportunities to connect with our children in the context of their struggles if we learn when and how to do that. They might slip back into blame in these moments, but we can let that go right by, and, after we listen to them, remind them that everyone in the home is learning to be patient, kind, gentle, and caring.

"But What Do I Do!?"

"I get it," exclaimed a frustrated parent. "I understand now that I need to respect their learning and frame the struggles with the virtues, but how does that stop our children from misbehaving or get them to listen to us? If I tell my child, 'You're having a hard time listening,' or 'It's hard to clean your room when you want to play outside,' they're going to look at me and say, 'Yes, duh!' Then what?"

⤞ Naming the struggle is doing something.

Naming the struggle is not the whole story. We need to do more, but naming the struggle needs to be part of our parenting response at all times. If our parenting is primarily barking orders or telling our children what to do, they will learn that love means telling people what to do. If we are constantly naming their struggles first, they will feel respected and will learn that love respects persons, no matter how they behave.

Naming the struggle is sometimes the only thing we can do, as we keep the limits firm. Sharing with Alexios, "It's hard to wait till after dinner," did not solve the problem. That is because this is not a problem to solve. There is no easy way for Alexios to learn patience and self-control. The only thing I can do as he's learning is join him in the struggle and communicate to him that I understand how hard it is by naming his struggle.

Only time will "fix the problem" of Alexios wanting cookies before dinner, provided I keep that limit firm and name his struggle. And time is on our side. I have eighteen years to walk alongside him as he learns. In the meantime, naming his struggle was what we did before I removed him from the room to calm himself down.

Naming our child's struggles helps us as parents as much as it helps our children to see the path before us. But it doesn't make it easy, and it does not change behavior in the short term. In fact, sometimes naming the struggle can seem to make things worse because we become vividly aware of the struggle. Our children will do fine with learning how to struggle if we walk with them. Naming our child's struggle communicates understanding, empathy, and respect as they internalize our messages about the path of life and love.

Yet those times are exactly when we are tempted the most to react. We're all busy, and it's hard to take the time to check in with our children. It's hard when we're tired, overwhelmed, frustrated, or in shock. It's easier to get angry than to name a child's struggle. It's particularly hard for single parents or those struggling through divorce.

In the end, it is hard for our children to learn what they have to learn, and it is hard for us as parents to respond to their misbehaviors in a way that helps them learn. Before we look more closely at how to respond, we need to take a moment to talk about our struggles as parents.

CHAPTER 6

Separate Your Struggle from Your Child's

So, let us raise our children in such a way that they can face any trouble, and not be surprised when difficulties come.
—St. John Chrysostom, *On Marriage and Family Life*

CHILDREN ARE NOT THE ONLY ONES IN THE HOME struggling to acquire the values and virtues of the Kingdom of God. Our kids' behaviors affect us in all sorts of ways. Our struggle as parents is to resist the temptation to react to misbehaviors and to respond at all times in the best interest of our children. Our struggle is to focus on our long-term goals in every interaction with our children, no matter how we're feeling. It's hard to stop ourselves, in the midst of our day, and reflect on what a good response might be, for example, when we hear the lamp crashing to the floor in the other room (true story for many parents). We might be too busy, overwhelmed, or upset because that was our favorite lamp.

Their misbehavior might disturb our peace and our plans when they misbehave in the home, or disappoint and embarrass us when they misbehave in public. That is our struggle, not theirs. It is not their fault they are children, and it is not their fault we struggle with their behaviors. Parenting is the intersection of our struggle as a parent and their struggle as a child.

Remember all the reasons children misbehave that we identified in Chapter 4? They're tired, hungry, upset, feeling disconnected or alone, or learning new skills. Parents struggle in the same way. In order to help our children, in order to succeed as parents, we need to keep our struggle separate from our child's struggle and respond based on our child's struggle, not our own. As we struggle to respond to our children, we model for them how to struggle and to respond to their challenges. As we cultivate the virtues of the Kingdom of God in our parenting, we teach our children how to live according to the virtues of the Kingdom of God.

———

You don't become holy by fighting evil. Let evil be.
Look towards Christ and that will save you. What
makes a person saintly is love.

—St. Porphyrios, *Wounded by Love*

———

The Struggle(s) and the Skinned Knee

We're all familiar with skinned knees. When Alexandra was five, she was running as fast as she could to catch up to her older sister. We watched as her upper body went faster than her feet and she fell. She didn't just scrape her knee but fell on her face, scraping her face from chin to forehead. She screamed.

Our first instinct as parents was to run over and pick her

up. We tend to think the loving thing to do is pick up a child when she falls. Our child is in pain and needs help, right? But is that really in their best interest?

When children fall, they experience a stinging pain for about thirty seconds. But after the pain subsides and they get their bearings, they are perfectly capable of getting up or asking for help, even if they have some pain in their knee (or their face).

Picking up children when they fall teaches them they need our help to get up. They learn to wait for us to pick them up and never learn how to get up by themselves. We've all seen children who have been taught this. When they fall, they look around for their parents, and when they see them, they begin to cry until the parent comes and picks them up. If there is no parent to be seen, they just get up.

The second most common reaction from parents (mostly from dads) is to tell the child, "You're okay. It's just a scrape." While this is true, this reaction dismisses the child's pain. In the moment, the child does not feel okay but is on the ground disoriented and in pain, thinking, "I'm not okay. You don't understand and you don't care." This response minimizes the distress and communicates a lack of care and understanding.

I want Alexandra to know I understand her pain and care about her when she falls. I also want her to learn how to get up on her own. She will need this skill the rest of her life. The only way to do that is to stay close and let her get up by herself.

Responding When Our Children Fall

I ran over to Alexandra and crouched down as she screamed. There was nothing to say, because she was screaming. Once she calmed down, I said, "Ouch, that looked like it hurt."

I stayed close, but I did not pick her up. I waited close by until she stopped crying and got herself up. She's learned from previous falls that she can get up by herself. After she stood up, I asked, "Do you want a hug?" She came into my arms.

If we want our children to learn, we need to give them the chance to work through their difficulties and get up on their own. If we love them, we will draw close to them without rescuing them as they learn.

Children need us to be close to them when they struggle, not to rescue them from the struggle. If we love our kids, we want to prepare them to succeed in life, which means helping them develop the capacity to get back up when they fall, dust themselves off, and ask for help if they need it. Alexandra will not always have me nearby when she falls, as a child or in life. It's impossible for me to protect her from every "fall" in life. It is possible for me to help her learn how to get up on her own. That's a great gift to give to a child.

When our children are old enough to walk, they're old enough to start learning how to get up when they fall. It's really hard when a one-year-old falls while learning to walk. It's not hard for them—they're wired to try to get up again. But it's hard for us as parents to let them learn how to do that. Unless the injury is serious, kids can get up by themselves. That's what happens in life. It's bad for children—and impossible—to protect them from falling down, no matter how hard some parents try. We want our children to learn, when they have painful and disorienting setbacks, to get their bearings, assess the situation, get back up, and ask for assistance if needed. There's only one way to learn those skills.

It's very painful for us to watch our children struggle and not rescue them. Just recently, our son Alexios, five years old and learning to ride his bike, fell in such a way that the bike landed on top of him. He cried. I panicked and ran over to him. "This time I need to pick him up. He's stuck," I thought to myself. I forced myself to follow the steps I know will help him the most. I drew close, crouched down nearby, and waited for him to stop crying. He looked at me, trapped under the bike, waiting for a rescue. In spite of my desires, I did not comply. "Ouch! Did that hurt?" I asked, which sounded like a dumb thing to say. Of course it hurt.

"Yes," he cried, remaining stuck. I did not know how much longer I could endure what seemed like ten minutes. It was actually closer to about thirty seconds. Just when I was about to crack, he pulled himself together, rolled out from under the bike, lifted his bike, and got right back on.

"Do you want a hug?" I asked desperately.

"Nope," he said as he rode off to catch up with his brothers.

Half of the time when my children fall and I run over, they don't even want a hug after they get up. But I want a hug! It hurts me to see them in pain. It hurts me to see them struggle. But I need to separate my needs from their needs. They are not here to fill my needs. I need to put my struggle aside and do what is best for them in the long term. They need to learn how to stand up, and I need to sacrifice my needs and desires in order to let them learn.

In the interest of full disclosure, my wife disagrees with me on this point. She believes if we love our children, we should help them up when they fall. I suggest the best way to help them, in the long run, is to stay close and let them get up, not to pick them up. Love is selfless, which means we have to suffer, selflessly, when they fall and do what is in our kids' best interest. It is in their long-term interest to have their parents close by as they learn to get back up again. My wife thinks when they are under a bike, that is too much. Alexios and I disagree.

Parents (and grandparents) love the results of this approach, but not the process.

"Your daughter was so strong. She fell off her bike and got

herself right back up," a mom reported to me about Kassiani, age eight at the time. My daughter is strong (so are your children), and I knew she had learned how to take care of herself through the many falls she'd already experienced in life.

⫷ Join your child in his struggle. Don't flee or rescue unnecessarily.

For Our Children to Thrive, They Need to Struggle

Getting up when we fall, like the very values and virtues we are trying to teach our children, can only be learned through struggling. Just as the only way to strengthen our muscles is by stressing them, the only way for children to become strong is through struggling. This is where growth happens. However, we don't need to abandon our kids in their trials or create trials for them. Life provides ample opportunities for children to struggle, learn, and grow. We need to learn how to join them in these struggles.

Children will struggle with the normal and appropriate limits we have to set for them. The list is endless of the opportunities life provides children to struggle and learn: keeping their hands to themselves in the supermarket, coming in for dinner when they want to play outside, waiting at the table until everyone has finished eating, doing their homework or cleaning their room when they would rather play or watch television, or sharing their toys, clothes, or even their bedroom, and so on.

Children are not supposed to understand or like the fact that struggles are essential for learning. In fact, they're supposed to pressure us to take away their struggle, solve their problems, rescue them, and even do their homework. Children don't like to struggle any more than we do. They might even blame us for their struggles. As parents, we have to know better and understand that if we love our children, we will stay close to them, but let them struggle.

❧ Children need to struggle in order to learn and grow as persons.

"Georgie (age eight), Mom said when your room is clean, you can go outside to play," I said one Saturday morning as my son was getting dressed to go outside.

"I can clean my room after I play outside," he said.

"Nope," I said, "you can play after your room is clean."

"That's just your rule," he continued, getting increasingly frustrated. "I'm not going to clean my room until you let me play outside."

First, you can tell he's definitely modeling the way I talk to him as a parent. Second, he's smart enough to twist my parenting reply to get what he wants. However, he does not understand yet that these rules are not really my rules. I would rather play than work, except that I know it would ultimately make me miserable. There are always things to do in life more fun than working, but if he does not learn how to work before he plays, he will end up unable to hold a job, have a family, or work toward meaningful endeavors in his life. That's just the way the world is. I did not create the rules; I just know that if we want to thrive in life, we need to live by them. George is still learning. And there's only one way for him to learn.

"It's hard to clean your room when you want to go outside to play. I know," I said, naming his struggle as sympathetically as possible, and then repeated, "When your room is clean, you can go outside."

I wish I could take that struggle away from him. I wish he never had to clean his room, because it is hard to clean your room at any age. I also wish he would just do what I say the first time and not argue with me. That's my struggle. These are, as you can see, only wishes, not reality. The reality is that he needs to struggle, and I need to struggle with him, in order to learn and grow. In fact, for George and many of us, the thought of cleaning a room is harder than actually cleaning it. Getting started is often the hardest part of doing chores or work. I want George to learn that fact and develop skills to navigate that challenge. He can't learn if I take the struggle away from him or react to him for having a tough time obeying.

George and I have these types of exchanges hundreds of times around emptying the dishwasher, putting his toys away, clearing his plate, and every other chore. No parenting strategy will get George to like cleaning his room or doing chores. That's not the goal. Our goal is to stay close to him as he learns how to navigate the struggle. If I name his struggle, break up the task into smaller steps, help him to get started, and require him to finish the chore before he does anything else, he will develop the skills and strength to resist his desires and impulses and do what needs to be done. I have eighteen years with him, and hundreds of chores, to teach him these things.

Keeping our limits clear and firm allows our children to stay in the struggle as they learn and grow. We'll talk more in Chapters 8–11 about how to do this. I knew that the better George gets at working before playing, the happier he'll be as an adult. It's my job to stay close and help him learn this.

≈ The goal of parenting is not to eliminate struggles, but to help our children learn to succeed in them.

Resist the Temptation to Make Their Lives Easy

Our children need to learn to succeed in these struggles while they are under our roof. Increasingly, I read articles or hear parents complain that children today are ill-equipped to handle the normal challenges of life as adults. Sometimes, the criticism is that parents are too focused on their children or love them too much. In fact, parents are not focused enough on actually helping their children prepare for life. It's easy to think we are being loving by making their lives easy. If we take away the struggle, we take away the learning. That's not loving or helpful.

> ❧ Children need to struggle *for* themselves,
> but not *by* themselves.

Children are far more capable than parents often give them credit for. I think this is because we see them make mistakes and bad decisions at times. That happens, but it does not mean they can't also make good decisions if they are given the chance. Sometimes children are forced to take on big responsibilities through, death, war, or immigration.

We've all heard stories of immigrant children who came to the United States with nothing. When these children grow up and become successful businessmen and women, they try to give their kids everything they wish they had, including an easy life. The result is their children are "lazy, unmotivated, unappreciative, and incompetent," an immigrant dad complained to me. "When I was his age, I didn't get to play sports and have my own car. I was running a restaurant."

What these adults fail to recognize is that it was exactly the struggles they experienced that enabled them to succeed. Unfortunately, many of them went through their tough struggles alone. Being alone in the struggle is what leaves lasting painful memories. If we want to raise disciplined and motivated children, we need to allow them to experience the normal hardships and struggles of life. If we love our children, we join them in those struggles. Children need struggles in order to thrive. They just don't need to go through them alone.

> **If we're afraid to see them struggle, they will learn to be afraid to struggle.**

Parents will read parenting books and talk to parenting "experts" with the hope that this will eliminate the struggles they face. That's impossible, no matter what any books or experts tell you. A real parenting expert will help you learn how to respond to the struggles. In fact, the best parenting experts understand that children need to be allowed to struggle and learn.

> **Learning how to parent is about learning how to respond to the struggles, not get rid of them.**

Respect Your Own Limitations and Pay Attention to Your Own Struggles

Although we need to learn how to respond, rather than react, we don't need to pretend we are super-parents or that this is easy. It's hard to raise children. It is hard to get kids up, get them fed, get them dressed, get them out, get them cleaned, and get them to bed. It's hard to deal with the whining and complaining around chores. We are not supposed to ignore our own struggles, but respect our struggles by attending to ourselves as we learn to attend to our children.

❧ Only pour as much milk as you want to clean up.

A meal rarely happens in our home without someone knocking over a cup of milk. This drives me crazy. Just when I'm sitting down to relax, someone knocks over a cup, disrupting the meal and forcing me to get up and clean. My children don't seem to mind this as much as I do. My struggle is to be patient as my kids struggle to master their fine motor skills. They are not to blame for this, and it would be disrespectful to get mad at them. I don't want to react, but I don't want to get up all the time, either. So, out of respect for our children and our own limitations, we only pour as much milk as we want to clean up.

❧ We teach our children how to struggle by the way we attend to our own struggles.

We teach the values and virtues of the Kingdom of God most dramatically by acting out of these virtues when we struggle. Everything we talk about in this book about our children applies to us as adults. Consider that parenting is about us learning or acquiring the values and virtues of the Kingdom of God in daily life. We need to learn new skills and change our own behaviors when we struggle.

We need to consider why we might be reacting the way we do. Remember all the ways we are tempted to react instead of respond to our children we mentioned in Chapter 3? These are our struggles, not our kids'. We might react because we are judging our children. They are not behaving the way we expect they should or respecting us the way they should. We might react because they are upsetting our peace—because we were hoping for a peaceful meal, a nice Christmas day, or a pleasant visit to grandma's house, and their fighting ruined it. They might embarrass us because everyone is looking at us in the supermarket or church when our children have a meltdown. We might believe their misbehaviors "make us look bad," and people might even criticize us for their misbehaviors. Our children might make us angry because they ruined our favorite garment, damaged our nice furniture, or broke our jewelry, which will now cost us money to repair. We may believe these things could have been avoided if our children had not misbehaved.

The fact is, accidents do happen, and our kids will act like kids. Each of these situations demands a parenting response, even though we are struggling. We can't react when our child is learning to work together with siblings, take care of property, or behave in public. They should be learning, and we need to be learning how to respond, not react. That's our struggle, not theirs. We need to identify and attend to our own struggles in order to learn to respond to theirs.

⟨⟩ Never react to a child for acting like a child.

Parenting reveals the areas where we need to heal and grow. There are things we need to learn that can only be learned in the struggle of parenting. We need to allow ourselves the freedom to fall and get back up again.

⟨⟩ When you fall as a parent, get yourself up, dust yourself off, and ask for a hug if you need one.

Taking time out to learn about parenting, giving yourself a time-out when you are about to react, and going to talk to someone about your struggles are great steps toward attending to your struggles. Once we recognize that the parenting problems we face are invitations for us as parents to grow, it opens up a whole pathway for our own healing. How we heal is outside the scope of this book, but it is necessary to mention that learning how to parent is a process of our growth and healing in Christ. As we learn to attend to our struggles, resist the temptation to react, and learn to respond, we walk the path of healing and salvation. In fact, it is through the struggles of parenting that we can acquire the Holy Spirit and the virtues of the Kingdom of Heaven.

We need to understand that God is working in us, transforming us, as we learn how to turn toward Him in the struggles. It is God who allows the struggles, for us and for our children. And it is He who draws close to us as we learn to get up on our own and ask Him for help.

⸙ God does not remove our struggles or flee from us but joins us in our struggles.

God's love is the very love we are trying to model and teach to our children. Attending to our own struggles means learning how to turn to God and others in the midst of all the daily challenges we face. We want to remember and teach our children that we are all learning how to love God and each other through the struggles of daily life.

We want our children to learn something invaluable through their struggles. We allow them to struggle because we want them to succeed. We must recognize that, in the struggles, they are acquiring the values and the skills that will enable them to succeed in life. We don't have bad kids or disobedient kids. We have kids who are learning.

To reach our long-term goals, we must separate our struggles from our children's struggles, our path from their path. We model this for our children as we struggle to respond to our children in their struggles. Once we are focused on our child's struggle, we can discuss how to respond.

≪≫ PRINCIPLE IV ≪≫

Separate Feelings
from Behaviors

CHAPTER 7

Take the Side of Feelings

Rejoice with those who rejoice, and weep with those who weep. (Romans 12:15)

IF WE WANT TO RESPOND RATHER THAN REACT to our kids' misbehaviors, we need to separate their feelings from their behaviors. Children's feelings require a different response than their behaviors do. Managing emotions is essential to good decision-making. Children typically know the right thing to do but misbehave because they can't control their desires, impulses, or emotions. To help our children learn to manage their emotions and control their desires, we need to learn to respond to their emotions, not just their misbehaviors.

❧ Responding means respecting their feelings and setting limits to their behaviors.

Remember, children learn respect by how we respect them. We need to respect the fact that their emotions can be all over the map and their behaviors crazy and out of control. That is part of childhood. A five-year-old should feel and act like a five-year-old. A twelve-year-old should feel and act like a twelve-year-old. It is okay for children to feel however they feel. It is not okay for them to act out destructively on those feelings.

❧ Children can't control their feelings, but they can learn not to be controlled by them.

We teach children how to manage their feelings in the same way we teach them how to get up when they fall: by drawing close to them as they learn how to pull themselves together and ask for help. They need to learn *for* themselves, but not *by* themselves, how to navigate the complex landscape of feelings so their behavior is guided by their good judgment rather than their feelings.

Really, feelings and behaviors go hand in hand. If we want to teach our children proper behavior, we need to attend to the feelings that often drive their misbehavior. And helping children learn to cope with their feelings requires that we set limits to their behaviors. I'm separating feelings and behaviors so we can explore each one more in depth, but you will notice we can't mention one without talking about the other.

Beware: if you are the type of parent who is attuned to your child's feelings but struggles to set limits to their behaviors (mothers often fall into this category), you might want to focus your attention more on the following chapters on behaviors. If you are the type of parent who naturally sets clear and firm limits (dads often fall into this category), I suggest you pay special attention to this chapter on attending to your child's feelings.

Bedtime and the Kingdom of God

One evening Georgia and I had company over, and it had gotten past our three boys' (ages eight, six, and three at the time) bedtimes. We had already stretched the bedtime, and I knew if we let them stay up much longer, we would pay the price the next day with overtired children. It's not fair to react to their misbehaviors the next day when we are the parents who let them stay up late the night before. Choosing the easier of two battles, I decided to take the three boys to bed but left Nikolia (age ten) to talk with the adults. As we headed up to bed, the boys' chorus began.

"Why does Nikolia get to stay up?! It's not fair!" the three of them protested, almost simultaneously.

"I don't want to go to bed," they wailed in painful harmony.

"Why do we have to go to bed?"

"I'm not going to bed!"

It is usually a struggle to get them to bed. It's even tougher when there's something fun going on downstairs. It's my struggle, and it's their struggle. None of us wanted to do this.

Based on what we talked about in earlier chapters, we can reflect for a moment about why my children were misbehaving. I'd guess they would rather be in the midst of their parents, siblings, and friends than all alone in a dark bedroom. Seems reasonable. Children can feel disconnected, alone, and sad when they are in bed. If everyone is downstairs having fun, they're also missing out on the fun. That's tough—but (and) they still need to go to bed.

If we frame this struggle in terms of our long-term goals, we might say they are learning to make good decisions, to do what needs to be done, even when they don't want to. They are learning how to resist their desires and do the right thing. They don't know they're doing this, but I do. I want them to learn this, and they're not going to learn it without a struggle. Just as we mentioned earlier, it is specifically in the struggle that they will learn everything we need them to learn.

✒ Recognize emotional meltdowns and reactions as learning opportunities.

There's no sense in trying to explain to my boys why they need to go to bed. They knew they had to go to bed. Statements like "You'll be too tired tomorrow" or "You need sleep" don't help, because my children are not disagreeing about the fact that kids need sleep. They just want to stay up. In fact, their desire to stay up is so strong that, if left unattended, they would stay up until they physically dropped. Their desires are stronger than their ability to make good decisions. They need to be put to bed, and they become sad and angry when they are forced to do something they do not want to do. We all know that struggle.

Just telling children what to do or explaining why they need to do it does not help them learn how to cope with their feelings and control their desires. In fact, by the time our children grow up a bit, they already know what they're supposed to do and how they're supposed to behave. We've told them hundreds of times. They simply don't want to do it. This is normal, and we can expect children to struggle with controlling their desires and managing their emotions. These struggles are not problems to be solved but opportunities to help them learn. Helping kids to do the right thing in the face of their strong desires and overwhelming feelings is more effective than reacting or lecturing.

We teach our children in these moments by separating their

feelings from their behaviors, keeping the limits firm, and taking the side of their feelings.

"Are you sad you have to go to bed?" I said to all three of them at the same time. "You don't want to go to bed? You'd rather stay and be with everyone else? It's hard to go to bed?" I continued to name their struggle with as much compassion as possible as I carried the three of them up the stairs.

"I wish you didn't have to go to bed."

Their reactions alternated back and forth between anger and sadness. I just repeated, as respectfully as possible, "It's hard to have to go to bed. Are you sad you have to go to bed? I wish you could stay up all night!" as I took them upstairs, got their pajamas on, brushed their teeth, said prayers—the whole bedtime routine, just as we do it every night. Eventually, after significant resistance, drama, and time, they got in bed, quieted down, and fell asleep.

This struggle will help them learn to manage their emotions and to do the right thing. I wanted them to know their dad was on their side, right by their side, as they struggled to do what they had to do. Just because they have to go to bed, and I'm the one making them, doesn't mean I have to ignore how hard it is for them. It's not me against them. It's me on their side as they learn and grow.

But wait, there's more. Nikolia was still sitting downstairs, and by the time I finished putting the boys to bed, it was also past her bedtime. So, predictably, the process started all over again. As I gently escorted Nikolia upstairs, she said, quietly at first, "Why do the girls get to stay up?" Her teenage sisters were still downstairs. "It's not fair!" she exclaimed. Of course, she seemed less concerned about this injustice when her brothers were suffering.

"I don't want to go to bed," she said, increasingly upset at her imminent demise. "Why do I have to go to bed? I'm not going to bed!" she continued, as if she'd studied her brothers' script.

And I repeated, on cue, as respectfully as possible, the exact same things I'd said to the boys as I took her upstairs, helped her put her pajamas on, got her teeth brushed, the whole bedtime routine, and tucked her in bed:

» "Are you sad you have to go to bed?"

» "You don't want to go to bed?"

» "You'd rather stay and be with everyone else?"

» "It's hard to go to bed?"

» "I wish you didn't have to go to bed."

Of course, these bedtime routines are painful and time-consuming ordeals, made more difficult when there are fun things going on downstairs. There's nothing we can do that will make kids want to go to bed. That's not our goal. There is a lot we can do to understand what's happening at bedtime and to learn how to respond appropriately by taking the side of their feelings as we physically escort them to bed. It's through responding to our children at bedtime that we work toward our long-term goals.

Naming Feelings

We manage our emotions by putting names to the various feelings with words. Feelings that we cannot name or identify tend to get out of control and end up controlling us. We stay in control of our behaviors, in part, by using words to share our feelings with others. Managing emotions is confusing because it's hard to know what's troubling us, and often we have mixed emotions. We might be sad and happy. We might be worried and excited at the same time. We learn to manage our emotions by sharing our feelings free of criticism, judgment, or blame. And many of us did not grow up in homes where we learned how to properly manage and express our emotions.

Naming feelings, when done respectfully, communicates respect for our children. By taking an interest in their feelings, we communicate that we are interested in them. If we respect our children as equal to us as persons, as icons of Christ, we need to respect their emotional world. We name their feelings with statements like:

» "You seem overwhelmed."
» "Are you mad?"
» "Are you sad the day is over?"
» "Do you miss your mother?
» "Are you mad at me?"
» "Are you frustrated with your brother?"

❧ Feelings need to be heard, not acted upon.

Bear one another's burdens, and so fulfill the law of Christ. (Galatians 6:2)

———◆———

Naming kids' feelings does not help when they are having a meltdown, and it doesn't work with teenagers, either. "Duh, of course I'm mad!" is a likely fourteen-year-old's response. What works in these cases is respecting their feelings by being silent and keeping firm limits. Maintaining a peaceful, calm presence, without giving in, communicates respect for their feelings and struggle. Parenting is about letting our children know we understand their struggles as we walk with them through life.

❧ Feelings are like children in the back seat on a road trip. If you ignore them, they will

be out of control, but they'd better not be allowed to drive the car.

Child development researchers and professionals have discovered the significant role feelings play in child development. The ability to manage emotions is a critical aspect of good decision-making, healthy relationships, and success in life. Managing emotions, also called affect regulation, plays a key role in impulse control, delayed gratification, motivation, reading social cues, and coping with life. Children need space and time to learn how to cope with their emotions. They do best in life when they have learned to manage their emotions and develop what's called emotional intelligence.

There are great parenting books devoted specifically to learning how to raise children who can navigate the emotional landscape. I've listed some of the best at the end of this book for parents interested in improving their skills in this area. While managing our feelings is not the only aspect of life, or even the most important, it is important to recognize that feelings are part of our humanity, and like the rest of our humanity, they are fallen and in need of transformation. Learning to control our emotions, desires, and drives is a key aspect of the spiritual life that we want our children to learn.

❧ Venerating our children as icons of Christ requires us to respect their feelings while not overindulging their desires.

Naming feelings is not a technique but an act of respect, an act of veneration of our children as icons of Christ. It might seem we're being lenient if we don't punish our children for their feelings or emotional outbursts and meltdowns. We're actually respecting them by allowing them to feel and helping them learn how to manage those feelings. We want to try to be strict about behaviors and lenient about feelings. In this way we communicate that we care about our children as persons as we're forcing them to get to bed.

Taking the side of their feelings affirms their struggle and affirms them as persons. This allows us to draw close to them as they struggle, as they learn to manage their emotions, control their desires, and do the right thing.

✎ Naming feelings doesn't solve very much, but it teaches a lot.

Naming feelings does not really work, and in fact may make things feel worse. As I took my children to bed, I named their feelings, and they increased their resistance. I resisted getting angry at them or letting them stay up later, and they resisted me. I can't take this struggle away, but I can draw close to them and respect them in the struggle by attending to their feelings.

As we discussed in Chapter 5, children learn how to interpret what's happening by what we say. They learn to name their feelings as they hear us naming them. They will learn "I am having a hard time," or "I'm sad that I have to go to bed."

Empathizing

After we name our child's feelings, we can always try to empathize with them. Empathizing with our children nurtures intimacy and connection when they need it the most. We want to communicate to our children that we understand how hard it is at times to do the right thing or to do what they have to do when they don't want to. That's kind and respectful. It's easy for parents to forget how hard it is to be a kid.

"It's hard to be patient with your sister," I said to Kassiani (twelve at the time) after she finished her tirade against her younger sister for taking her sweater without asking.

"But she takes it all the time, Dad!" she argued.

"I know. It's hard to be patient," I replied as compassionately as possible.

We need to remember that it's hard to wait until after dinner for a cookie. It's sad to be left at home when your older siblings leave for school. It's hard to find something to do at home on a Saturday when you're bored, you have no one to play with, or it's raining outside. It's hard to stop playing video games and clean your room or pick up your toys. It's hard to put the bikes away. It's hard to take off your soccer uniform after the game. You get the idea. Life is hard, and we can't change that, but we can try to empathize with our child by kindly and compassionately affirming the difficulty of the struggle. We're on their side.

If these statements are not made with a genuine understanding and compassion, they come off as dismissive, sarcastic, and manipulative. Empathizing is an expression of compassion, not a technique, although it can be learned. If we don't have compassion, empathic statements seem empty. That is our struggle, not our child's.

Sharing a Wish

A third way to show them you understand their desires or feelings is to share a wish. Children genuinely wish the fun would never end, you never had to go to work, or they got to play without ever having to clean, sleep, or even go to the bathroom.

» "I wish you never had to go to bed."

» "I wish we could play all the time."

» "I wish you did not have to sit in a car seat."

» "I wish your room cleaned itself like in *Mary Poppins*."

While we know, as adults, that these are fantasies, they are the real desires of our children. We want our children to learn that life doesn't work that way. But as importantly, we want them to know that we understand their struggles and desires. They will learn about how life works by the limits we set to their behaviors. We don't need to tell them. Sharing a wish simply communicates that we understand what's on their hearts. This communicates respect.

By sharing a wish, I can take the side of my children as we all struggle with real life. Plus, most parents wish parenting were easy. I wish my kids listened, always got along, and always did what they needed to do without a struggle. That is my wish. But as an adult, I've figured out that it is only that: a wish. Succeeding in life comes from following God's path, not following a wish. Parents don't make the rules of nature: we need sleep, children need to struggle to learn, struggle is hard, and love means selfless sacrifice. I don't expect my children to know that, but I do expect parents to, and we want to teach that success and happiness come from following God's path, not our wishes.

A respectful bedtime routine might sound like:
» "Tell me what you did at your friend's house," while putting their pajamas on.
» "Did you have a fun day?" while you brush their teeth.
» "Are you sad the day has to end?" while you walk them to bed.
» "It's hard to have to go to bed," while you slip them into their beds.
» "I wish you did not have to go to bed," as you give them a kiss goodnight.

"Why do you have to go to work? Why can't you stay home?" I was asked almost every Monday morning by Alexios when he was five years old. I could have explained that there was work to be done and that if I did not go to work we would not eat, but his questions were based on his desire to have me around all the time, not on his sense of economics. Respecting his childlike desires communicates respect for him as a person.

> » "Do you want me to stay home?"
> » "Are you sad I have to go to work?"
> » "I wish I could stay home all day and play."
> » "I can't wait to see you tonight."

These were my standard responses, accompanied with a hug, before I left each morning. While I do have to go to work, I do not have to ignore my children and their desires. And I don't always have to go to work.

Alexios's New Year's resolution one year was, "That Dad stays home from work more." That's tough to hear because I think I'm home a lot. "I wish I could stay home all year!" was my reply.

It is important to beware of the temptation of always having something "more important" to do than to play or connect with our kids. Children will learn that sometimes you have to go to work or get something done, but we don't always have to go to work, and we don't always have something more important to do. They need to see there are other times when they are most important and other things get put aside, such as evenings, weekends, and vacations. And when we are home, we need to try to be attentive to them, get to know them, check in with them, and take care of them. Having said that, I have found the more time I spend with my children, the more they want me home all the time. That is a wish, not reality, and the only thing I can do with that wish is name it.

Taking the Side of Feelings Is the Solution

Parents are tempted to try to fix kids' feelings and desires. It never works because kids' desires are not problems to be solved, but part of their humanity that needs to be transformed in a relationship of love. They cannot control their feelings and desires. They don't have to like going to bed or picking up their toys; they just need to learn how to do it, and we support them in this process by attending to their desires. An effective response attends to their desires as they learn to do what needs to be done.

⋘ Taking the side of feelings does not stop children's misbehaviors. It stops parents' misbehaviors.

We can't solve the problem of our kids' feelings, because they need to learn how to do that themselves. We are not here to cheer them up or solve their boredom but to draw close as they learn how to manage their emotions and figure things out. Life will provide many limits that our children need to learn how to navigate. We can do our best to focus on drawing close to them as they learn by taking the side of their feelings.

⋘ If you can't solve the problem, listen to the feelings.

Parenting is not about solving problems but about loving persons, and it is particularly important that we listen to our child's feelings. Most misbehavior can be understood, as we talked about in Chapter 4, in terms of children learning how to acquire the values and virtues of the Kingdom of God. This is hard. We support them by asking about their feelings and listening to them. Asking about feelings and taking the side of feelings is a powerful way to communicate respect.

» "Are you sad you have to go to bed?"
» "Are you frustrated that your brother knocked over your block tower?"

» "I'm sorry you got cut from the team. Are you sad? That's disappointing. It hurts to get cut."
» "I'm sorry your coach said you can't travel with the team. That's a bummer."
» "I'm sorry you did not get the lead in the play. I would be hurt by that. Are you upset?"
» Or even worse, "I'm sorry you did not get invited to the party." Silence. I wouldn't want to touch this one right away.

Paying a little attention to our child's inner world is far more effective at helping our children navigate the disappointments of life than saying something like, "Why are you in such a foul mood?" or "What's wrong with you?" or making statements of fact, like "Life's not fair." "Not everyone can make the team." Or worse yet, "Did you upset the coach?" Nothing hurts more than when your parents seem to turn against you when you're in pain.

These statements might be met with reactions like "I am mad," or "Yes, I'm frustrated," and we can respond with simple silence or some of the responses discussed. We are not supposed to fix or solve their feelings, just try to sit close as they work through them. Parenting is not about always voicing the right answer but about communicating care and respect. This can happen in a variety of ways with a variety of statements.

❧ We ask about feelings not to get information but to communicate respect and care.

"It's hard to clean your room. I wish it cleaned itself," I said to George (seven).

"If you really cared, you'd clean my room for me!" he retorted. Which is to say, if I really cared, I'd make his life easy and do all his chores for him. That makes sense when you're seven. However, if we really care, we do whatever it takes to help our children learn the skills and virtues that will enable them to succeed in life, and we support them in the process. We didn't create reality; we just want to help our children learn how to succeed in it.

❧ Naming their feelings equips them to navigate life and the spiritual path.

As children learn to manage their feelings and desires, they develop self-awareness and a capacity to reflect on their feelings and their inner world. Taking the side of their feelings helps them learn emotional self-regulation, to calm themselves in the midst of strong feelings. This nurtures empathy for others as our children learn how to read emotions in other people. It allows them to learn self-restraint so they can respond and not react to life's events. It helps them learn to postpone gratification, problem-solve, and think clearly. As kids learn to manage their own emotions, they are able to see beyond their short-term feelings toward long-term goals and do what's true, right, and good, no matter what they feel.

Ask, Don't Tell, Children about Their Feelings

Statements like "You're mad" or "You're frustrated" often get reactions from children. Nobody likes to be told what he's feeling, as if we have figured him out. The goal of attending and naming feelings is to communicate "I care," "I understand," not, "I have you figured out."

Instead, try to ask children about specific feelings, or share what you see, with statements such as "You seem mad" or "Are you frustrated?" Your child might not be able to articulate what he is feeling because he's learning.

If we can make this a habit, we create a culture of respect and learning within which our child can learn what he's feeling and how to articulate it. Remember, you're going to have this conversation a lot. They will learn to associate their inner experiences with the words you use to describe them.

If you're not sure what your child is feeling, take a guess. Sometimes parents worry that if they guess, they might be putting ideas into their children's heads, or might bring things up that will make the child feel a certain way. That is not true. Usually children can tell you if your guess is right or wrong. When you're wrong, they'll let you know, and when you're right, they will respond instinctively.

"Do you miss Mom?" I asked George (age five) at bedtime one night when Georgia was out.

"No," he replied, "I'm sad I don't get a glass of water. Mommy always lets me have a glass of water."

I had just denied his water request, thinking he was stalling. "I can get you some water." After his glass of water, he calmed down, and we continued our routine.

Beware of Disregarding or Trying to Control Their Feelings

✎ Dismissing or disrespecting our children's feelings or their struggles disrespects them.

Sometimes parents disrespect children by condemning or trying to control their kids' feelings.

"Why can't you just appreciate that I already let you stay up past your bedtime?" I could have snapped at my children as they protested going to bed.

My kids might respond, if they could verbalize like adults, "Why can't you respect the fact that I'm eight, and no matter how late you let me stay up, I still don't like going to bed?"

Sometimes when we give treats or privileges to our children, like letting them stay up late or play at a friend's house all day, we expect them to respond with appreciation and obedience. In fact, the more we indulge our kids' desires, the more difficult it is for them to give up their desires. Parents dismiss or disrespect their children's feelings, thinking they are helping their children, with statements like:

» "I don't care how hard it is—we all go to church in this house."

» "There is no reason to be upset."

» "You should be happy you got to stay up late."

» "Big boys don't cry."

» "We don't hate in this house."

» "How dare you feel that way!"

» "Why can't you just be happy for your sister?"

» "Why can't you be thankful you got to play at your friend's house today?"

» "I don't care how you feel—you have to clean your room!"

» "I don't care if you're upset—we don't talk like that in this house!"

» "I don't want to hear if it's hard. You have to share!"

It's disrespectful to condemn, criticize, or try to control our kids' feelings. Children can't control how they feel, but they can learn how to express or manage those feelings. Condemning their feelings communicates to children that there is something wrong with them, which is a lie. There might be something wrong with their behavior, but not with them.

Beware of Giving in to Feelings

Children can only learn how to manage their emotions if we allow them to. If we try to protect them from hard feelings, or give in to their feelings by relaxing or changing the limits, we undermine their learning and our long-term goals.

» "Okay, you can have a cookie before dinner, but just one."

» "Okay, but promise me the next time you play video games you'll ask first."

» "Okay, you can stay up for ten more minutes, but that's it."

Each time we give in to our children's desires, they become a little more enslaved to their desires, making it harder for them the next time we set a limit. In each of these examples, you will eventually have to set a limit, and your child will, predictably, protest. This is frustrating for parents who might assume that giving in to their kids' desires will result in more compliance. In fact, the opposite is true. They will have a harder time stopping on the second cookie, asking the next time for video games, or going to bed in ten minutes than if we just set the limit right away. If we love them, we will try to help them learn to manage their emotions by keeping the limits firm and respecting their feelings.

Respecting Feelings Allows Us to Connect with Our Children

Children learn best when their parents are by their side. They are less oppositional and defiant when they feel we are on their side. The best way to stay on their side is to take the side of their feelings. We want them to experience us as being on their side even when we are the ones setting the limits. We do not choose between setting firm limits and naming feelings; rather, we name feelings within firm limits. We'll talk more about this in the next chapter.

As we've talked about in Chapter 6, children are learning in these struggles. Taking the side of their feelings, even as we try to keep the limits firm, allows us to connect with our children in the struggles. It is easy to miss the fact that we don't connect with our kids only when things are calm. We connect with them in the struggles. Responding to our children in the difficulties allows us to connect with them even when things are hard.

"I don't have time to sit and ask them all day about their feelings," parents say to me when we discuss feelings. Attending to our kids' feelings is about being attentive even when we don't have time, and learning how to make time for their feelings.

Sometimes we can't sit down and check in with our children. Sometimes we have to get dinner on the table or get out the door, but not all the time. In the normal cycle of family life, sometimes we have the time and sometimes we don't. We should do our best to make time for feelings when we have the time and learn to attend to feelings when we don't have much time. Attending to feelings, when it becomes a habit, takes very little time. Trying to name feelings as we're making dinner or getting children dressed, in the car, or into bed takes paying attention, not time, and nurtures a culture of respect in the midst of daily life. Parents can learn how to do this. Try to make time for attending to feelings at bedtime, at dinnertime, in the car, and during other natural downtimes in family life.

The real challenge parents face is learning how to attend to our child's feelings. It takes ten minutes at night to read a little on parenting and emotions or fifteen minutes to discuss this with your spouse.

"I wish I had my own room," my daughter says every time she gets in a fight with her sister. I listen to her struggle.

"It's hard to have to share a room," I admitted, and I made

a mental note to myself to comment the next time I see them making an effort to share.

"How Do I Know What My Child Is Feeling?"

You don't have to be a therapist to name your child's feelings, but you do have to learn how to express and manage your own emotions if you want to help your children learn to do the same. Kids don't need therapist parents, just parents who care enough to learn how to do this. When your child reacts or is upset, try to step back for a moment and reflect. Consider what your child might be feeling. Talk to other parents or professionals about what your children might be feeling and the effective ways to respect their feelings.

Just the act of considering what a child might be feeling instead of reacting is an act of veneration that shows a deep respect for the person of your child. Try to reflect on how you might feel if you were in your child's shoes. Consider what your child has been doing or seeing just before the reaction. What kind of day has your child been having? Have there been any major changes in his or her life? Consider what virtues your child is struggling to acquire and how difficult that might be for someone his age.

Attending to Your Own Feelings

We teach how to properly express and manage emotions by modeling these behaviors for our children. Plus, if we don't know how to pay attention to our own inner world of the heart, it is difficult to attend to our child's inner world. If we grew up in a home that disregarded the inner life and world of feelings, this might require some learning.

I find that most couples struggle to attend to each other's feelings in marriage. While we might fear opening up a can of worms, attending to our spouse's feelings nurtures intimacy in marriage and makes marriages stronger. Don't let your marriage or life become a series of tasks to be accomplished. That's not what you wanted on your wedding day, and that is not God's plan for marriage or family life.

Feelings are an important aspect of our humanity that we disregard or ignore at our own peril. God created us as feeling human beings and heals us in our broken humanity with our feelings. He invites us to confess, not deny, our feelings and fallen desires. This requires that we learn to attend to our inner world and offer it up to Him.

If you've read this chapter and are thinking that listening to feelings constitutes pampering your children or indulging them, and you fear you'll raise weak children who can't struggle, it's quite the opposite. Naming feelings is crucial to raising strong, confident, self-aware children.

Boys grow into strong men by mastering their feelings, not ignoring them. If you want to raise a strong boy, don't teach him how to dismiss or ignore his feelings, because he'll grow up unable to navigate his inner world. Try to teach your son how to express and manage the full array of emotions, so that as an adult he will not be cut off from or controlled by his emotions. Children can only learn how to master their emotions if they are allowed to struggle with them. We need to help them name their feelings as they struggle with them. That produces not only strong children but insightful, empathic, intuitive strong children.

Attending to our kids' feelings is not all we do, but it can always be part of what we do. Trying to attend to our kids' inner world is essential for our long-term goals, and so is learning how to set limits.

CHAPTER 8

Set Limits to Behaviors

"But let your 'Yes' be 'Yes,' and your 'No,' 'No.'"

—Matthew 5:37

I TOOK MARKOS, ABOUT TWO-AND-A-HALF AT THE TIME, on a shopping errand. I let him play with some trucks on a shelf while I looked for something. I suspected it would be tough to pull him away but indulged myself in some peace while I shopped. When the time came, I gave Markos a two-minute warning.

"Markos, we're leaving in two minutes." He barely noticed.

In about two minutes, I had finished my work and headed toward my two-year-old, who was surrounded by trucks. I was not looking forward to what I had to do.

"Markos, time to go," I said as I went to pick him up.

"I don't want to go!" he began.

"You want to stay and play with the trucks?" I named his struggle.

"Yes," he answered.

"It's hard to have to leave the trucks," I said gently as I started putting the trucks back on the shelf.

"I want this truck!" he said. He loved trucks, and, you can imagine, he had a bunch of his own at home. But, as we all know, there is nothing like a new toy no matter how many toys we have at home.

"You like that truck?" I asked.

"Yes!"

"I wish you could take that truck home with you. Time to go. Put the truck away," I said, entering into the heart of the struggle.

"I want to get this truck!" His protest began in earnest.

"You have a bunch of trucks at home," I reasoned with him, forgetting the very things I write about in my own parenting book. He was not thinking. He was struggling with his desires.

He did not miss a beat. "I want to get that truck."

I picked him up and headed out the door.

"I want that truck!" he protested.

"You want that truck? Do you wish you could take that home with you?" I said calmly as I carried him out. For the next few minutes, as I carried him out the door and put him in his car seat, I repeated alternately,

» "Did you want that truck?"

» "I wish you could get that truck."

» "Are you sad you can't have that truck?"

❦ **Setting limits is something we do, not *to* our children, but *for* our children.**

It got worse before he calmed himself down. He got mad and sad. I stayed firm in my response and empathized with his feelings. The fact is that it *is* hard to be two and not be able to have a truck that you "love." As I drove away, he quieted down and sat with a sad look on his face.

"Markos, what is it?" I asked after he quieted down.

"I'm sad I can't have that truck," he reported meekly, modeling my language.

Markos did not need a consequence for his "misbehavior" or "defiance." As a two-year-old, he did not have the discipline or self-control to say no to that truck. He needed a parent who loved him enough to say no for him and empathize with his struggle. He was not undermining my authority and did not get a consequence. I was still in charge, and he was learning.

It would have been easier for me to buy him the truck than to keep that limit firm. I could have gotten mad at him and promised myself never to take my kid to a store again, or I could have silently endured his tantrum, wondering why I have such a materialistic and strong-willed child. These reactions do not respect the fact that Markos was two-and-a-half years old. He needed me by his side as he struggled to learn to live within the limits I set. I knew that the sooner he learned this, the happier he would be. The only thing worse than a two-year-old throwing a temper tantrum until he gets his way is a sixteen- or seventeen-year-old who throws a temper tantrum until he gets his way. Then it is dangerous. We can't pick up a seventeen-year-old and carry him out of a store, a party, or a destructive relationship.

When children misbehave, the temptation is to look for a consequence to stop the behavior. Consequences are the "hammer" of the parenting toolbox. The problem with consequences is that, as the saying goes, if the only tool you have is a hammer, everything looks like a nail. Parents need to use consequences, but that should not be the first or the only thing we do when children misbehave. Consequences may stop their misbehaviors in the short term but undermine our long-term goals. Our goal is to raise kids who know how to set limits to their own behaviors and live their lives within God's limits for salvation. We need to learn how to give consequences in ways that work toward these long-term goals for our children. To do that, our consequences need to be part of a bigger process of how we set limits to our kids' behaviors.

⋙ Children don't always need consequences, but they always need limits.

Setting limits respects the fact that our children do not yet have the capacity to set their own limits. Clear and firm boundaries protect our children from their own powerful drives and desires and provide them with a safe place to thrive, to learn, and to grow naturally into adults. A number of other parenting tools are available for setting effective limits with our children besides the hammer of consequences. In fact, the more skilled you become at using different tools to set limits, the less you'll find yourself needing to come up with consequences.

Although parenting cannot be reduced to techniques or skills, children learn best when parents set limits well, which requires skill and technique. Kids need limits to their behaviors in order to grow and thrive, and there are good and bad ways to set limits. Setting limits well gives our children the best opportunity to learn, over time, how to set limits to their own behaviors. These are essential skills that parents can and must learn.

Limits as Love

The goal of setting limits and giving consequences is not to punish our children or stop bad behavior. Setting limits is about teaching the values and virtues of the Kingdom of God, the greatest of which is love. Beware: as parents learn the skills and techniques of parenting, it is easy to lose sight of the heart of parenting—loving our children as persons. It is important also to understand that setting limits well is an act of love toward our children.

❧ Children feel cared for and loved as they experience the peaceful presence of adults who love them enough to set clear limits to their behavior.

Rather than giving our children love *and* limits, we need to think in terms of love *as* limits. Setting appropriate limits communicates love to our children. Kids should be left neither alone nor in charge. They do best when they experience our love as unconditional and our limits as non-negotiable. Children will thrive by feeling connected to us as they run into those limits and learn to live within them. Kids will feel unloved by us, or feel that our love is conditional, not if we set limits to their behaviors, but if we withdraw our love by reacting against them when we set limits.

❧ We set limits as a response to a child's behaviors, not as a reaction.

The limits we set on our children must be informed and shaped by God, His Church, and His limits. When children are raised in this way, within the life of the Church, they come to understand our relationship with God. We were not created to be alone or in charge. God created the universe and reveals to us how to thrive in this reality. He knows us deeply and is intimately close to us. He loves us first (1 John 4:19). He offered Himself to us, offering His very Son, and we love Him in response by choosing to obey His commandments and live within His limits. God's commandments are an expression of love because they provide for us the pathway to an eternal loving relationship with Him and others. We believe everything God does is an expression of His love, including His commandments, because He is love (1 John 4:8). His rules are not negotiable, but we have a choice whether to follow them or not. His love is unconditional, no matter which choice we make. We thrive as persons when we respond to His love with our love by walking in His ways.

Helping our children thrive within our limits teaches them how to set limits to their own behaviors and equips them to live within God's limits. We'll talk more about this in Chapter 10, but for now it's important to understand that firm limits communicate love and are an act of love toward our children that prepares them to thrive in life.

⋘ Good limits are essential for children to thrive.

The sooner our children learn this and experience the peace, joy, and love that come from this path, the happier they will be. We have eighteen years and hundreds of interactions each day to help them do this. We can learn to set limits effectively and stay close to our children as they learn to live within our limits.

Effective Limit-Setting

I can't make setting limits easy to do, but it is easy to learn how to set limits once we understand how children think and learn. If we respect the way kids function, we can learn to set up limits that are respectful and effective. I can't make children like limits, but that is not our goal. Our goal is to set effective limits that work toward our long-term goals. This is not complicated, but it does take some thought, and for some of us, a change in our approach.

To understand limit-setting, imagine yourself getting pulled over by a police officer for speeding.

Scenario One: The officer simply says, "I clocked you at seventeen over." He asks you if you knew you were speeding and listens to you. Then he gives you a ticket, politely says, "Please slow down," and sends you on your way.

Scenario Two: The officer comes to the car and, instead of giving you a ticket, lectures you about how dangerous it is to speed. He seems to be in a good mood. He doesn't ask you why you were speeding, but goes on and on about the number of people who die in accidents every year, and how it is a privilege, not a right, to drive. He asks you to promise him you won't speed anymore and, instead of giving you a ticket, tells you he's sure you won't do that again. You say, "Of course not," and drive off as he heads back to his car.

Scenario Three: The officer approaches you and begins to yell at you. "Why can't you just drive slower?!" He continues to yell at you about what a busy day he's having and how he doesn't have time for handing out speeding tickets. He says he's sick and tired of always pulling people over for speeding and demands that you never speed again. However, instead of a ticket, he gives you fifty dollars, stomps back to his car, and speeds off.

We might say Scenario Two has the "nicest" police officer, because he didn't get mad or give you a ticket, but it's hard to take him very seriously.

Scenario Three, with the angry officer, is likely to leave you confused and hurt. He obviously has a problem. His behavior is abusive and disrespectful. You might even report his behavior to his boss. It's also confusing because it hurts to be attacked, but you did get fifty dollars.

Only the first officer is clear and respectful to you and your choice to speed. Only the first officer was really doing his job. The first officer kept his actions focused on your speeding, followed through on the posted speed limit, and issued you a ticket at a determined amount. Only the first officer will help us change our driving habits. In fact, no matter how many times the first officer pulls us over, we are likely to respect him as we learn there is a speed limit we have to follow. He is nice about it and consistently gives us a ticket.

≪≫ The key to setting good limits is to be clear, consistent, firm, and matter of fact.

Vague commands, instructions, and limits, inconsistently enforced or based on our mood at the time, are ineffective at helping children learn. Imagine playing tennis or volleyball and not being able to see the lines on the court. Imagine trying to learn a sport and not knowing the rules. Imagine how confusing it would be if the rules of a game changed during the game, or if the referee was lax on the rules when he was in a good mood but added rules arbitrarily when he was upset. In order to learn how to play a sport, children need clear lines and rules, consistently enforced.

Good limits keep the focus on the child's decisions in such a way that the child learns to change her behaviors. Low emotional intensity and consistently issuing consequences based on posted limits allow children to learn that the consequences are the result of their behavior, not of our mood or opinions.

Children learn from our actions, not from our words. No matter what we say, they will wait patiently to see if we're serious enough to act before they reflect on their behaviors.

⫷ Connection with parents is the currency that rewards children for their actions.

Whether we respond or react when our children misbehave makes the difference between positive connection and negative connection. When we react or spend time patiently lecturing, we connect with them, subtly rewarding their misbehavior. When we get angry, we connect with our children but hurt them, leaving them wounded and confused. If we pay attention to our children only when they misbehave, we set up a system that subtly rewards misbehavior with connection. Why would you stop speeding if you got fifty dollars every time you were stopped?

Now imagine if the first officer told you, "If you speed, I will fine you, but if you go the whole day without speeding, I'll give you a hundred dollars." That would give you not only a consequence for speeding but an incentive not to speed. When we pay attention and connect with our children when they make good decisions and behave well, we encourage good behavior. The best reward we can offer our children is to connect with them. That's money in the bank! We need to learn how to reward our children for good behaviors by connecting with them throughout the day whenever they are making good decisions. This reduces the number of "speeding tickets" we need to give our kids.

Children are natural speeders. All kids need to learn to slow down and follow the rules of the road. Typically, children who are labeled as difficult are children with strong engines and poor brakes (see Hal Edward Runkel, *Scream-free Parenting*).

Some kids will need to be pulled over many times before they learn how to control their speed. A good police officer will never resort to lectures or yelling or handing out cash but will just hand over a ticket each time. In fact, simply seeing a police car by the side of the road leads to slower driving. And if the good police officer were following you, it would be easier for you to control your speed. In this way, good supervision with clear and consistent limits actually helps a child learn to control herself.

Simply giving tickets does not teach someone how to drive. In the same way, just having limits and consequences does not teach a child how he should behave. However, clear and consistent limits are a necessary part of the parenting equation.

One difference between good police officers and good parents is that parents also spend time with their children, play with them, and take an interest in them as persons. Cops don't typically say things like "Let's go outside and play catch," or "How did your math test go today?" Children need more from us than just limits and consequences. They need to connect with us all the time. However, we need to learn how to be like the first officer in terms of setting limits and giving consequences.

CHAPTER 9

Strategies for Setting Limits

Instruct your son, and he shall give you rest, / And he will delight your soul. (Proverbs 29:17, OSB)

ONE CHAPTER CANNOT CAPTURE ALL THE ASPECTS and examples of setting limits. Numerous parenting books detail the aspects of good limit-setting. I list some of the best at the end of this book. What they all have in common are the characteristics of good limits. Good limits are clear, consistent, and firm, and are enforced in a matter-of-fact way.

Because we will need to set limits for our children hundreds of times, taking the time to learn a variety of ways to set limits is respectful to our children and reduces the number of power struggles we experience.

Just Say No

"No" is a complete sentence and an appropriate way to set a limit. Some parents say no too quickly and too often. Children build up a resistance and resentment when they hear it too much. Other parents fear saying no because of the tension it creates in our children. Saying no invites a quick "Why not?" reaction, which invites the classic parenting response, "Because I said so," and then you're locked in a power struggle with your child.

Because it is so easy to slip into this power struggle, "no" is not, typically, the best thing to say first. It is an important tool, but we want to reserve this tool for special cases. It usually works best after we've set a limit in some of the following ways.

Instead of No, Say "Not Yet"

When your child wants something reasonable, but it is not the right time, saying "not yet" is a more effective limit than just saying no.

- » "May I go to Sarah's house to play?"
- » "May I play my video games?"
- » "May I stay out later?"
- » "May I have a piece of candy?"
- » "May I be excused from the table?"

All these are reasonable requests that might need to be contained. Saying "not yet" allows a child to understand that we are not opposed to these desires or requests, but they need to find their appropriate time.

- » "Not yet. You may go to Sarah's on the weekend."
- » "You may play video games in the evening."
- » "You may stay out later when you don't have school the next day."
- » "You may have a piece of candy after dinner."

» "When everyone is finished eating, you may be excused." Our children will not like hearing "not yet" any more than hearing "no," but saying "not yet" teaches a child that we are not against good and fun things, but there is a time and a place for these things. We should expect the appropriate resistance because your child needs to make sure you really love him, so he will need to test that limit. Another way to set a limit is the next strategy.

Instead of Saying No, Give Children a Pathway to Yes

Children love ice cream, and rarely does a meal end in our home without a request for ice cream or some sort of dessert. There is not much my kids won't do for ice cream. We want to make use of that opportunity and not give the ice cream away for free. Make appropriate privileges and treats contingent on things you want your children to learn. The more they desire something, the greater opportunity we have as parents to teach them skills that will last longer than a bowl of ice cream.

"When the kitchen is clean, you may have ice cream," Georgia replies, predictably. They have learned Mom is strict about a clean kitchen before ice cream. Their desire for ice cream motivates them to clean the kitchen in record time. They grumble, but if we stay firm, their desire for ice cream is greater than their disinclination to clean the kitchen. Our long-term goal is to help our children develop the skills to clean a kitchen when they don't feel like it. We can use their desire for ice cream to motivate that learning.

Giving children a pathway to yes is a way to help them learn while avoiding the head-on confrontation and power struggles of just saying no. As kids learn your limits are firm, they quickly learn that the easiest way to get what they want is to meet your conditions and terms. Set them wisely.

Children don't like this limit any more than they like hearing us say no, but giving them a pathway to yes shifts the focus from power and control toward doing what needs to be done. We're not saying no. We're saying yes, with a few conditions.

- » "Yes, you may go to Sarah's when your homework is done."
- » "Yes, after you walk the dog, you may play thirty minutes of video games."
- » "Yes, when your room is clean, you may go outside to play."

As children learn to take the pathways to yes, they improve their skills at struggling to do what needs to be done, and they experience the inherent joy and sense of accomplishment from being responsible. It doesn't stop them from being kids, but over time allows them to acquire the skills to be adults. These skills last longer than the bowl of ice cream. If you give children a pathway to yes, try to stick to your words when your child does what you asked. Adding on more conditions after the fact confuses and frustrates a child and sends the message that your words cannot be trusted.

Pathways to yes work well not only with short-term requests but also with larger requests, like doing extracurricular activities or earning major privileges.

- » "If you keep your GPA above a 3.0, you may play soccer."
- » "If you raise half the cost, you may go to that summer camp."
- » "If I see you being kind to your sister, you may go to your friend's house Friday night."

It's important for children to learn to work for privileges, but we can't be super rigid about this. There are times when we can give the ice cream away for free. If an exceptional situation arises, like going outside to play in the snow on a snow day before they do their homework or clean their room, kids still learn that work comes before play, but that in some cases we make an exception.

Give Directions and Instructions

One of the most basic ways to set limits is to give directions and instructions. These range from "Time to get up. Get dressed. Clean your room. Mow the lawn. Say please. Say thank you. Be home by 11:00 pm" all the way to bedtime: "Brush your teeth. Go to bed." Too often, the most common interaction parents have with their children is telling them what to do.

Giving instructions is an important and necessary tool we have for setting limits. However, because it takes the least amount of effort, it is often misused or overused. It should not be all we do or what we do the most. If the only way we know to set limits is by giving commands, we'll find ourselves constantly giving commands. "Do this." "Do that." This can quickly become the only way we communicate with our children. Do your best to avoid that.

✷ Check in with your child before you tell him what to do.

When I come home at night, or walk into my kids' bedrooms, the first things I notice are all the things that need to be done instead of my children themselves. Their rooms are usually messy. They have left chores unfinished. Shoes are typically all over the floor. It is always tempting, particularly as a dad, to see the mess before I see the child and to give instructions and directions before I greet or check in with my child. We want to resist this temptation. Try to acknowledge your child before you tell him what to do, because we want to be focused on persons more than on behaviors.

"Hi, Markos" (age eight), I said, biting my tongue as he came in the door, soccer cleats tracking mud, dropped his shoes in the middle of the floor and his shirt on the couch, and started dribbling his ball. I gave him a hug and asked, "How was soccer?"

"Good," he reported.

Then I said, "Please put your stuff away. Ball: outside. Cleats: off."

If we correct, command, direct, or react to our children before connecting with them, it communicates that we are more concerned about where cleats and balls go than about who they are.

Telling our children what to do is necessary at times, but it is not the most effective way to work toward our long-term goals. Telling children what to do is dangerous because it does not necessarily invite them to think for themselves, and, when overused, can communicate to our children that they are not capable of thinking for themselves. Plus, they probably know what to do, because we've told them hundreds of times. They just don't want to do it or aren't thinking about it. Beware of overusing this tool. Instead, after you've connected with your child, consider some of the following options.

Describe What You See
» "I see shoes on the floor."
» "I see a shirt on the couch."
» "The dishwasher is still full."
» "I see Legos all over the floor still."

Say It with One Word
» "Shoes."
» "Shirt."
» "Dishwasher."
» "Legos."

Describe How You Feel

I was carrying my daughter Nikolia, age three at the time, on my shoulders. She was playing with my hair and decided to grab the hair on my temples and pull it. Maybe it made for great handlebars.

"Ouch," I gasped. "That hurts."

"Sorry," she said and never did it again.

Setting limits in this way, instead of telling children what to do, nurtures a sense of empathy and teaches our kids how their behaviors affect others. It nurtures a sense of our being on the same side with our child.

» "I am so upset about the report from your teacher today."

» "I am frustrated that you did not walk the dog again today."

» "It's overwhelming to see the kitchen such a mess."

Beware. Our children are not here to care for us or our feelings. However, when appropriate, it's important for them to learn how their actions affect us and others around them.

> ❧ The more our children feel cared for by us, the more they will care how we feel.

Share Information

» "If you eat upstairs, it will attract insects."

» "Dirty cleats ruin the rug."

» "If you eat in the living room, food will get all over the floor."

» "If you don't put your stuff away, you won't be able to find it when you need it."

Comments like these serve as gentle reminders of the limits we have set and as alternatives to constantly telling our children what to do. Kids know the limits, but sometimes they forget.

They are easily distracted. Or rather, they are learning how to pay attention as they learn to become responsible adults. Sharing information helps children understand the rationale behind our limits. Notice, these are short statements. Beware of nagging or lecturing.

Direct Children Toward the Behaviors You Want to See

We are all tempted to notice our children more when they misbehave than when they behave. We are also tempted to set limits that draw attention to the behaviors we don't want to see rather than the virtues or behaviors we do want to see. It's good to resist those temptations.

Telling a two-year-old, "Don't touch the outlet," as we point at the outlet, only draws a child's attention to the electrical outlet. "Don't draw with markers on the wall" only invites children to focus on drawing on the wall. "Yeah, that is fun," he might think.

Instead, try to set limits that direct kids toward the behaviors you want to see. "You can play with these toys over here on the carpet" or "We draw on paper" are statements that set limits and focus a child's attention where it should be.

If we want our children to internalize the values and virtues of the Kingdom of God, we should try to set limits using these virtues. This will draw our kids' attention toward the good rather than just away from the bad. Remember that we'll be making these types of statements a lot. We want to fill our home, and our children's souls, with positive statements.

Say:	Instead of:
"Take turns. Share. Be patient."	"Quit fighting."
"Walk quietly."	"No running."
"Four legs on the floor."	"Don't rock the chair."
"Be gentle."	"Don't hit."

You get the idea. More than just a parenting technique, speaking in this way to our children shifts the orientation of all our interactions. It focuses or refocuses our children toward appropriate behavior. It also makes it easier for parents to recognize and comment when children do take turns, draw on paper instead of on a wall, share, sit at the table, and treat others gently.

The goal of the Christian life is not to resist temptation but to acquire virtue. We are called to seek the Kingdom of God, not just to avoid hell. This subtle change of focus allows our home to be a place where we are learning how to love rather than trying not to hurt. Remember, the gospel is called the Good News, not the List of Things We Should Not Do.

Break the Task Down into Smaller Steps

I have not found a good way to get my children to clean their rooms, empty the dishwasher, or do chores they do not like to do. It is a constant struggle for all of us. Statements like "Go clean your room" or "Empty the dishwasher" are met with complacency and inaction or disobedience. Sometimes these tasks seem too overwhelming to our kids. Starting a chore is often the hardest part of completing it, even for us adults. If you break the tasks down into smaller steps, and stay close to the children as they complete each step, the whole task seems less overwhelming, and they learn an important life skill. Breaking down a large task into steps makes it easier to accomplish.

"Make your bed, and come back to me. Put all the clothes from the floor onto the bed, and then come back to me. Now put the toys away. Now fold the pants. Now go put the shoes away," and so on. These smaller tasks are far more manageable than the global "Clean your room." I follow up with "If you want my help, you need to do the small task; otherwise, you're on your own." In this way, we keep our expectations high and our limits firm, and we help children accomplish the task.

"Take out five dishes, and then come back to me. Now take out five more dishes and come back to me." Naturally, your child will figure out what is happening, but they have also figured out that taking out five dishes is easier than doing the whole thing, and they did it. They will learn how to break down large tasks into smaller steps. If we make the smaller steps mandatory and stay close, they will also complete the whole task.

I can never resist commenting, once the task is done, that it took longer to complain about doing the task than it did to simply complete the task. That is also something I want them to learn.

A Teaspoon of Sugar

Just doing what needs to get done in the mornings, around meals, or in the evenings can feel like a chore when our children struggle to cooperate. I can't count how many times, once the kids were asleep, I wondered to myself why it takes two hours to put a few kids to bed. It's called a chore for a reason, because it is one. Adding a "teaspoon of sugar" to the normal routines of life by incorporating songs, play, and games goes a long way toward getting things done, if not making them fun.

"Go get Mr. Toothbrush," I told Kassiani (then age four). Once I discovered that if I made Mr. Toothbrush talk, Kassiani would happily open her mouth and let me brush her teeth, Mr. Toothbrush and I became very close for many years.

"Let's see how long it takes the three of you to get your clothes put away. Can you break your record?" I asked my three boys regularly when they were younger. While competing against siblings can be problematic, competing together to complete a task or a chore can help turn the mundane jobs of family life into a positive experience. We are all familiar with the classic "airplane" spoonful of food that gains entry into a toddler's mouth. Easing our children's burdens by making daily tasks and chores more enjoyable is respectful to their development and creates a powerful connection.

Be Specific with Directions and Instructions

"I want you to behave in the supermarket," you might think to tell your four-year-old on the way to the store. First, sharing your desire is different from giving instructions, and it's confusing.

"That's nice," your child might say, "and I want to run around." And of course, they will behave just like a four-year-old who wants to run around and touch everything he sees. Specific directions or instructions are more clear and effective:

"Stay next to me in the supermarket," or even better, "Keep one hand on the shopping cart at all times."

"Walk quietly and use inside voices" is a much more specific limit and guideline to children than simply saying, "Behave." What's even better, if you know what your child will struggle with—because it always happens when you shop—try to be very specific about the limits.

"If you see something you want, you can tell me or ask me."

Avoid Instructions Disguised as Questions

When is a question not a question? When your parent is asking. Then it's really an instruction, or a command, disguised as a question. Some parents ask questions, give suggestions, or make requests when they really mean to give direction and instruction.

- » "Can you help clear the table?"
- » "Would you mind picking up your things off the floor before you go upstairs?"

» "Can you help me empty the groceries from the car?"

» "Would you mind cleaning your room before you go out to play?"

A child's answer to the question:

» "Not right now, I'm busy."

» "Yes, I would mind, thanks for asking."

Sometimes we give instructions disguised as suggestions or preferences:

» "It would be nice if you thanked Grandma for that gift."

» "I'd prefer if you cleaned your room before you go out to play."

» "I'd like to leave in five minutes."

Boy, these sound nice, and boy, are they confusing for children. A child might answer, "I don't," or "Not me."

We might think we are being kind or gentle, but we're just being confusing. Asking children a question gives them a choice. If they really don't have a choice, then we should not make it sound as if they do. Otherwise, they will learn that we don't mean what we are saying. Try not to ask a question when you really mean to give an instruction or direction.

Respectful directives:

» "Please clear the table."

» "Please pick your things up off the floor before you go upstairs."

» "Come out and help me empty the car, please."

» "First you need to clean your room. Then you can go out to play."

» "Please write Grandma a thank-you note."

Being clear is not the opposite of being nice. We should give directions in a nice way, but we need to be clear. Children are strong, and they can handle a command. You can ask a question, but you better mean it to be a question and respect the choice you just gave your child. If you mean to give a directive, then avoid asking a question or making a suggestion. Try giving a clear command nicely. You can say please, but it should be at the end of a direction, not a question.

⋙ **It's okay to say please, but it's confusing to ask a question when you are really giving a command.**

"But I want my child to want to be helpful without being told," a mother shared with me. "I want my child to say thank you without being told." Our children will learn to be helpful and respectful as they acquire those skills and virtues. It's disrespectful to their learning to expect them already to have these habits, manners, and virtues, and it's confusing to give them a choice when we really don't mean it. They will acquire good habits as they learn to respond to our clear, firm, and kind directions.

It is appropriate for grandparents, neighbors, or extended family members to make requests rather than giving directions to our children. The more we, as parents, are direct and kind, the better our children will learn to respond appropriately to the requests of other adults.

Giving clear directions is one way we point the right way for our children. This is more than just changing the way we speak, although it is important to watch how we speak. We don't need to be afraid to give instructions and directions. We need to be concerned if that's all we do.

Get your child's attention before repeating your directions. When your child does not listen to your words or directions, he might be tuned out or distracted. We've all experienced the selective deafness of our children, who can hear their siblings whisper but can't seem to hear us when we're asking them to do something. Rather than repeat ourselves, it might be best to get our child's attention by drawing close, gently touching her, making eye contact, and repeating the direction in a calm voice.

Avoid Baby Talk

Using that high-pitched, sing-songy tone is great with cooing babies, but children will soon notice that you use a different tone to talk to adults. If you talked to an adult with that tone, it would be disrespectful and condescending. When should we begin talking to our children with the same respectful tone we use with adults? If we want our children to understand that we respect them as much as we respect adults, although they have different needs, they deserve the same respectful tone of voice starting when they're old enough to speak—before they're two years old. When we use an adult tone of voice with our children, we communicate to them that we do respect them just the same way we respect adults. Children may not protest being talked down to with baby talk when they are young, but they grow to resent it.

Give Five-Minute Warnings

Transitions are usually tough for children. They get sad or upset when they have to shift gears or change tasks, particularly when they're having fun. It's also hard to stop abruptly when they're focusing on something or they have it in their minds to do something, and we put a stop to it. We can ease their burden a bit by giving them a little warning about an imminent transition.

- » "Dinner is in five minutes."
- » "We're leaving in five minutes."
- » "Cleanup time in five minutes."

» "Bedtime in five minutes."

It's respectful, and effective in the long term, to give a five-minute warning for transitions, but be prepared to act when the five minutes are up. Five-minute warnings don't make stopping an activity any easier, but they respect the fact that our child is going to struggle to stop one thing and transition to another. Children don't need a consequence in these cases, just parental involvement and action. If we are consistent and act in five minutes, they will learn how to transition on their own when we give a five-minute warning.

Take Action

My children, in general, do not listen to my words. More accurately, they are still learning to listen to my words. They do listen to my actions. The best way to teach our children to listen to our words is to accompany them with action. When I say something, I need to be prepared to act. The more my kids know that my words will be followed by action, the more quickly they will learn to listen when I speak.

Sometimes children cannot listen to our words. It's just too tough. There's no easy way to get kids away from a video game, a playground, or a birthday party. Those things are just too enticing for our children to remove themselves from. No matter how many times we tell them it's time to go, sometimes it's just too hard to stop doing something fun. Rather than repeating ourselves, we need to physically remove the child. Fortunately, particularly when they're young, they are much smaller than we are and we can lift them up and remove them.

❧ **Children don't always need a consequence, but they always need us to follow up our words with action.**

Taking action is the way we teach children to listen to our words. Taking action is often more effective than empty threats, repeated requests or demands, or consequences. Remember Markos and the toy store? Remember the kids and bedtime? We don't need to give consequences, just take action to enforce the limits we set.

Parents can be tempted to be strict about behavior in public but relax rules at home or at the dinner table. This is a mistake. Try to take action following an instruction when you're at home, because in public it's not always possible. It's easier to remove our child from the dinner table at home than at a restaurant or at the grandparents' home. We can separate children until they are ready to be patient much more easily at home than on a road trip or in someone else's home. We can give a child a time-out at home more easily than in church. Try to take advantage of the time at home to follow through with your words, because sometimes in public all we have is our words. Consistently following through with our words at home teaches our children that our words are real, and we'll need that at church, at a restaurant, on a road trip, or at the grandparents' home.

"Why is someone always getting sent away from the dinner table?" Nikolia (age eleven) asked as another brother was sent away from the table to calm down.

"Because this is where they'll learn how to eat respectfully. I can't teach them that in public," I replied. If we're lenient at home, our children misbehave in public. If we recognize that the dinner table is the practice field, and we're prepared to act, they will do better in public.

Children quickly learn when we are making empty threats or setting limits that we cannot, or will not, follow up on. Be careful not to set a limit you cannot follow up on. If we're going to state things in positive terms, it might be better to say, only set limits you are prepared to follow up on. And when you set the limit, prepare yourself, because you'll likely be acting on it.

"If you're not ready, I'm going to leave without you" or "One more fight and I'm getting rid of the video games" are meaningless threats if we are not able or have no intention to follow up. Our children are less likely to listen to our words if they believe those words are unrealistic or empty.

Instead, consider something like, "If I have to wait for you/ if you are late this morning, I will wake you up fifteen minutes earlier next time." Or "One more fight and you lose the video game for an hour."

Beware: Don't Get Mad and Don't Give In

❧ We don't have to be mean or angry when
we set limits, but we need to be firm.

Setting limits for our children creates tension in our relationships with them. The temptation is to be lenient until we get mad. Children will feel connected to us in positive ways if we stay peaceful when we set firm limits. They feel safe and cared for when they experience firm limits from their parents, but they get hurt when those limits are accompanied by anger or meanness. Children learn that we care, specifically, as we stay calm and firm when we set limits. Expect them to challenge the limits we set. They want to make sure we really do love them. But resist the temptation to accompany the limits with anger. Remember, our anger is our struggle, not theirs. We'll talk more in Chapter 11 about responding to pushback.

Children will feel unconditional love when they attack us, disobey us, react to us, or defy us, and we return their disobedience with gentle but firm limits. They feel loved when they are not condemned for pushing hard against the limits, and they feel safe when the limits hold strong. We communicate love by being unflappable in our interactions, gentle in our manner, and firm in our resolve. In this way, limit-setting communicates love and is a powerful means of connecting with our children through the struggles of daily life.

❧ You can't love your child too much, but you can express your love in the wrong way.

Parental limits create a tension in a child between doing what he wants to do and what we require. They also create tension between us and our children. This tension is creative because in it a child acquires the values and virtues of the Kingdom of God and the skills to thrive as an adult. This tension is the struggle children need to experience that we discussed in Chapter 6. Children who do not experience this tension never acquire the skills they need to thrive as adults. When we stay peaceful in the tension, we can draw close to them as they are learning.

❧ Children need to experience limits in order to grow strong, but they don't need to go through it alone.

Much as we are tempted to pick up children when they fall, parents are tempted to rescue their children when they struggle to live within our appropriate limits. Too often, parental love is equated with soft limits or low expectations for our kids. It is hard work to set limits for our children. Kids do not like limits. Parents don't like the pushback or resistance. It might seem mean or cruel to create this tension for our kids. "I love my child too much to see him suffer!" is a common parental misunderstanding of love. However, if we love our children, we need to care for them in the tension rather than rescuing them. Setting no limits or soft limits undermines their learning and harms our children.

When parents give in to their children or do things to protect them from this tension, children grow up unable to manage life. It takes real care to allow our kids to struggle with our limits without rescuing them or getting angry.

⟨⟨⟩⟩ Setting limits well communicates respect for our children and teaches them how to respect themselves and others.

Children lose respect for themselves and their parents when they grow up without appropriate limits to their behaviors. We all would lose respect for the nice police officer in the second of the three scenarios we sketched in Chapter 8. This is particularly frustrating to parents who tell me how they tried to give their child everything he wanted, and now their child is unappreciative and disrespectful to them. Indulging a child's desires undermines his capacity to learn how to control his own desires. The result is a selfish, impulsive, demanding, and disrespectful child who is unable to thrive in healthy relationships that require selflessness and respect.

Using our words to give instructions and directions and following up with action is an essential parenting tool, particularly when children are young. But as they grow, if we want them to learn, we need to expand the ways we set limits.

CHAPTER 10

Setting Limits with Your Child

But the chief thing is that one should form in children an attitude of conscientiousness and awareness. Awareness is something extraordinarily important in life, but however easy it is to form it, it is just as easy to stifle it in children.
—St. Theophan the Recluse, *Raising Them Right*

IF OUR LONG-TERM GOAL IS TO TEACH OUR CHILDREN to think for themselves, make good decisions, and set limits by themselves when they go off to college or out into the world, we need to do more than give instructions, directions, and reminders. We need to give them opportunities to learn these things on their own. It is best if they learn how to do this with us by their side, while they are under our watch.

As children grow, they are able to take on more responsibilities and make more of their own decisions. Even if we don't respect this fact, as they grow we will have less and less control over their lives and their behaviors. They will be on their own after high school, and our goal is that they be able to set limits to their own behaviors by that time. If we don't allow them to make choices while they are under our watch, they will be on their own without the skills to make good choices. We need to give them age-appropriate freedom and responsibility while they are under our care.

❧ Setting limits is something we do not *to* our children but *with* our children.

Setting limits with our children helps them learn to set limits to themselves as they grow. Working with our children around our limits helps them understand that we are on their side, that we care about them as we set and enforce the limits. The better you get at setting limits with your kids, the less you'll have to tell them what to do.

Age-Appropriate Choices and Responsibilities

Children need enough freedom to learn how to make decisions but not so much freedom that they are overwhelmed or at risk of harm. It is difficult to know what age-appropriate limits should be. And, just to complicate matters a bit more, we need to expand the limits as a child matures and becomes able to handle more responsibilities. Dr. Sylvia Rimm, author of *How to Parent so Kids Will Learn*, calls this the "V" of parental limits.

When children are young, they need tight limits to their behaviors and few choices. As they grow, they need more freedom and choices. We set the expanding outside limits for their decisions and allow them to make choices within those limits. Giving children age-appropriate freedom and responsibility means letting go of control while still remaining in charge.

A two-year-old can have the freedom to choose between two outfits to wear. A teenager should be free to arrange her own schedule, with our approval, even as we require her to tell us where she is, with whom, and when she will return.

Every child will eventually be totally in control of her own life, and our job is to prepare her for that. We cannot control kids all through high school and then expect them to make good decisions when they have total freedom later on. They do best as they acquire the skills they need to live on their own gradually, over time. This means allowing as much independence as possible while they're under our roof. The more kids are running their own lives as seniors in high school, with us close by, the more likely they are to succeed with all the freedoms, choices, and responsibilities, as well as the crazy, destructive temptations, of college or life on their own.

It is outside the scope of this chapter to detail all the different choices and responsibilities we can and should allow our children to have. However, a good rule of thumb is that it is important to give our kids as many choices and responsibilities as they can handle at their age.

———◆———

Never do for a child what he can do for himself.
—Rudolf Dreikurs, *Children: The Challenge*

———◆———

Stay Involved and Informed, but Not in Control

Children do best when parents stay informed and involved in, but not in control of, their decisions as they grow. Some parents know how to make all their kids' decisions. The mantra is, "As long as you're in my house, I decide what you do. When you're on your own, you can do whatever you want." That's fine when our children are two years old. However, if our limits are too tight, our kids cannot learn and thrive. This approach dis-respects their growing age-appropriate abilities, encourages them to sneak around, and communicates to them that they have poor judgment. They will eventually escape our limits without good decision-making skills.

Some parents choose to let go completely. That's good when your child is twenty-five. However, limits that are too broad are also disrespectful to children. Kids can feel unsafe and uncared for, and they may get into situations where their desires are too much for their ability to make good choices. The challenge of parenting is to stay involved without making all our kids' decisions, which is what they need between the ages of two and twenty-five. The better parents are at staying involved but not in control, the less children mind having us close by as they learn. The more our children feel respected by us, the more we can remain informed and involved, if not in control.

It is not sufficient for the parents to be devout. They mustn't oppress the children to make them good by force. We may repel our children from Christ when we pursue the things of our religion with egotism.

St. Porphyrios, *Wounded by Love*

Strategies for Setting Limits with Your Children

Give Choices

Being in charge is not the opposite of giving choices. There are many times when children don't have choices. They have to get up and dressed in the morning, and they have to go to bed at night. In between there are a lot of things they simply have to do. If we want our children to learn how to make good decisions, we need to look for opportunities to give them age-appropriate choices. We show them respect by giving them choices within our firm limits.

> » To a four-year-old girl: "Which of these three dresses would you like to wear?"
> » To an eight-year-old: "You may sweep the floor or put in the dishes."
> » To my two boys, ages nine and eleven: "You may read quietly or come with me to the store. No football in the house."

⤳ Not making a choice is not an option.

Naturally, giving children two or three choices they don't like still invites resistance and non-compliance.

"You may sweep the floor or put in the dishes," I offered to George, age nine.

"I don't want either. I want to play outside," he retorted.

If we're going to give choices, it is best if the child knows what we will do if they refuse the choices.

"Okay, if you can't decide, then you can put in the dishes," I responded.

Giving choices does not make children like limits any more, but it gives them a little room to breathe and exercise their growing autonomy. They will quickly learn, if we are firm, that they can choose the least painful option.

Collaborate

Being in charge is not the opposite of collaborating with your children. Collaborating with your children in setting limits nurtures clear thinking, invites responsibility, and helps you connect with them as you set limits.

❧ Instead of telling your child what to do, consider inviting him to think about what he needs to do.

Before you tell your child what to do, you might want to ask yourself if he already knows what to do. It's common for parents to fall into the trap of constantly telling their children things they already know. So many of our instructions to our children are things we've said hundreds of times. By the time your child is old enough to think through limits with you, he's probably heard the limits many times before. You can't collaborate with a two-year-old, but by the time he's four, he's ready to make a plan with you.

» "Your bedroom's a mess. What do you need to do?"
» "What has to be done before you can go out to play?"
» "What are the three things we need to do at bedtime?"
» "What do we do when we wake up in the morning?"
» "What do we do when we're finished playing with the Legos?"
» "What do you have to do before you can play video games?"
» "Where do the bikes go when you're finished riding?"
» "What do you do when you come home from soccer?"
» "What do you do if you're finished eating?"
» "What do we do before church on Sundays?"

There are hundreds of examples of things we say to our children that they already know. They know what they have to do but just don't want to do it or don't want to think about it. Asking them instead of telling them sends the message that we expect them to think and to already know.

Brainstorm Solutions

Asking our children to think about what to do develops their decision-making skills. That's one of our long-term goals. When our children are struggling with what to do or are doing the wrong thing, we can brainstorm possible solutions with them as an alternative to telling them what to do. Brainstorming solutions with our kids communicates respect for them and their growing capacity to think. It helps them understand that the problem is not the limits we set, but their struggle to live by those limits.

Brainstorming works best when we name their feelings and their struggles as part of the process. We can let them come up with their own ideas and solutions by allowing them to figure things out within our limits. Brainstorming with our children in the struggle allows us to join them in the struggle while keeping the limits firm. We can't change the limits, but we can help our child figure out what she can do.

> » "I'm sorry you can't play outside. What's a good thing to do when you're bored inside on a rainy day?"

> » "It is frustrating to share a room with your sister. What's a good thing to do if you're frustrated with your sister?"

> » "That is upsetting. What can you do if you both want to play with the same toy?"

> » "I'm sorry. What can you do if you're bored in church?"

When children are young, brainstorming consists of us identifying the various options. As they grow and have experienced brainstorming with us, they will know all the options on their own. When they're young, we suggest:

> » "You can read a book. You can color. You can play with your toys, or you can stay next to me."

> » "You can ask her nicely not to touch your things. Or you can remind her to ask you before taking something."

> » "You can take turns. You can play together with the toy. Or one of you can play with a different toy."
> » "You can follow along in the book. You can pay attention. It's hard to pay attention, but the more you do, the more interesting church is."

Children will still struggle even if we brainstorm with them. In the moment, they are overcome by their feelings and desires and just want what they want. It's hard to be stuck indoors on a rainy day. Brainstorming does not take that struggle away, and that's upsetting. That's their struggle. If they refuse to brainstorm, that is their choice. We just do our best to keep the limits firm, name their struggle, and let the limits do the teaching. They might refuse to brainstorm with us, or they might give bad answers.

> » "There is nothing fun to do!"
> » "She should just live with another family!"
> » "He should just play with another toy!"
> » "I don't know!"

When they give bad choices, we can ignore these answers and remain silent. We can name their struggle, or we can simply identify the consequences of these bad choices.

> » "It's a bummer when we want to play outside and it's raining."
> » "If you yell at your sister, you will lose the privilege of going out with your friends this evening."
> » "It's hard to share. If you can't figure this out, I'll have to take the toy away."
> » "The less you pay attention in church, the more boring it is."

◆ Respond to bad suggestions with silence, naming their struggle, or reminding them of the consequences.

Essentially, we want to attend to them in their struggle, not solve their problem for them. If they're too tired or upset to brainstorm, that's good information for us to have. We should respect that and allow them to work through their feelings. When our children are struggling, they're not really interested in our great suggestions, anyway. They are interested in knowing we understand, and they need us close by while they learn to figure things out on their own.

◆ Resist the temptation to solve your child's problem.

Our child's problem is not our problem to solve. Our goal is to be a peaceful presence and keep the limits firm as they figure out what to do. We can try to be patient while they figure out how to cope and what to do. Brainstorming while naming feelings and keeping limits firm sends the message that we care about them and they are capable of learning how to take care of themselves.

◆ Let children figure things out *for* themselves, but not *by* themselves.

Just like the way we help our children when they fall down, drawing close to our children but not solving their problems teaches them that we care and that they can figure things out. With clear expectations in place, we can get on their side and give our children the time and space to calm themselves down and make their choices. We set the limits and expectations and let them figure out how to live within them. No consequences needed yet.

Prepare Your Children Beforehand

The most difficult parenting situations typically happen over and over again. How many times are you going to go to the supermarket with your children? How many times do we need to get them up, dressed, and out the door or to bed? How many times do they have to clean up their room, or clean up after dinner, or get their homework done? The list of the repetitive challenges of parenting can seem endless. This can be either a frustration or an opportunity for intentional parenting.

Consider making a plan with your child for the perennial challenges you face. Making a plan before things happen invites children into the process of getting things done and learning how to behave. We set the limits concerning what needs to be done, but that does not mean we need to set them alone.

Taking time when things are calm to share your expectations in a discussion with your child creates a powerful connecting moment that invites a child to participate in the process of learning how to behave. They tune us out if they hear us constantly repeating ourselves. Going over the guidelines the night before a school morning, or on the way to school, the store, a restaurant, grandma's house, or church, invites our children to think for themselves about the limits we've set numerous times before.

"If you want to come shopping with me, what are the rules?" I ask my three boys (ages ten, eight, and five) each time on the way to the store.

"No running. No touching things. No asking for anything," they list once I get their attention.

"Stay next to you the whole time," Markos, the ten-year-old, adds.

"Got it?" I ask.

"Yes," they reply.

Other examples:

» "Remember what happened last time at Grandma's. What do you think we need to do this time?"

» "How do we behave in church?"

» "What's our plan tomorrow morning?"

» "You can go outside to play, but tell me the rules."

» "How are you going to treat the other students today?"

Children behave better when we've prepared them ahead of time. This encourages children to pay attention to their behavior. They will understand and attend to our expectations and feel connected to us. As we involve our kids in setting the limits, they will come to understand that these limits are not about us. They still won't like it, and they will struggle. In that struggle they will learn how to think and behave, and they will know their dad or mom cares and is close by.

Making a plan with our child and setting limits together allows us to ask questions or give gentle reminders rather than commands. If you have a plan for the tough times, you can use many of the tools from Chapter 9: describe what you see, say it with a word, describe how you feel, share information, and focus on the behaviors you want to see.

Preparing children beforehand does not eliminate misbe-haviors, but it maximizes learning and allows us to connect with our kids in the process. This is particularly true if we choose to follow up afterward on how things went.

Follow Up with Them Later

My temptation, after I go somewhere with my children, is to be frustrated with them on the way home because of their misbehavior and to make exasperated, meaningless statements.

> » "Why can't you guys sit still at a restaurant?"
> » "I'm never taking anyone shopping again."

Other parents are tempted to lecture or share their anger or disappointment.

> » "I can't believe how you behaved!"
> » "I've told you a hundred times we don't run around like that!"

The other temptation for parents is to react in the moment when children misbehave and then forget about it later. However, as we mentioned in Chapter 5, when things are calm is the best time to discuss their struggles. Learning happens when we talk calmly about their behaviors and struggles after the fact. On the way home is a great time to check in calmly about how things went at the restaurant, shopping, Grandma's house, or church.

> » "How did it go at the store?"
> » "How did we do at Grandma's?"

Beware of following up solely on misbehaviors. Try to focus on their efforts and their successes as well. Collaborating in this way connects us with our children as we teach and they learn. This nurtures in our children an awareness of their behaviors and our expectations and communicates that we are working with them as they learn.

Follow up at bedtime. Naturally, I don't want to bring up the struggles of the day at bedtime when I would rather have a nice, peaceful connecting time with my children. However, bedtime can be a valuable opportunity to reflect on the day in a calm environment. Be careful not to criticize or shame your child at bedtime. Rather, make an effort to comment on their good decisions and behaviors. Take the side of their feelings. Share your expectations. This is more effective at teaching than trying to give consequences in the heat of the moment.

"What happened today with your sister?" or "You had a hard time listening to Mom today?" you might ask at bedtime.

"I know it's hard to be patient with your sister/listen to your mother, but what would happen if nobody listened to anyone in this house?" you might say, after you listen to her.

If we want to teach children how to think, we have to invite them to think for themselves. Following up later, including at bedtime, is a great way to engage our children in thinking about their feelings and behaviors, the reasons for the limits we set, and our love and the expectations we have for them. It's a great time to explore the reasons for their misbehaviors (see Chapter 4). Many of the challenging behaviors happen repeatedly. It doesn't mean we have to keep giving the same instructions or increasing the consequences, but we do have to follow up later. Preparing children beforehand and following up afterward with the chronic problems creates a culture of respectful attentiveness and learning in the home.

The challenge of planning ahead and reflecting back is that usually, when we're rushing to get ready in the morning or on the way to the supermarket, we're thinking about all the things we need to do and how little time we have to do them. We get distracted with our worries and responsibilities and forget about our children—until they're making us late or running around the store. We also might be tempted to avoid bringing things up later because it is difficult to do and might create tension. It might seem too difficult, but it is a lot easier than constantly reacting in the moment and always telling them what to do. If we want to raise up children who think through their behaviors, we have to make time in our busy schedules to ask them about these things.

Collaborating with our children around limits requires us to pay attention to our children and to what we're teaching them before they misbehave and afterward. And it's the only way to reach our long-term goals.

"Where Do I Set the Limits?"

This is another common question I get that does not have a precise answer. In fact, effective parenting requires that we constantly ask ourselves this question. Each child struggles with different things and learns at a different pace. The art of parenting is attending to the ever-expanding, age-appropriate limits on an ongoing basis.

This is a chapter on *how* to set limits more than *where* to set them. Different parents have different ideas about appropriate limits. However, if we want our children to grow in the life in Christ, our limits should be set according to the values and virtues of the Kingdom of God. At a minimum, we must set limits around sinful conduct and sinful impulses such that a child grows to set these limits himself.

———

One must act in such a way that this attitude in the growing Christian will grow by itself, even though under the guidance of someone else, and that he will more and more become accustomed to prevail over sin and conquer it for the sake of pleasing God, and will grow accustomed to exercise his powers of spirit and body in such a way that they will work not for sin but for service to God.

Bishop Irenaius of Ekaterinburg,
On the Upbringing of Children

———

However, the appropriate choices, responsibilities, and autonomy a child is given depend on each parent and child. Age-appropriate limits are those that do not overwhelm our children emotionally or overtax their ability to make good choices. Listening to them through their struggles allows us to understand what they are struggling with and where to set appropriate limits.

⋘ Set the bar high and be patient as they learn to get over it.

Children will meet the expectations we set for them if we are patiently present with them in the process. As a parent, I know that my fear tells me to set very narrow limits on my child's behavior. It can feel like a very scary world, and our children will make mistakes. However, our fear, emotional intensity, criticism, or judgment undermines their capacity to learn. Our peaceful, listening presence will help them navigate and help us discern.

Patiently allowing children room to fail or misbehave while calmly setting limits communicates our expectations for good decision-making and respectful behavior. If we're too afraid to give them autonomy or too critical of them when they fail, how can we expect them to learn? Of course, all parents make mistakes, being either too strict or too lenient or sometimes both, but we can adjust. Children will make mistakes, and they will adjust. The goal is to do this together.

Giving children freedoms and responsibilities means having a stomach for failure. Some parents react to their children's failures by tightening the limits. "Look what happened the last time I let you have a little freedom," I hear parents say. Setting appropriate limits means giving your kids room to fail while you're close by. They cannot learn how to make good decisions if they are not free to fail. Failures or poor decisions on their part might mean you need to tighten the limits, but it might also be part of growing up and the only way for your child to develop good judgment.

Children Need Firm, Not Suffocating, Limits

Having a firm curfew is different from having a curfew that is too early or too late for your child. Being strict about the limits we set is good. Being overly restrictive is not.

◈ Children do best with firm, age-appropriate limits and responsibilities.

With broader limits and more choices come greater responsibilities. Some parents struggle to give children age-appropriate responsibilities. Children are capable of helping around the house, getting themselves up and fed in the morning, and taking care of themselves, starting at a very young age. While each child is different, children do best when parents have high expectations in terms of responsibilities as well as behaviors, but do not react when kids struggle or fail. Beware of having low expectations in terms of children taking responsibility for their own schoolwork, helping around the house, having a job, or caring for siblings. Our children will meet our expectations no matter where we set them, so set your expectations high, and stay calm as they struggle to meet those expectations.

Children Need Firm, Not Cold, Limits

Firm limits without attention to a child's struggle or feelings will feel like cold and uncaring limits. Too often, parents with firm limits do not attend to their child's feelings, and the parents who attend to feelings tend to have soft limits. Firm limits are most effective when we also attend to our child's feelings. Naming kids' struggles and naming their feelings, from Chapter 5, go hand in hand with setting firm limits. "I am so sad you can't have your lawnmower for the walk. It's hard to listen," I said after taking Markos's lawnmower away when he headed to the street.

It is disrespectful to ignore our kids' struggles or to rescue them from the struggle with low expectations and soft limits. Children will internalize a healthy, godly self-image and feel respected when they experience firm, age-appropriate limits and responsibilities from parents who empathize with their struggles. In this way, they learn that they are loved and they have to make good choices.

There are a variety of ways to set limits for and with our children beyond those I've mentioned. The limits we set and the way we set them create the framework within which our children can learn. They will learn as they struggle to live within these limits. We do not need to make them into adults. They will naturally become adults and acquire the values and virtues they see modeled in the adults around them as we create the framework for them to make their decisions, exercise their judgment, and grow.

Setting limits, however, does not stop children from misbehaving. We should not expect compliance, but pushback. Children need and desire firm limits, and they are wired to make sure our limits are not going to move. The only way to see if a boundary is firm is to push against it. The only way to teach our children that our limits are firm is by responding effectively when they push against them.

CHAPTER 11

Responding to Pushback

When the children are traumatized and hurt on account of some serious situation, don't let it affect you when they react negatively and speak rudely. In reality, they don't want to, but can't help themselves at difficult times. They are remorseful afterwards. But if you become irritated and enraged, you become one with the evil spirit and it makes a mockery of you all.

—St. Porphyrios, *Wounded by Love*

Pushback—when our children resist, argue, or protest our limits—is a child's way to make sure that our rules are firm. Like all their misbehavior, it's a normal part of childhood. We should expect it but not accept it. When our kids struggle with the limits we set, they don't need us to react, get angry, or give in. In the face of pushback, they need to know our boundaries are solid, and we love them even when they struggle. We should expect resistance and pushback and respond to it appropriately.

❧ Pushback is not a problem to solve. It's an important part of the learning process.

This past year we arrived home close to midnight from a Christmas party filled with food and sweets. We were all exhausted and wanted to go right to bed. However, everyone needed to brush teeth. Ordinarily I would not have set this limit, but I could practically see the candy still stuck to our son's teeth.

"I don't want to brush my teeth," said Alexios (seven years old) as I carried him to the bathroom.

Using everything I've discussed in this book, I replied, "You don't want to brush your teeth? I wish you didn't have to brush your teeth." I set him down, put toothpaste on the toothbrush, and, with a bit of struggle, brushed his teeth. He didn't like that very much. His exhaustion only strengthened his resistance. He screamed, and I brushed.

Not wanting to concede defeat, he continued to scream as I carried him to bed, put his pajamas on, and lay down next to him for a few minutes. When I left, Georgia took over. In the spirit of Christmas, his screaming echoed all through the house and stirred all creatures who were trying to go to sleep. Cuddling with his mother, he eventually tired out and fell asleep.

The next morning, Alexios woke up later than normal in a great mood. When I asked how it went going to bed so late last night, he replied nonchalantly, "Good," unaware of the drama and tension he created for the whole family. It's important to note that anger, lectures, or giving a consequence to an over-tired seven-year-old would not have made much sense.

It's easy to get overwhelmed, frustrated, upset, or stressed when children test our limits. It's easy to react when we feel like we have no other choice but to escalate conflict when our kids resist our instructions. The temptation is to look for a consequence to stop that behavior, or to "crush the resistance." But giving a consequence tends to escalate conflict between parents and kids.

"I've taken everything I can think of away from my son (eight years old), and he's still not listening," a desperate mother shared with me. Sometimes we imagine that there is a consequence that will stop our children from misbehaving or testing our limits. Parents quickly get stuck because we can't figure out good responses for our child's misbehavior. Then we resort to empty threats or piling on more consequences that we would never actually follow through on. If you can't think of a consequence to give, maybe you should not give one. Instead, respond with some of the different ways we'll talk about in this chapter.

Parents are tempted to think they must give a child a consequence when he pushes back or the child won't learn. "He can't just get away with that!" I hear. Actually, your child can still learn even if we don't give a consequence for every push-back. Or we might believe that it is wrong for children to push back. Kids should just do what we say, the first time, without complaining, arguing, or getting upset, right? While that's true, what's more accurate is that our children are learning to live within our limits. In order to learn, they are going to push back. We need to resist the temptation to react and be prepared to respond in a variety of ways that work toward our long-term goals.

❧ **Children don't always need a consequence, but they always need firm limits.**

We have too many interactions with our children to give a consequence each time they are struggling to do what we've asked them to do. What kind of consequence can we give for a child struggling to sit still in church or a restaurant? Should we threaten that if they don't sit still, they will have to go out? That's going to feel like a reward, and it is not always an option! Consequences might stop their misbehaviors in the short term while undermining our long-term goals. Sometimes we can't give a consequence, it won't help, or there is no good option for us to give. No amount of consequences will stop siblings from fighting. Parents need to use consequences, but it should not be the first or the only thing we do when our children misbehave, test our limits, or push back. In fact, the more skilled you become at using different tools to respond to pushback, the less you'll find yourself needing to come up with consequences.

✎ Giving consequences is not the first, or only, thing we do. But when children push back, it is the most tempting thing to do.

Strategies for Responding to Pushback
Check In
Before giving a consequence to pushback, we can ask ourselves why our child might be pushing back and address the underlying reason. This will stop us from instinctively reacting. Remember, no Wild West parenting: "Shoot first, ask questions later." Instead, you can ask a question.

» "What's going on?"
» "How come you guys are not emptying the dishwasher/ putting your clothes away?"
» "Did you guys hear what your mom just said?"

Checking in with them de-escalates the situation. We need to pay attention to why our child is misbehaving before we can figure out the best response. From my experience, most of the time they simply don't want to do what needs to be done. However, sometimes there might be something else going on. They could just be distracted. They could be distressed about something entirely unrelated. They could be really tired. In order to avoid reducing parenting to manipulating our kids' behavior, try to check in with them first, before you do anything else when they push back. If they simply don't want to do something, consider one of the following responses:

Do Nothing and Keep the Limits Firm

What we can do each time our child argues or resists our instructions is be clear with our words and firm with our expectations. Sometimes, firm limits are the only consequence we can and should give. We must set limits to their misbehaviors, and if your limits are firm, sometimes you might not need to give a consequence.

    ✥ **We exercise our authority as parents by keeping limits firm and taking the side of their feelings as much as by giving consequences.**

My children, like most, are great at taking toys and bikes out to play with but are still learning how to put things back when they're finished. They play until they're exhausted, and then the last thing they want to do is pick up their stuff. Because they need to clean up, we need to be firm about expecting them to. Because it's hard to do, we can expect pushback.

"Boys, bikes and baseball stuff need to go back in the shed,"

I directed them before dinner one Saturday. (I could have used other ways to communicate this from the previous chapter but decided on my default mode.) Naturally, they did not seem to hear me, walked right by me into the house, and dropped on the couch.

Then I set a limit: "Before you can eat dinner, everything needs to be back in the shed."

"We can't! I'm too tired! Why can't we do it later?" they cried out in protest.

Keeping our limits firm when children push back sends the message that we are paying attention to them and they are worth struggling for. Kids can tell we are serious when we remain resolute when they argue or resist us. They can tell we care and respect them when we remain calm and caring.

❧ We venerate our children by keeping our limits firm when we experience pushback.

When you keep the limits firm, you can let the limits do the teaching.

If we are unclear, inconsistent, or change our minds a lot, we should expect more pushback than if our children learn that when we speak, we mean what we say. If we are thoughtful about how we set limits, we have firmer ground to stand on when they push back than if we say things we don't really mean. If it's time to end the video game, then stick to it. Avoid giving them "just one more minute," "one more game," or "just one more try." This is when a five-minute warning is good to use.

To keep our limits firm, we need to remind ourselves that it is okay for our children to struggle and that it is worth our effort to stay strong in the face of pushback. They will struggle because they are learning, and having firm limits allows them a safe space to learn and grow. If we stay as peaceful as we can while we keep solid boundaries, our children will learn that we love them and we mean what we say.

❧ If we love our children, we will keep limits firm as they protest.

My children have gotten better at putting their bikes away because they know they always lose that battle. I still have to remind them. They still complain, and I still name their feelings. I don't always need to give them consequences for resisting, but I do always need to stay firm. That is the most loving thing I can do for them, because the more unwavering I am on that expectation, the sooner they'll learn that there is no use struggling. Resistance is futile. That's not mean; that's respectful. They need to learn to put their bikes and stuff away. I'm not always consistent, but the more consistent I am, the quicker they develop the discipline of being responsible for their things. If I resist the temptations to get upset, give in, or threaten consequences, they know I care for them, and they feel connected to me even as they "lose" and march out to put their bikes away.

———◆———

At the time of conflict, keep your mouth shut and act.

Rudolf Dreikurs, *Children: The Challenge*

———◆———

I try to have game night with my three boys (ages eleven, nine, and six) every Wednesday night. Although we don't spend as much time with each other as we'd like, being together every Wednesday night helps them know that they are a priority in my life. Inevitably, game night ends. Typically, it ends with a lot of whining and complaining that they don't want game night to end.

"Can't we play one more game?" Alexi (six) will predictably plead.

"Yeah," his brothers will join in, "one more game."

Because I'm not a perfect parent, and I want to play one more game, too, I will often concede a final game, but that just postpones the inevitable drama that ends each game night. I'm not as consistent as I want to be. Since they know I'm vulnerable to their pleadings, they are great at pushing back on my limits.

"I didn't get a turn. I want to play one more game!" George (age nine) will exclaim as he begins a meltdown.

I could give in, react ("Why do you guys always ruin the night by complaining?"), or try to control their feelings ("Why can't you guys be happy that we had such a nice evening?"). However, my job is not to make them happy at all costs in the short term, but to teach them how to attain happiness in the long term. I need them to learn how to manage their emotions and do the right thing. They'll be most happy in life if they learn those skills. We want to think long-term about them, not short-term about us. Following through my statements with actions is the only effective choice I have at that moment. I collect the game and escort each of them to bed.

Removing a child from a fight, walking a child to bed, taking your child by the hand to go clean up, physically removing him from the dinner table, turning off the television or video game, and taking away the iPod or toy are ways that teach our children that we mean what we say. Being as peaceful as possible while we do this communicates that we love them even though they struggle. That's unconditional love. It's not always possible for us to respond in this way, so when we can, we should use this option. This comes in handy when we need them to do what we say and we can't follow up physically.

✥ In the face of pushback, try to keep the limits firm.

Describe the Process

"Boys," I said one evening as they were resisting the end of game night, "Do you know how I can tell that game night is over?"

"How?" Markos asked through teary eyes.

"Because everyone is sad and upset. Have you noticed that it is always hard to end game night?"

Respectfully describing the struggles or the process that happens to our children allows them, over time, to understand the nature of life and struggle. It certainly does not stop them from struggling or get them to behave in the short term. But in the long term, they become more aware of their inner world and the nature of temptations. Now Markos (twelve) makes the same reflection whenever anyone struggles at the end of game night.

"Yup, it means game night is over," he said kindly with an insightful smile as his two younger brothers began to cry and complain while I collected the cards.

"Alexandra" (eight at the time), "do you notice that the more you play that computer game, the harder it is to stop? Do you notice how they designed those games to get you to keep coming back? Does it work?"

"Do you guys notice how hard it is to clean the kitchen right after dinner? It is even harder to leave the kitchen dirty and have to come back later to clean it up," I said at the end of dinner one night.

"Do you guys see how hard it is today to listen to Mom, be

patient with each other, and do your chores when we're all so tired after staying up so late last night?" I say to my kids all the time.

"I'm not crying because I'm tired!" George (age eight at the time) retorted, after melting down in tears for the fifth time before noon. "I'm crying because Markos is mean to me all the time."

He did not agree with me, because he cannot see what I see. He's eight. I'm trying to be patient, and he will remember my statements as he discovers, on his own, that it's hard to be patient when we're exhausted.

Helping children develop the ability to reflect on their inner struggles requires us, as parents, to take a moment to reflect on the patterns of misbehavior. We're modeling for them by taking a moment to reflect on when, why, and how they struggle and sharing this with them in a calm but clear way. Children do great in life and in spiritual struggles when they are aware of the process and equipped with the skills to succeed.

Walk Away

We need to give our children the time and space to pull themselves together as they learn to live within our limits. We don't need to react or reply to every comment, frustration, or difficulty they have. We stay in charge by staying in control and staying firm.

If we know we're going to stay firm and they know we're going to stay firm, we can be peaceful and allow them to blow off some steam as they struggle to do what has to be done. When they're upset, we should take their frustrations seriously, but not necessarily their words. Sometimes it's best just to ignore their words when they talk back or argue. Reacting, or even responding, to their pushback rewards their misbehavior with our connection and attention. We can follow up on their words later when things calm down. Walking away, when feasible, communicates that we are not going to waiver, we're not going to lose our cool, and we're not going to engage. Remaining peaceful when we walk away communicates that we are not withdrawing our love, just ourselves.

You can state what needs to be done. You can set a limit or simply state the rule, but then you just walk away.

» "There's no back talk in this house."

» "There's no yelling in this house."

» "Game night is over. It's bedtime."

» "It's not okay to leave your room a mess."

The more they know your limits are real, the less you need to engage in their drama. The less you engage, the fewer escalations you will have.

When your child does get it together and does what he needs to do, reward him with the powerful connection of a smile, a touch, a word—"Good job pulling yourself back together and doing what you needed to do"—without giving a consequence. Stay focused on effort or the virtues you are trying to instill. When children see that we are not mad at them for struggling, they learn that our love is unconditional and our expectations real. We'll talk in a moment about what to do if they follow you around with pushback.

Use the Full Parenting "Toolbox"

❧ Taking action and naming their struggle is usually more effective than giving a consequence.

Of all the parenting challenges I face, the toughest, and most chronic, is getting children to do their chores. They hate chores, as we all do, and it is always difficult to get my kids to clean their rooms, pick up their stuff, put things away, or do chores. They always resist, and we usually struggle.

"George" (age eight), "you need to empty the dishwasher," I will say to him right after breakfast.

He will, typically, either just ignore me or present me with a barrage of resistance: "Why do I always have to do it? Why me? It's not fair! Why can't Markos do it? I did it yesterday. Why do I have to do it now?!" He likes emptying the dishwasher almost as much as I like hearing him complain, whine, and resist.

Because there are so many different types of misbehaviors and situations, there are a variety of possible responses. Many of the strategies we discussed with setting limits in Chapters 9 and 10 are appropriate responses to back talk and pushback. We can learn to use these same strategies when we are faced with resistance, defiance, and noncompliance. While keeping the boundaries strong, we can name their struggles, take the side of their feelings, empathize with them, or share a wish.

» "It's hard to have to empty the dishwasher."

» "You don't think it's fair?"

» "I wish the dishwasher emptied itself."

We can prepare children ahead of time for chores by having a chart or making our expectations clear on a daily, or weekly, basis. We can follow up with them after they've finally completed the chore or at the end of the day. We can also simply describe the process.

» "George, did you notice that the hardest part of emptying the dishwasher is just getting started?"

» "George, was it hard to empty the dishwasher? I noticed it took you longer to complain about it than to actually do it."

Reinforce Positive Effort

❧ **Comment on any effort they make, even when it's not perfect.**

My children don't need a consequence for melting down at the end of game night. No need to take out the "hammer" for having a hard time emptying the dishwasher, although whining and pushback are annoying. They will learn more if I walk with them in their struggle and keep my resolve. I can ignore some of their drama but pay attention to their effort. If they act out and yell at me or hit, I need to set a limit or "take out the hammer" and give a consequence. It's respectful to comment on any effort you see them making to control themselves, their words or their actions, even if they're not perfect. They might be misbehaving, but they are also going through a battle and might be trying hard to keep things together. It's respectful to recognize their effort.

"Good job not swearing," I said to my daughter (twelve) as she stomped off and slammed her bedroom door. We were working on appropriate pushback, and she'd been battling to control her mouth. She did control her mouth, even though slamming the door was not appropriate. We don't need to expect perfect children, and I made a note to talk to her later about slamming doors.

Give Your Rationale Once

"Why do I have to?" "But why?" or simply "Why?" are common resistance statements.

Instead of "Because I said so," give your reasons one time, but only one time.

- » "Because if you don't go to bed, you'll be exhausted tomorrow."

» "Because eating dessert first will ruin your appetite."

» "Because we work before we play."

When you notice they really don't care why, try, "I'd be happy to tell you why after you do what I asked." This is a gentle but firm response that closes the door to noncompliance but keeps the door open if they really want to know what we're thinking. (See MacKensie, *Setting Limits to your Strong-Willed Child*.)

Giving reasons for the limits does not get children to like them, but it helps them to understand that the rules are not random or arbitrary. They do not have to agree with our rationale or our limits, only live by them. But telling them what we're thinking is respectful and encourages their thinking. We should only give our rationale once, because if they're asking more than once, they're not really interested in the rationale; they're just trying to resist the rules.

We might not have a good rationale for the limits we set. That's okay sometimes but not all the time. We are responsible to set limits that we are comfortable with, and we can't always explain that, but if setting limits is something we want our children to learn how to do, helping them understand them is essential. Reflecting on our limits and revising them teaches our children how adults make decisions. They see that we are not perfect, but we are responsible for the rules of the home.

These types of responses to pushback work best if children know that we are going to act and that our resolve is strong. When they know that we mean what we say and that we will act, these responses are effective in communicating respect and care for our children as they are learning and growing. We want to connect in a positive way with our children as we set limits, because we'll be setting a lot of them. The more they feel connected to us and respected by us, the more likely they are to model our lifestyles and adopt our values and virtues.

Give a Time-Out

Sometimes children misbehave because they are overstimulated and need some quiet time or downtime. They might be in a bad mood, upset, or just too worked up or excited to behave. I know that my kids fight more with each other when they are overtired, hungry, or have been spending a lot of time with each other. Having children play alone when they are fighting a lot or upset is an appropriate response. They don't need a consequence for that behavior; they just need someone to contain them a bit and a quiet place to pull themselves together.

✎ **Time out is not a consequence, just a good thing to do sometimes.**

Time-outs are most often misused as consequences by parents. We say things like, "If you don't stop, you're getting a time- out." A time-out is not a consequence, just a good idea. It is, in fact, exactly what a child might need at that moment, and we want our children to learn to give themselves a break when they need it. Sports teams don't take time-outs as punishment but as an opportunity to slow down, regroup, and make a plan for going forward. Of course, you might say that hockey players get a time-out as a consequence for misbehavior. It's not really a time-out, but time in a penalty box. The real consequence is that their team is playing a man down. Kids need time-outs when they cannot control themselves or their behaviors. In fact, taking a time-out is something we all need to learn to do when we feel out of control.

"Go take a two-minute time-out until you are ready to sit still/listen to what I'm asking/talk respectfully/treat your brother calmly/stop hitting." You get the idea. This approach works best when children are clear about the limits and are given a time-out until they're ready to live within them.

You will get frustrated if you use time-outs as a punishment, because time-outs don't stop children from misbehaving. They do help kids slow down, regroup, and prepare to get back in the game, no matter how many times they need it. Time-out chairs or corners should be quiet places with no entertainment, away from the action of the family, for a specified amount of time. It is not a punishment, although it might feel like it. It is a tool we want our children to learn to use on their own. We are not withdrawing our love but are teaching a child how to separate himself and pull himself together. It is our emotional reactions that communicate withdrawing love, not the time-out.

❧ Firm limits won't stop the misbehavior but will help children to learn.

Setting Limits to Pushback

We need to allow pushback and resistance but should set limits to excessive or inappropriate pushback. Children need to be free to feel but should not be free to act out in destructive ways. We should allow them to struggle but not to swear, hit, or throw things, for example. Giving our children room to struggle is respectful to them, and setting limits to the amount and type of pushback we receive is an important part of their learning.

We should be patient with our children, but we can only endure so much of their struggle, and we do not have to be around them when they're in this state. Put a stop to the pushback when you start to feel yourself getting worn down, frustrated, disoriented, or weak. Remember what we said in Chapter 3: Set a limit before you get angry. Children should be free to struggle, but they are not free to wear you down or disturb the peace of the whole home.

We don't withdraw our love when we cannot endure any more, because our love is not dependent on their behaviors. They need to know that we love them unconditionally, which means we need to do our best to respond, not react, when a situation gets to this point.

Once the pushback becomes excessive or inappropriate, the parenting issue has now changed from the original misbehavior to their reactions to our rules. It is appropriate to give a consequence for inappropriate pushback. However, before you give a consequence, consider some of the other options you have. Restrict the pushback by naming their struggle and stating the limit:

> » "I understand you're upset, but it's not okay to use those words."
> » "It's okay to be upset, but it's not okay to talk to me like that/behave like that."
> » "I know you're upset, but you need to go to your room until you're ready to speak respectfully."

We can describe what we see, say it with a word, describe how we feel, or share information:

> » "We don't talk like that."
> » "That's backtalk."
> » "It's rude to speak like that."
> » "I'm sad you're speaking like that."
> » "If you don't clean your room, you'll never be able to find anything."

Naming their struggle or describing what we see can deescalate the situation. That's a good practice. Sometimes, however, the situation has already escalated, and we need to set a limit by removing the child from the scene:

> » "Either pull yourself together, or go to your room to calm yourself down."
> » "If you want to scream, you can scream in your room."

Naturally, saying these types of things to an upset child is not going to be effective at calming him down or getting compliance. However, if we're calm about it, and because it happens often, our children will internalize our inner state and our words, and this works toward our long-term goals.

If your child does not respect the limits you set with your words or follows you around when you've established a clear boundary, disengage or disconnect from your child. Cutting off your communication and ignoring your child essentially disengages you from the conversation and cuts off the connection that they feed on. Before you do that, be clear that this is what you are doing, and be clear about what the child needs to do to re-engage with you.

> » "When you do what I ask, I will speak to you again."
> » "When you are done speaking to me with that tone of voice, we can talk about your concerns."

You follow through with this statement by shifting your focus and attention off your child and onto the other tasks you need to do. Your child's behavior might escalate, and you can give a consequence for that, but it is appropriate to ignore your child until he is calm. You might reinforce this limit to the pushback by sharing a wish or naming his struggle:

> » "I wish you were calm enough, because I'd love to talk to you."
> » "I know it's hard to listen to what I said," while remaining detached.

Resist even making eye contact. The more your child knows that this is a firm limit, the more he will become frustrated that he cannot control you, and the more quickly he will learn that the pathway to connecting with you is listening to your instructions. It is appropriate to remove yourself from his presence, if this is feasible. The more peaceful you can be, the more your child learns that your love is unconditional and his behavior is unacceptable.

Consequences are necessary for responding to inappropriate pushback, but before we talk about giving consequences, we need to be aware of three of the most common ways children push back and how to respond.

Avoid the "Trust" Trap

As children grow they desire and deserve more autonomy. In fact, they demand more autonomy, and one common pushback to our limits is, "Why don't you trust me?" Parents can get caught in that trap by saying "We don't trust you," "We want to trust you," "We've lost our trust in you," or, "Yes, we trust you." Often parents will tell children they need to earn our trust. It is never clear and always a mistake to identify what it takes to earn our trust.

It is a trap to talk in terms of trust, because it is disrespectful to tell a child we don't trust him to make good decisions, and it's a mistake to trust him to make good decisions all the time. It shifts the focus from our child's behavior to our feelings as parents. That's a mistake. They don't need to earn our trust. In fact, we should trust a ten-year-old to act like a ten-year-old and a sixteen-year-old to act like a sixteen-year-old. They will make good and bad decisions. Either way, the trust discussion is bad, because we are either giving our children a vote of no confidence or giving them no room to make mistakes. Talking about trust ignores the fact that they are learning, and they learn best with age-appropriate limits and supervision.

Imagine if the police officer told you, "I'm going to trust

that you will go the speed limit the rest of your drive." Essentially, he's telling you that he will not be watching you. That would make it harder for a speedy driver to control himself. It would be rude for the police officer to say he does not trust you. A good police officer needs to let us drive within the speed limit and should give us a ticket if we speed. The issue is not really trust. It's being clear about the rules and consequences and supervising properly.

Children need to be respected rather than trusted. We should respect our children by putting in place a system for them to develop good judgment: age-appropriate responsibilities, clear rules and consequences, and proper supervision.

The best way to answer a child's challenge about trust is to say something like, "This has nothing to do with trust. This has to do with respect. You need to respect these guidelines, and I need to respect your ability to make good decisions within these guidelines."

"No One Else Has These Limits!"

Setting limits can be tough to do when your child complains that you are stricter than every other parent. Strict parents have no trouble dismissing this challenge by stating, "I don't care what your friends do; these are my rules." That's good in terms of keeping your limits firm, but we can respond to this charge with empathy *and* firm limits. How about:

"I'm sorry I'm the strictest parent. I know that's hard. These are our rules."

We can also challenge them on this. The fact is, while families do have different rules, most families require children to listen, do chores, treat each other respectfully, and do homework before television. They monitor kids' movies and music and have curfews. And most kids make this same claim to their parents. We could point out that our rules are reasonable and other families have similar expectations, but children are not interested in these facts. They're struggling to live within our rules.

However, there is typically some truth to this claim. Different parents set different boundaries with their children. Some parents are less strict about their kids' activities than we might be or supervise their children less than we do. Most children can point to one friend who has more toys and technology and less supervision. Many families do not make their kids get up for church or even sit down for dinner together, and some parents permit practices that we are not comfortable with. This can be difficult for our children, and we can empathize with that struggle.

It is respectful to identify the rationale for our rules and our chosen lifestyle to growing children. If we want our children to internalize the values and virtues of the Kingdom of God, it is important that they have contact with other families and have friends from families who share our values and vision of family life. This goes a long way toward helping our children understand that our rules are more than just about the will of their parents.

"I Hate You!"

Technically, hate is a feeling, and children should be free to feel hate, because they cannot control their feelings. However, it's easy for parents to be very hurt when kids yell this in anger.

In much the same way, statements like, "You're mean!" "You're the worst mother!" "This is the worst family on the planet!" or "I hate this family!" are reactive, angry statements children will hurl at us. When these types of comments hook us, we react with angry punishments or statements like:

» "That's it. You lose your (fill in the blank)!"

> » "You don't talk to your mother like that!"
> » "How dare you talk like that!"

I have found that the best response to these painful statements is to ignore them in the moment and bring them up later when things are calm. We should take our kids' frustrations seriously, but if we allow ourselves to react to these childish, angry statements, we give them more credence than they deserve. It is not okay for children to talk to parents like this, but reacting in the moment is not the best way to teach.

It's also not okay to let this statement go without following up later. But we want to keep our focus on the person of our child rather than her crazy actions and words. Make sure to gently check in with your child when things are calm and ask what she was feeling or thinking when she said those things.

> » "What happened today when you said that you hate me? What's wrong?"
> » "What should you do when you're that upset?"
> » "We don't talk like that."

When things are calm it is very effective to name her struggles, remind her how we speak in the home, and share how sad you felt when hearing those things. We need to remember that she doesn't really mean them. Teach your child, in a quiet moment, to apologize for those things. This will help her learn how to struggle without saying hurtful things the next time she gets upset.

Remember, responding with kindness is the best way to prove to a child that you are not the meanest parent in the world. It's harder to make that case if you react negatively. You might be the meanest mother in the house, but you're not likely the meanest mother in the world! You also happen to be the kindest, most respectful, most understanding, and most loving mother in the house.

The Final Straw

In the heat of the moment, our children are not likely to care what limits we set and are not likely to be able to control their words and actions. When they, predictably, cross the line we've established with excessive pushback, it's time to take out the "hammer" of consequences.

If we allow our children to talk or behave rudely to us, they will talk and behave rudely to others. In the moment, if they continue to escalate, we need to set the limit. If they cross that limit, then we issue a consequence.

In the home children learn how to behave. In fact, the home is specifically where they will learn what to do when they are having a hard time, if we use their struggles to teach them. Giving consequences for inappropriate actions and words while allowing kids the freedom to struggle and push back teaches them how to control themselves, even when they're upset.

In fact, I have found that unless children experience consequences for their misbehaviors, they will not learn how firm the limits are or how to stay within them. When we respond with consequences instead of reacting, they learn that we love them unconditionally and that their choices have repercussions. The effective use of consequences, when the time is right, allows all the other alternatives that we've discussed so far to be effective. Without the real threat of a consequence, all the strategies I've presented, such as checking in with a child, describing what we see, or sharing a wish, are less effective.

CHAPTER 12

Understanding Consequences

And you, fathers, do not provoke your children to wrath, but bring them up in the training and admonition of the Lord. (Ephesians 6:4)

WHAT CAN I DO TO STOP MY CHILD'S MISBEHAVIORS?" This is the most common question I get from parents and the reason some people might read this chapter first.

When children misbehave, most parents look first for a consequence, something they can do to their child so he does not misbehave again. However, consequences should be our last resort. They work best when they are used as a deterrent to kids' bad choices rather than as a punishment once they've already made a bad choice.

Consequences work best when they are used to reinforce the limits rather than to stop kids from misbehaving. We want our children to develop good judgment and learn to live the path of life in Christ. Consequences alone cannot do this.

Keep Limits Firm by Giving Consequences

Speeding tickets do not teach people how to drive, and consequences are not enough to teach our children how to succeed. Because it's so easy to focus on stopping bad behavior instead of teaching life skills, it is easy to misuse or overuse them.

Consequences serve to maintain the firm limits around behaviors, but they are ineffective if they are the primary way we interact with our children. Parenting is not about manipulating our children to behave a certain way; it is about taking a real interest in our children within a clear framework of expectations and choices. Our consequences need to be part of a bigger process of how we set boundaries to our kids' behaviors throughout the day and part of a deep relationship of love and caring with our children. Firm limits and consequences make for happy children only when they feel their parents really care for and respect them. If our children don't feel connected to us or respected by us, the same consequences can seem mean and uncaring. If your relationship with your child is strong, a look or a word is enough, and consequences are hardly needed.

However, consequences are a critical part of parenting, because they are essential for setting clear expectations and teaching self-control and good decision-making. The sooner children learn that there will be negative outcomes for bad decisions and positive results or rewards for good decisions and that we love them independent of their choices, the quicker they will learn to make better choices. Giving consequences should not be the first thing we do—which is why this is Chapter 12 and not Chapter 1—but they are an essential part of teaching.

❧ Consequences are not meant to stop bad behavior but to teach that our limits are firm.

By Chapter 12 it should be clear that it's not our goal to get children to behave. The only thing we can do is to help them learn from their misbehaviors. It is hard for children to live within our rules. They have to give up doing what they want and resist the powerful urge to act on their impulses and desires. If our kids don't experience any negative consequences for crossing our limits, they will have little incentive to stay within those limits. But if children think we love them only if they make the right choices, that is destructive. Consequences provide the incentive to stay within the boundaries or, rather, a disincentive to step outside them. In this way, giving consequences helps our children learn to control themselves. Kids need firm limits, not just consequences; but consequences teach them that the limits are firm.

Consequences are like the United States military. It is good to have it, and it is best to have the strongest military in the world, but military force can only do so much. If it is used recklessly, without diplomacy and negotiation, a military response can cause more problems than it solves. However, the fear of military action can help nations negotiate non-military solutions. In the same way, consequences work best when the very fear of them helps children stay within the boundaries. Our job is to teach our children to live within the limits, not just to hand out consequences when we don't like what we see.

❧ If we love our children, we will keep limits firm and issue consequences consistently.

The more consistent we are with consequences, the more effective they are in teaching our children. If, however, consequences are unclear or arbitrary, or there is a fifty–fifty chance that there will be no consequence, our children might choose to play those odds and indulge their desires.

Why do people play slot machines, even though most of the time there is a negative consequence? Because there is a remote chance of a positive reward. If you knew that a slot machine never paid out, you would be less tempted to play. The more consistent we are at giving children consequences, the more quickly they learn that their misbehaviors are a bad bet.

✥ Consequences are not meant just to stop bad behavior but to teach about life.

Life is filled with payback for both good decisions and bad decisions. There's no escaping this fact. If life is about choices and their aftermath, so is our parenting. Typically, the best choices in the long term are the hardest choices in the short term. It's always easier to act out, react, or indulge our desires and impulses in the short term than to control ourselves and do what is right and good for the long term.

At the heart of the spiritual life is learning to make the hard choice in the short term—to deny ourselves, take up our cross, and follow Christ—so that we will experience joy, life, and love over the long term. In a fallen world, we are inclined toward sin. We can't change that fact of life. God invites us to turn away from serving ourselves and our desires and to turn toward Him as the path of life. The Christian life is an invitation to follow Him and His ways and experience life.

———◆———

"If anyone desires to come after Me, let him deny himself, and take up his cross, and follow Me." *(Matthew 16:24)*

⤳ **The Art of Parenting:** Helping our children to deny their impulses and desires in the short term to experience the joy that comes from choosing the path of life in the long term.

The struggles our children face are the basic battles they will face in living lives of righteousness. Many of our parenting challenges can be boiled down to this process: Getting up in the morning when we don't want to. Sharing our toys when we don't want to. Drawing on paper when we want to draw on the wall. Coming in for dinner when we want to play. Going to bed when we want to stay up. Waiting until after dinner when we want a cookie right now.

If we love our children, we will prepare them to succeed in this journey by putting in place a system that makes it easy for them to learn to make good choices. We do that by having clear and firm limits, with clear and consistent consequences. Kids will learn that our love is unconditional as we learn to respond with consequences rather than react to their misbehavior.

⤳ If we love our children, we take the side of their feelings as we give consequences to behaviors.

Confessions of a Difficult Child

At this time in the book, I can share with you that I was what could be called a difficult child. I was disruptive, non-compliant, and impulsive. I would talk back, sneak around, and rarely sit still. Maybe this book should be called *Raising Philip: Lessons from a Difficult Child*. My teachers and my poor mother tried to contain my behavior as best they could. I don't remember being difficult, but I remember seeing what difficulties my teachers and parents had in dealing with me. Children are typically unaware of their own difficulties but very aware of the emotional state of the adults around them.

What I remember is that I was not difficult all the time. There were adults, I noticed, who seemed to draw out of me my good judgment, self-control, and responsibility. I remember that I enjoyed taking on big responsibilities at a young age, caring for my younger siblings, helping teachers, and earning my own money. I noticed that when I was given responsibilities, I thrived.

I remember regularly getting in trouble in the sixth grade and being sent down to the principal's office for disrupting class, talking out of turn, or not sitting in my seat. There I would spend a few hours quietly talking with the secretary, who smiled at me. With the secretary I was calm, did what I was told, sat quietly, and helped out like a mature, responsible child. Even the principal was nice after giving me a gentle smile and a look that said, "Philip, what did you do this time?" I also felt better about myself when I was in that quiet environment, talked to respectfully, and given age-appropriate responsibilities.

When teachers reacted to my misbehaviors, I felt like they didn't like me, and I started to believe what some of them told me: that I was a disruptive, difficult child. But in the principal's office, I connected with the secretary. She thought I was mature and responsible. How could I be the same boy in those two situations?

Essentially, the principal's office was a positive connecting experience. It was much better than being in the stale afternoon air of the classroom, bored and disconnected from the other twenty-five students, waiting until everyone learned what I had learned the first time it was explained. I loved going to the principal's office, and it felt like a treat or privilege. I remember being a little confused. I couldn't understand how the principal's office was considered a bad thing. It was much more interesting than the boring classroom. I would return to class feeling calm, connected, and engaged.

I didn't understand my own behavior when I was in sixth grade, and I certainly could not control myself. It did not seem fair that I was a "bad kid" because I had a harder time sitting still than the nice, quiet girls in class. And it was confusing, because I was not a "bad kid" in the principal's office. I was neither a good boy nor a bad boy. I was a person, and this is how I functioned. If you wanted compliance from me, you wouldn't try to force me to sit but instead would recognize what I needed to thrive and provide it for me. Lectures, anger, and threats never worked. They confused and excited me, because I perceived them as negative and as a challenge to face. No amount of consequences could get me to sit quietly and focus when I was bored and distracted. Engaging me could, though. You can imagine how many teachers I drove crazy.

As a parent, I have learned that when children are bored and feeling disconnected, they have a hard time sitting still and controlling their behavior. When they are engaged in what they're doing and feel connected, they can sit still and stay on task. Engaging our kids invites compliance and enables them to thrive and experience success in a way that giving consequences cannot do. I remember learning best on my own as

I experienced the adults in charge being on my side, smiling, encouraging me, and letting me use my natural but unrefined talents. I desired to follow the guidelines and instructions of adults who seemed to delight in both my strengths and my shortcomings, who kept limits firm but never got mad at me for struggling.

Parenting is about setting up the conditions for our children to thrive. They need to feel connected to us. They need to know we care and that we take an interest in who they are, what they're learning, and why they're misbehaving. And they need to be contained, calmly, with real limits to behaviors and effective consequences.

Some parents might fear the damaging effects of consequences on their children. Getting angry, reacting, withdrawing love, or indulging our kids can damage them. Learning to respond by connecting with our children before, during, and after consequences teaches them that our love is unconditional and that their choices matter. There are a number of different ways to give consequences. Like setting limits, it is a critical parenting skill that can be learned.

Natural Consequences

Natural consequences are the results that children can experience without requiring us, as parents, to do anything. Our goal is to have our children learn, but we don't always have to be the ones teaching them. Sometimes all we have to do is let the teaching happen.

Good natural consequences are things that happen to our children through their own decisions that are not so devastating that they damage them, but are difficult enough to cause our children to think. Whenever possible, we should allow for natural consequences instead of giving instructions or directions.

» "Put a jacket on. It's cold outside."

» "Come in and go to the bathroom."

» "Eat dinner now, or you'll be hungry later."

These are all reasonable statements, but they are also things that children can learn naturally without us telling them what to do. Never make decisions for your children or tell them what to do when they can figure things out by themselves. Letting children experience the effects of their decisions respects their intelligence, their ability to learn, and their developing judgment and autonomy. Kids learn better from first-hand experience than from our telling them what to do, anyway.

❧ Set limits to your own behaviors so your children can learn to set limits to theirs.

We don't need to be mean or angry. We just need to set limits for ourselves, step back, and as much as possible, let our children make decisions. You could force your child to put a coat on, or you could force yourself not to intervene and allow your child to learn by herself when she needs to put a coat on.

The natural consequences need to be acceptable to us and immediate for children. Allowing them not to brush their teeth because it's hard to do at night will result in rotted teeth, which is a natural consequence. However, a five-year-old will not make that connection until it is much too late. On the other hand, there is little harm in letting your five-year-old learn what happens when you go outside without a coat or wait too long to go to the bathroom. If your child does not want to wear a jacket when you're going to be away from the house, however, it is best to require him to bring one along, even if he doesn't put it on. That way, he can choose to put it on when he gets cold.

Decide what you will do instead of what you will make your child do.

Jane Nelsen, *Positive Discipline*

———◦—◦———

We need to resist the temptation to rescue our children from the repercussions of their decisions. If a child decides not to eat dinner, we don't need to give a consequence. The natural consequence is going to bed hungry. You could force your child to eat (good luck) or force yourself not to give in when they're hungry after dinner (difficult, but possible). If we give a child a snack after dinner, we are blocking a natural result, and our child will learn that there is no fallout for skipping dinner. If we love our children and want them to learn to eat at dinnertime, we should set the rule, "The kitchen closes after dinner," and allow them to experience the consequence of not eating. Set a limit for yourself and do not give any snacks after mealtimes. Children won't die from going to bed hungry, once. If our limits are firm, they will learn not to make that choice again.

Natural consequences should not harm our children. If the worst thing that can happen is that our child gets cold, that's appropriate. When we can deal with the result, we should allow them to experience it. If a child is sick and wants to play out in the cold, we should say no, because the natural result could be more than we are prepared to deal with.

Because we have to set so many limits for our children, we should look for opportunities to let nature set the consequence, just like letting our kids get up on their own when they fall. This helps them learn and allows us to join them as they struggle with the aftermath of their own decisions.

» "It's hard to have to come in when we have to go to the bathroom."

» "It's no fun playing outside when we're freezing."

» "I don't like going to bed hungry either."

These are all empathic statements that support the child as he makes his own decisions.

Effective consequences are intended to allow children to learn, on their own, that good choices lead to good outcomes and bad choices lead to bad outcomes, not whether they are good kids or bad kids or whether their parents like them or not. We want our children to develop a sense that they have control over outcomes based on their decisions, and we like them and are on their side no matter what they choose.

Natural consequences are at the heart of the spiritual life. God is always on our side, present and desiring to draw us close to Him. He allows us the freedom to choose to walk in His ways or to choose to follow our own desires. There are natural consequences for choosing to turn toward or away from Him. He loves us deeply no matter what we choose. He is not punishing us or rewarding us, loving us or hating us; He is simply revealing Himself to us, showing the way, allowing us to choose, and staying close to us through the process.

Logical Consequences

When there are no appropriate natural consequences, we must choose to give consequences ourselves. Children don't need to be punished for their bad choices, but they need to learn that all choices have ramifications, good or bad. Good consequences are meant to teach, not just cause pain.

✎ Logical consequences are related, respectful, reasonable, and revealed in advance.

Dr. Jane Nelsen, author of *Positive Discipline*, identifies what she calls "the Four Rs for Logical Consequences." In order to be effective, logical consequences must be related, respectful, reasonable, and revealed in advance.

Related

"You're not going to your friend's birthday party!" one mom declared after her five-year-old hit a sibling. Why would a child lose a birthday party because of a sibling fight? If your child is unable to get along with a sibling, it makes more sense to say, "If you cannot play nicely together, you need to play alone."

"If you don't sit still at the table, you're going to go to bed early," we might be tempted to say. What, however, is the connection between the sitting at the table and sleep? Going to bed early is a logical consequence if we see our child is overtired. Plus, if your child is tired, putting her to bed earlier is not a consequence; it's just a smart thing to do.

When there is no connection between the misbehavior and the consequence, it is probably a reaction, not a response, to the child's actions.

"If you talk back, I'm taking your video games away!" we might threaten. What's the connection? It seems like a punishment that is intended to cause pain, not teach. It's easy to pile on consequences or try to figure out the most painful consequence we can think of just to get our children to submit. This invites resentment and defiance from our children and creates an atmosphere of "us against them." "If you cannot turn off the video game when I call you, I will take the video game away." That makes sense. Look back at Chapter 11 for responding to back talk.

"So? I didn't want that anyway," or "I don't care if you take that away," our child might say, because he doesn't want us to "win" by letting us know that it hurts. The more we try to get her to submit, the more she increases her resistance and defiance. Our children can tell when our reactions are intended to hurt them, and that's confusing. Children learn not to tell us what they like or what's meaningful for fear that we will just take it away. Plus, we end up in situations where we've taken everything away and now have an angry and non-compliant child. That's not working together toward the Kingdom.

Respectful

When a child draws on a wall, the logical consequence is to have the child clean up the wall and lose use of the markers. They don't need to be criticized, disrespected, humiliated, or hurt. Getting mad disrespects the fact that your child just made a choice. We should respect that choice by issuing a consequence, not getting upset, frustrated, or even disappointed, although such behavior is often upsetting, frustrating, and disappointing. But that's our struggle, not theirs. The consequence will teach the child to make a better choice, eventually. We don't need to drive home the point with emotional intensity but give the consequence in a firm and respectful way. Our anger or frustration will communicate that we don't like our child or that he is bad. Our children are practicing their decision-making, and, while they might have made a bad choice, the choice is theirs, and we need to respect it by following through with the consequence rather than reacting with our emotions.

Naturally, avoid helping your child clean the wall or making it a fun cleaning project. That rewards your child with connection and will encourage him or her to draw on the wall again. Leave the child alone with the cleaning supplies, to struggle to clean the wall. It should be difficult and boring. Keeping permanent markers out of their reach is also a good idea.

"It's too hard to clean," my four-year-old, Alexios,

protested as he scrubbed the pencil marks off the wall. "It's hard to clean a wall," I affirmed. "Boys who draw on walls need to clean walls." I kept my distance and allowed him to struggle. We can still take the side of their feelings as we keep the consequence in place. We need to be strict but not heartless. The wall was, eventually, clean, and he has never drawn on it again. If he did, he would be cleaning it again. I would try not to get mad or make him do other chores, just clean it again. That is one reason I don't write on walls. I don't want to have to clean the mess. Children don't need us to get upset and react. They need to experience the results of crossing our boundaries. Respectful consequences allow each misbehavior to be a difficult but positive learning experience, not a negative one.

Reasonable

When you give a consequence, make sure the punishment fits the crime. While punishment is not what we're doing, and we're not talking about crimes, you get the idea.

"If you don't clean your room, you're not going on the camping trip this weekend," we might cry out in desperation. Really? Beware of cruel and unusual punishments. We don't give consequences just to inflict pain, although consequences can be painful. Avoid consequences that are too severe, extreme, simple, or painless. My kids typically forget to put their bikes away when they're finished biking. Losing a bike for a week might be severe for failing to put a bike away. Nagging kids to put their bikes away is tiring. Not being able to sit down for dinner until all the bikes are away seems reasonable.

A logical consequence to a dirty room might be not playing outside. However, if your child has a soccer game, it might be excessive to pull him or her from the team because of a dirty room, no matter how frustrated we are that the room is a mess.

"If you can't sit still at the table, there will be no movie tonight!" This threat seems to be intended to give a painful consequence. However, what is the connection between dinner and watching a movie? It makes more sense to say, "If you cannot sit still at the table, you can sit in a time-out or eat after everyone else is finished." No after-dinner activities, such as a movie, until the kitchen is clean seems reasonable.

Instead of looking for the most painful consequence because we're overwhelmed or frustrated, consider a reasonable consequence. We need to patiently allow for time and repetition to do the teaching.

Effective consequences are respectful and reasonable. If a child fails to brush his teeth at bedtime, rather than getting angry or taking away a play date the next day, your child might lose part of the bedtime routine, like a story. If your child refuses to wear a bike helmet, he should not lose dessert or a play date, just the privilege of riding the bike.

Revealed ahead of Time
This is a key difference between a reaction and a response to a child's misbehavior. If we really want to teach a child how to make good choices, they need to know the consequences of their choices before they choose. Roads have posted speed limits. In fact, we all feel a sense of outrage or injustice if we are pulled over for speeding when there are no posted speed limits.

Markos, eight at the time, was walking through the house dribbling his basketball. "Markos, no dribbling in the house," I said. He stopped for almost a minute and then continued dribbling. I could take the ball away, which is a logical consequence. However, if I want him to learn to make choices, I should inform him ahead of time about the consequences for that behavior.

"If you dribble in the house, I will take the ball away." At this point, the criteria for a logical consequence are in place. Now, it's my job to follow through, respectfully and peacefully, each time he dribbles the ball in the house. I don't need to get angry, withdraw my love, or even give him another chance. I never need to say another thing. In fact, the less I say and the more I simply respond with the consequence, the more quickly he will learn that I love him unconditionally and that balls are bounced outside.

CHAPTER 13

Giving Consequences

It is better to pray devoutly for your neighbor than to rebuke him every time he sins.

—St. Mark the Ascetic, "On the Spiritual Law: Two Hundred Texts" in *The Philokalia*

W E DON'T NEED TO REACT TO MISBEHAVIORS or react when our children push back on our limits, but we need to respond by giving consequences when necessary. Sometimes I struggle, as a dad, with giving too many warnings before I act, and sometimes I give consequences too quickly. Our goal is not to be perfect, but we can continue to improve our parenting skills.

✺ Say it once. Say it a second time with a consequence. Give the consequence.

If your child doesn't put away her bike, she shouldn't lose the privilege of going to her friend's house. Instead, she will lose her bike, and she should know that before she takes her bike out to play. She might still be allowed to go to her friend's house, but she'll have to walk there. Or maybe she just needs to put her bike away before she can go. Or, she might lose a visit to her friend's house if her chores are not done. That makes more sense. Work before play.

Tightening the Limits as a Logical Consequence

If your child is mishandling or misusing a privilege or a responsibility, he might not need a specific consequence, just a tightening up of the limits of his freedom and choices. Tightening the limits is not so much a consequence but an act of respect and is more effective than punishing a child.

"If you can't play outside nicely together, you need to come inside." They don't need to lose dessert or go to bed early. They might just be too tired to keep playing nicely and need to be contained a little bit with some quiet time.

If your child watches TV or uses technology before doing homework, losing the technology is a logical consequence. She knows this ahead of time, and you respond respectfully. If your child continues to struggle with this limit, it might be best to prohibit technology on the weekdays and make screens available only for a certain amount of time on the weekends. Your child might not have the self-control yet to stay off the video games if they are accessible. Tightening the limits might be better than giving a consequence, and it is certainly better than repeating ourselves or getting mad.

Asking for Forgiveness as a Logical Consequence

"And the glory which You gave Me I have given them, that they may be one just as We are one." (John 17:22)

At the heart of the Christian gospel is God's radical love for each of us. He is a just and loving God, and His justice is expressed by His radical love. He is not looking to punish us into submission but to draw us close to Him through love. At the heart of His love is His overwhelming forgiveness of us. His forgiveness is unending and unconditional and in many ways is hard for us as humans to understand. How can God forgive those who persecute Him? He is the Father of the prodigal son who waits, longing for his son to return. Notice how the father in the parable allows his son to suffer the natural consequences of his decisions, though. He does not look to give the prodigal son a consequence when he returns but welcomes him back. We'll talk more about the centrality of forgiveness in parenting and in our homes in Chapters 16–18, but for now, I want to mention that giving our children the path back by teaching them forgiveness is often the only consequence necessary.

When Markos, age five, returned after being removed from the dinner table, Georgia simply said, "Please ask your sister for forgiveness for taking her food."

We might be tempted to think we need to punish a child for every transgression, but if we consider that our goal is to help our child learn the right way, if he asks for forgiveness, we've accomplished our goal. No more consequences are necessary to teach. Asking forgiveness is humbling and very difficult. Admitting I am wrong is a type of consequence. It does not feel good but leads to good. Teach and encourage this as often as possible, and beware of adding additional consequences once a child has taken responsibility.

Beware of Overusing Logical Consequences

Logical consequences are effective teaching responses to children, but beware of overusing this good tool. Our goal is not to be great manipulators of their behaviors, but parents who teach and love their children. Before you give a logical consequence, consider why your child is misbehaving, and think about the variety of other responses from earlier chapters in this book. It might be a logical consequence to lose dessert if your child can't sit quietly until everyone finishes dinner. But before you give that consequence, you might consider checking in with your child and realize that asking a five- to fifteen-year-old boy to sit quietly listening to boring adult conversation is a tall order. It might be more effective to engage the children at the table in the conversation as you require them to sit still.

⫸ Don't "up the ante" if it happens again. Allow time and repetition to teach.

It's tempting to look for more intense consequences when our children repeat the same misbehaviors so that "he never does that again!" Parents need to resist the temptation of adding onto these consequences with a lecture, a lesson, or emotional intensity. Logical consequences work well when we implement them consistently as often as needed. No matter how many times Markos dribbles the ball in the house, simply taking it away each time is better than upping the ante after a few times with anger or more punishments. Children learn best from logical and natural consequences when we issue them the same way each time. They will learn, over time, that it is not worth it to disobey. More importantly, they will learn that we love and respect them. If we respect our children and want to teach them that their choices have effects, we simply issue the consequence patiently and consistently each time. Or, actually, as patiently and consistently as we can.

The benefit of natural and logical consequences is that they allow us to teach our kids through experiencing the results firsthand.

Beware of Punishments Disguised as Logical Consequences

We might think we are giving a logical consequence when we're, in fact, giving out a punishment as a reaction to our child's misbehavior. We're often tempted to do this when siblings fight.

"I'm so sick of you guys fighting all the time," I yelled at Markos and George, squabbling over a croquet mallet. "That's it—everyone inside." And as they made their way in, I added, nagging and lecturing, as if my reaction were not good enough, "Why can't you guys just play together nicely? There is no reason for fighting all the time." You get the idea—bad parenting.

While a logical consequence for not being able to play together without fighting is to end the game, when we do not include the four elements of logical consequences, it becomes a parental reaction and a punishment. They were paying little attention to my words, but I'm sure my emotional reaction was hurtful and my punishment ineffective.

It would have been far more effective to tell them the consequence, "You'll lose time playing together if you cannot get along," and then respectfully take the mallets away, even if the end result, coming inside the house, is the same. Punishments are about my mood. Logical consequences are about their choices. One is bad and the other good.

Avoid Vague or Empty Threats

One of the signs that we are relying too much on consequences and have gotten off our game as parents is when we find ourselves issuing empty or vague threats. As we mentioned in

Chapter 9, vague threats or threats of consequences that we have no ability or intention of acting on undermine our authority and teach our children to pay no attention to what we say.

» "If you don't come down now, I'm leaving without you!" You can't do this, so don't say it.

» "You'll lose your video games for a month if you play them again without permission."

» "You're not going to the birthday party if your room isn't clean." That's cruel and unusual punishment, and when we calm down, we'll realize it.

» "If you touch something in the store, you're in big trouble." I've said this, and I'm still not sure what it means.

While this is an attempt to give a warning, it is a vague threat that your child, likely, has learned will be followed by anger or frustration, but not a consequence. Be specific about the limits and the consequences.

"Okay, but Next Time . . ."

The power of logical consequences lies in keeping the limits or consequences in place when we issue them. If we let her off the hook, a child learns that she can get out of the consequences of her decisions. That's a bad thing to teach. If you've followed the four Rs of logical consequences (related, respectful, reasonable, and revealed in advance), avoid letting your child off the hook. If she begs for one more chance, remind her that she will have another chance the next time she has a choice, not this time. She will always have more chances to make a better choice, just not this time.

Saying to your child, "Okay, but promise me you won't do that again" is another, similar temptation.

This is a variation of the same parenting mistake. And yes, it's a mistake. Parents might feel better about letting a kid off the hook because we got him to promise us he will behave. But it is disrespectful to extract a promise from a child who is still learning how to control his behavior. Even if children have the intention to comply, often they do not have the ability to keep their word. Kids will promise quickly just about anything to avoid facing the consequences of their actions. But by asking a child to promise that he will not act like a child and misbehave, parents set him up for failure and and set themselves up for frustration. If a child is learning to control his behavior, we should expect him to struggle and make mistakes no matter what he promises. If we want to help him, we should give the consequence. Avoid letting him off the hook, even with a promise.

⁂ Have a short memory for their mistakes and take the long view on their learning.

Clear and consistent consequences are an act of love toward our child. They are an act of veneration. We don't give consequences because we're mad, fed up, or disappointed, even if we feel these things. We give consequences so our children will learn. Consequences are the way we venerate our children, because we respect the growing and learning that they are doing through their decisions and misbehaviors.

If we're following the four Rs of giving consequences that are related, respectful, reasonable, and revealed in advance, we can connect with our children as we give them. We want to connect quickly with our children when they've completed their consequence. They don't need prolonged drama over their bad choices. Be quick to forgive your children as soon as they get themselves back together. Every consequence can end with kindness.

Removing Privileges

Removing privileges is very effective when it is a logical consequence but not effective as a punishment. When removing a privilege follows the four requirements of a logical consequence, it communicates that your love is unconditional, your limits are firm, and your words are true. When one of the four elements is missing, it becomes a punishment and invites hostility and resentment. It can seem to a child that you do not love him anymore. That hurts, and it's confusing. When in doubt, or in the heat of the moment, try to give your child one warning, indicating what privilege will be lost and how. Then, when the misbehavior is repeated, remove the privilege.

Privileges are the reward for being responsible. As a child grows, she should be allowed more privileges and take on more responsibilities. Children like to be treated like adults but are still learning how to behave like adults. If a child fails to uphold some of the responsibilities, removing some of the privileges makes sense. We want to help children make the connection between the privileges and the responsibilities that come with being older.

Beware of removing once-in-a-lifetime privileges. That denies the "reasonable" requirement of a logical consequence. It is one thing to lose a play date. It is another thing to lose a birthday party, special outing, or field trip. Play dates can happen all the time, but birthdays are rare. There should be some things that should not be taken away, like special time with Mom or Dad, so don't threaten that. "If you guys don't quit fighting, I'm not going to go to the ballgame with you!" That is unfair.

Earning Privileges Back

If you're going to remove a rare privilege, in addition to giving advance notice of the pending loss, give your child a chance to earn the privilege back once it's lost. This, I have found, is the most effective way to remove privileges. When children are clear about why they lost a privilege and what they must do to earn it back, we can recruit them to work hard to make good choices.

Anyone who has played tennis or another racquet sport knows that there is a sweet spot in a racquet. When the ball hits that sweet spot, it takes very little effort to get great speed and ball movement. The sweet spot in parenting is when our children are working hard to do what we want them to do without prodding and pressure from us.

We hit that sweet spot with our children when they are motivated to do what they need to do to earn back a privilege they have lost. They are more likely to work hard to do the right thing if they are clear about why they lost something, clear about what they need to do to earn it back, and convinced that you are going to be true to your word.

If the child thinks you'll cut him some slack and give the privilege back anyway or will add on additional requirements, he is not likely to do what needs to be done. Sometimes the only way a child can learn whether you're serious is when she chooses not to earn a privilege back, and then she doesn't get it back.

"I'm so sorry you cannot go to your friend's house today. I told you that in order to earn back that privilege, you needed to clean your room and fix the toy you broke. You must not have really wanted to go, because that did not happen. You can earn it back when I see a clean room and a fixed toy."

We need to remember that children do not need to earn our love. They should know we love them no matter what they choose or how they behave. If we are angry at them while they are making mistakes and kind to them when they've earned a privilege, this sends a message that our love is conditional. It is good for them to learn to earn privileges but bad for them to believe they need to earn our love.

Earning New Privileges

My children are constantly requesting privileges: to go outside to play, watch a movie, use the computer or video games, or stay up late. Kids do best when their lives are rich with interactions and activities, but not if they are overindulged with all these things. The flip-side of losing a privilege as a consequence is a pattern of earning privileges as rewards. Setting limits around earning privileges as rewards is more effective at teaching children than removing privileges as a consequence.

We discussed this in Chapter 9, when we talked about not giving away the ice cream for free. Children do best when they want something so badly that they are willing to do almost anything to get it. This is that sweet spot of parenting again. Look for ways to say "yes" to your children's desires, and tie the values and the virtues you want to teach into earning these privileges. If they know what they need to do to earn a privilege, and they know that you will be firm about this, they will amaze you, and themselves, by demonstrating great maturity and responsibility.

» "If you want that new video game, here's what you need to do."

» "If you want to go to the baseball game, here's what you need to do."

The best thing about hitting that sweet spot in parenting is that children acquire something eternal (discipline, postponing gratification, work before play) on the path of trying to earn something temporal (a video game, play time, or a bowl of ice cream).

They will discover their own potential to be responsible and feel good about that as they clean their room, share their toys, talk respectfully to each other, or do the hard thing without a parent prodding them along the whole way. We can join them in their pursuit of something important to them as they do what is important to us.

Remember, however, if you told your child what she needs to do to earn a privilege, and she does it, do not add any extra requirements later. That is confusing and discouraging. Rather, be clear about what needs to happen, and celebrate with your child when she steps up to do what needs to be done.

Naturally, there are some things we give to our children that they do not have to earn, as well as things we cannot give our kids no matter what they do. Sometimes they just need to go out and play, and there might be nothing they can do to earn the privilege of staying up too late or staying outside too long.

Spanking

If consequences are like the U.S. military, spanking is like a nuclear weapon. Some might argue that nuclear weapons have a role to play in our military, but they are rarely used because they have so much collateral damage. It is important to be aware of the limited benefit, the real risks, and the damaging effects of corporal punishment. However, as a parent, I'm not going to disarm unilaterally.

The problem with spanking is that it is minimally useful and rarely appropriate, yet so easy to misuse. We have discussed how we don't want our words to shame, humiliate, belittle, or discourage our children. Spanking lends itself to communicating all these negative, destructive messages toward our children.

Spanking is a consequence that is, usually, not related to the misbehavior. It is disrespectful because we're tempted to spank when we're angry, and it is unreasonable because it is much too severe a consequence. It's hard enough for us, as parents, to resist the temptation to react and punish our children rather than follow the four Rs of logical consequences. Once we allow ourselves the option of causing physical pain, it opens the door to more destructive parenting. It is one thing to react with an empty threat but quite another to react and hit our child.

Parents tend to spank when they're frustrated, overwhelmed, and angry. That's a bad way to issue any consequence. Children do great when loving, engaged parents set clear and firm limits and issue consequences consistently. Without these parameters, they are more likely to act out and misbehave. They don't need a spanking; they just need clear and firm limits from parents who are checking in with them.

He who spares his rod hates his son, but he who loves him instructs him with care. (Proverbs 13:26, OSB)

It is clear that the Old Testament refers to corporal punishment as part of the discipline process. This has led many parents to support spanking. The truth is, children don't need to be spanked to thrive, but they need firm limits. Kids who do not have firm limits grow up spoiled. As our first "rod," we should discipline our children with firm limits and clear consequences, issued promptly without negative emotional intensity. Remember, God's rod and staff comfort us because they keep us safe, not because they cause bruises!

Your rod and Your staff, they comfort me. (Psalm 22:4, OSB)

Lose the Battle to Win the War

Although it's dangerous to think of parenting in terms of war, sometimes it can feel like we are losing when we try to set limits and issue consequences. I can't always think of a logical consequence. Many of my kids' misbehaviors catch me off guard, in part because I struggle to pay good attention to my kids. When they do misbehave, I don't want to react with a punishment, because that is destructive. But I can't always think of how to respond. Sometimes I've let the limit slide or have not been consistent in what I say. They've escaped over the wall of my limits, and now I'm stuck with their misbehavior.

If you can't think of a logical consequence, maybe there isn't one. Consider, instead, checking in with your child, reflecting on why they might be misbehaving, naming their struggle, connecting with them, letting it go in the moment and bringing it up again at bedtime. Even if we lose the battle, they're still learning from how we keep our cool and respond when we're stuck. It might feel like we're losing, and maybe we did lose, but because this isn't really a war, and we're on their side, we can keep a long-term perspective and not react. We can lose the battle but win the war of modeling the values and the virtues we want them to internalize.

Instead of giving a consequence, I can always live to parent another day with a renewed commitment to keep limits firm. Yes, my children get off the hook without a consequence, but there are ways to lose the battle that set us up to do a better job being firm next time.

"I thought I said you could have Brittany over only if your room was clean," a mom said to her ten-year-old daughter, Nina, as she noticed the two of them playing in Nina's messy room.

Sometimes children figure out ways to get around or through our limits just because they're designed with that skill. Rather than giving a consequence or making a scene, it is far better to make a note of it, follow up later with a conversation, and double our efforts at clear and firm boundaries next time.

Do consequences work? Not really, in the short term. Children still misbehave, fight, and don't listen, but if we are clear and consistent within a loving relationship with our children, consequences work well in the long term to help them learn what they need to thrive as adults. And that's our goal.

Beware: As you learn to give consequences effectively, it's easy to lose sight of the person of your child, why he's misbehaving, and how you can connect with him. Children are not the objects of our parenting techniques or manipulations. They are persons to be loved.

Consequences serve to enforce the limits and help children decide, on their own, to stay within those boundaries. But our children need to learn more than this. Our goal is to raise up children of God. The goal of the Christian life is not to stay within God's limits, or "act like a Christian." The goal of the Christian life is holiness, union with God, deification. We are seeking the Kingdom of God, not avoiding God's wrath.

Having conquered all sinful desires, we pursue a spiritual life both thinking and doing all things that are pleasing to you.

Prayer before the reading of the Gospel
in *The Divine Liturgy of St. John Chrysostom*

God's commandments are the guidelines, not the goal. Our role is to love our children as God loves, to walk in God's love with them, and to teach them to walk in His love as they experience firsthand the joys of this path. What begins when we're young as following the rules needs to grow into pursuing love and walking in love. While it is essential to improve our skills at giving consequences, we can't lose sight of the Kingdom of God.

Teach the Joy of Obedience

CHAPTER 14

The Joy of Obedience

Like frost to a flower, so is a child's disobedience to a parent harmful to his growth.

—St. Theophan the Recluse, *Raising Them Right*

FOR ALL THE TOOLS WE HAVE AS PARENTS for setting limits, giving consequences, and guiding our children, sometimes they just need to do what we say. We can't avoid that fact. Whether it's time to get up, eat, or go to bed; whether it's cleaning their rooms, picking up toys, doing homework, or turning off the video game, we can name their struggles, share a wish, and give choices—but it always comes back to them learning to live within our guidelines.

Alexios, age seven, loves his baseball pants. They are his most comfortable, favorite pants to wear. He cannot understand why he cannot wear those pants everywhere, including to bed, to church, and to a wedding we attended recently.

"Alexi, you need to wear nice pants to the wedding," I stated.

"Why can't I wear my baseball pants?" he asked with real confusion and curiosity.

"Because we dress nicely for weddings and baseball pants are not nice enough for a wedding," I replied.

"But why not?" he continued. It was clear that I did not have any reason that would make sense to a seven-year-old who loved his baseball pants. I sensed a storm brewing on the parenting horizon.

"I wish you could wear your baseball pants all the time. You can choose between your blue or your tan dress pants. We wear baseball pants for baseball and nice pants for weddings," I clarified.

"I wanna wear my baseball pants!" he demanded. "Why can't I?"

There are few more common challenges parents face than getting our children to listen to us. In spite of how it can feel a lot of the time, parenting is not about getting our kids to do anything, including listen to us, because that is a short-term goal. Children need to learn obedience just like they need to learn patience, kindness, and self-control. Because they are learning, we need to be teaching, not just demanding, obedience.

Children, obey your parents in all things, for this is well pleasing to the Lord. (Colossians 3:20)

Obedience Is Necessary, but It Is Not the Goal

Some parents value obedience in children and feel justified demanding it. It's easy to see the impulsive, immature, and strong will of a child as a problem that needs to be solved through force of our will. It's easy to use the virtue of obedience as a means to control our children with very firm and very tight limits. This is dangerous, because if children do not feel close to their parents, do not understand the rules, or do not feel respected as they grow and are able to make some decisions on their own, they become resentful and rebel when they're old enough to escape our control.

———·•·———

When we teach discipline and obedience to a child, we should allow for the child's personal development and character. Our pedagogical aim is not to crush the child's will, or to "break it in" like a young pony we are training, so that we subordinate its personality to our own. Although when a child is young he has to learn simply to do what he is told, our ultimate goal is that he develops unselfishness and consideration for others.

Sister Magdalen, *Children in the Church Today*

———·•·———

Demanding obedience does not work in the long term because, while we do have authority over our children, we do not have the authority to crush their wills. That is disrespectful. They will need their wills to be strong as adults to make good decisions and to follow God, which is our long-term goal.

———·•·———

If we crush a child's will we deprive him of something which is a necessary part of his make-up as a free human person, and a necessary weapon of survival in the Christian struggle.

Sister Magdalen, *Children in the Church Today*

Having obedient children cannot be our goal, even if it is our desire. Our goal is not to raise up robots who just do what they are told. Our goal is to have our children internalize a spirit, a disposition, of obedience to God and His commandments by the time they leave our homes so that they will choose, with their own will, to be obedient to God.

———

Do you want your child to be obedient? Then from the beginning, bring him up in the discipline and instruction of the Lord.

St. John Chrysostom, "Address on Vainglory and the Upbringing of Children"

———

Some parents are uncomfortable with the idea of obedience. Obedience can seem harsh and oppressive, and some parents fear that obedience will harm a child and inhibit his capacity to think for himself. This thinking leads parents to give children plenty of choices, do lots of cajoling and convincing, and struggle to set clear and firm limits. The end result is kids who are impulsive and demanding and parents who are resentful of their children.

Some secular parenting experts have an aversion to talking about obedience and a negative view of parental authority. Many have an egalitarian approach to family life, viewing it as a democracy. Obedience seems like an outdated idea, associated with a time in history when children should be seen but not heard. The father of parent education, Dr. Rudolf Dreikurs, who has influenced many contemporary parenting books, writes that "since democracy implies equality, parents can no longer assume the role of the authority. Authority implies dominance: One individual having power over another."

Parental Authority in the Christian Home

Unfortunately, this does not work in the home. Parents are in charge, and we are one hundred percent responsible for how things run in our homes. We have the responsibility to take care of our children, to protect them, and to create the atmosphere in the home for them to thrive. We can only do this if we are clear about our authority and comfortable exercising it. Any good parenting book must recognize this basic fact.

However, there's a good reason obedience gets a bad rap, because it is often abused. Trying to control our children by demanding obedience is disrespectful to their learning and destructive to their development. Learning obedience, however, is essential to developing good judgment. We want our children to learn how to control their selfish desires, resist any impulses to react, manage their emotions, and grow up to obey God's commandments. Beyond simply knowing what is right, a child must learn how to do what's right, no matter what she wants. This is at the heart of having successful relationships and thriving as adults. Our children develop these skills as we teach the joy of obedience.

Obedience is the gateway through which knowledge enters the mind of a child.
    Annie Sullivan in William Gibson's *The Miracle Worker*

As Orthodox Christians, we recognize that God has established in the family, as in the Church, an equality of persons within a hierarchy of authority. However, this is an authority of selfless, loving service, not of power, control, and oppression. Those with more authority have a greater responsibility to love and serve the best interests of those under their care.

Christ, the ultimate authority, taught that he who is first is called to be the servant of all. He modeled this by washing the feet of His disciples and commanding them to go and do likewise. Christ modeled His ultimate authority by giving up His life for the salvation of the world as an act of obedience to His Father. This is the model for parental authority.

Parental authority is about dedicating ourselves selflessly to doing whatever is in the best interest of our children. It is about being in control of the routines, rituals, rules, and regulations of the home more than in control of our children. One is an act of love and the other an act of oppression. We need to use our authority to nurture a loving, respectful, peaceful home that allows our children to learn and grow as we've discussed in the previous chapters. We cannot exercise our authority arbitrarily, impulsively, or disrespectfully. We do not have the authority to react selfishly or disrespectfully to our children no matter how they behave toward us. We do have the authority to establish a culture and atmosphere in the home that allows our child to acquire all the values and the virtues of the Kingdom of God, including obedience.

The Art of Parenting: Parental authority is expressed as living a godly life and nurturing a loving home environment rather than by controlling our children.

Obedience and Our Long-Term Goals

The truth about obedience is that it sets us free. Learning obedience is how we develop good judgment, because our impulses, desires, or out-of-control feelings obstruct good judgment. Obedience teaches our children to let go of getting what they want, when they want it. Our long-term goal is to raise children who align their wills with God's will, rather than live enslaved to their impulses and desires.

—⊷⊷—

From obedience comes humility, and from humility comes discernment. From discernment comes insight, and from insight comes foresight.
St. John Climacus, *The Ladder of Divine Ascent*

—⊷⊷—

Learning obedience frees up our children to make good decisions later in life as they learn in their youth how to resist their own impulses, desires, and even their own thoughts, and do what we say.

—⊷⊷—

Obedience develops with maturity. In the beginning it has to mean: "Do what you are told"; but for an adult it means: "Prefer the will of another out of love."
Sister Magdalen, *Children in the Church Today*

—⊷⊷—

We want to raise up disciples of Christ, and obedience to God is central to the Christian life. To be a Christian is to follow Christ and to model our lives after Him who was obedient unto death, overturning the consequences of Adam's disobedience. Obedience to God is an invitation to life.

—⊷⊷—

He who says he abides in Him ought himself also to walk just as He walked. (1 John 2:6)

—⊷⊷—

Those who submit to the Lord with a simple heart will run the good race.

St. John Climacus, The Ladder of Divine Ascent

———◆———

Obedience and Love

Our obedience to God is in the context of, and specifically in response to, God's self-giving love for us. He loves us first and loves us completely, and we respond by our obedience to His commandments. "If you love Me, keep My commandments" (John 14:15).

Obedience to God is an act of love and is an expression of love. It is our path for participating in the love of God. "He who has My commandments and keeps them, it is he who loves Me. And he who loves Me will be loved by My Father, and I will love him and manifest Myself to him" (John 14:21). By our obedience to God, we grow in His love and in holiness and perfection. "But whoever keeps His word, truly the love of God is perfected in him. By this we know that we are in Him" (1 John 2:5). We express our love for God by turning away from sin and temptations and obeying His commandments.

———◆———

Blessed is the man who fears the Lord; He will delight exceedingly in His commandments. (Psalm 111:1 OSB)

———◆———

We can say unequivocally that we value obedience. It is an act of faith and love. It is an inner disposition of a heart turned toward God. We cannot overstate the importance of obedience in the Christian life and in the lives of our children, but we can overemphasize it. It is not our obedience that marks us as Christians, but our love. Yet it is our obedience to God that enables us to participate in His love. God's greatest commandment is not to obey, but to love. But notice, it is a commandment. We might say then that obedience is essential but not primary in the Christian life. It is a means to an end and not the end of the Christian life. In the same way, teaching obedience to our children is essential, but it cannot be primary in our parenting. Learning obedience is not the end goal but a means to our end of raising up children who love God and one another. Only when children know and experience our selfless love can they understand the proper place for obedience.

The Joy of Obedience

Most people don't associate obedience with joy. When parents demand obedience with cold, hard, or excessive control, it is hard to experience any joy. Yet, obedience is at the heart of a peaceful home, a happy marriage, and a blessed life. More than that: "Blessed are those who hear the word of God and keep it!" (Luke 11:28). There is chaos and conflict in a home if each person expects to get his or her way or gets to do what he or she wants. What happens in marriage when the husband or wife demands to get his or her way? The absence of obedience leads to conflict and disharmony as each person tries to impose his or her will on the other. A spirit of obedience in the home nurtures peace.

Children can only learn the joy of obedience if they experience the joy of being in a home where everyone is loved and respected or, rather, learning how to love and be respectful. If they are told to be obedient but do not experience love, intimacy, caring, and connection from their parents, obedience will feel oppressive and mean. Children will not experience joy if parents spend more time demanding obedience from them than connecting with them or demand obedience while invalidating their feelings, prohibiting their expression of thoughts and feelings, or criticizing or attacking them. Any parental actions that are manipulative, angry, or critical toward a child are disrespectful and teach disrespect. Demanding obedience with anger, impatience, hostility, ridicule, embarrassment, shame, or withdrawing our love undermines our long-term goals. The child development research is clear that disrespectful or emotionally manipulative parental controls are destructive to a child, no matter how important obedience is.

Children will experience the joy of obedience if they feel cared for and respected by their parents even as parents make age-appropriate demands, set rules and limits, issue consequences, and monitor behaviors with kindness and gentleness. Our children need to know that, first and foremost, we respect and love them, and then they need to learn to listen to us.

The reward of obedience is joy, and our children should have plenty of opportunities to experience joy when they are with us. If there is no obedience in the home, there can be no peace. If there is no joy, our children will not experience God's love. God's love should fill our homes with joy even in the midst of our struggles. The gospel is called the Good News, not the Oppressive Rules. Our job is to try to parent in joy, with joy, as our children struggle in learning to listen.

Modeling the Joy of Obedience

If the husband and wife order their lives according to God's law, their children will also submit willingly to the same law.

St. John Chrysostom, "Address on Vainglory
and the Upbringing of Children"

More effective than demanding obedience is modeling obedi-ence and having close relationships with our children. Teach-ing the joy of obedience requires that we, as parents, model obedience toward our spouse, our own parents, those in authority, and God, reflecting God's love toward our children in all that we do. When our children feel connected to us, they naturally model our behaviors and acquire our values and virtues.

We all know that it is easier to obey someone for whom we feel love and respect. We fear obeying someone we do not trust, and it's hard to obey someone we don't respect. This is at the heart of teaching the joy of obedience. The more our children know and experience our care, respect, and love, the easier it is for them to follow our instructions and live within our limits. We make obedience an easy task for our children when the parent who is telling them what to do is the same parent who plays with them, understands their struggles, and responds instead of reacting when they misbehave.

⤳ Do not try to control your children. Try to control yourself.

Teaching the joy of obedience requires that we, as parents, follow God's commandments as we teach our children to fol-low our way. This means that our wills, as parents, need to be aligned with God's will. A father who demands control of the TV remote is teaching selfishness, not obedience. A father who lives according to God's commandments and loves and cares for his children teaches obedience to God as the path of life. The obedience we teach in the home needs to be connected to the path of life revealed through Christ and His Church. We model obedience by being obedient to God and the Church.

When we transmit life to another generation, our task is to transmit not only the life of the body, but also the spiritual life. It is important to work hard to feed and clothe a child; it is more important to ensure a healthy mental and emotional development; and more important still to enhance the spiritual growth of a child. Spiritual life is the most precious thing for a child to inherit.

Sister Magdalen, *Children in the Church Today*

Connect Your Home to the Church

We teach the joy of obedience by helping our children see that obedience is not something just for children. Obedience to God's commandments is the path for all, parents and children alike. Children learn obedience by learning to live within the limits we set in the home. They internalize an inner disposition of obedience to God as they make the connections between the rules of the home and the commandments of God. When children feel connected to their parents and see their parents living in obedience to God, they internalize obedience to God as the path of life.

✥ We teach the joy of obedience by connecting with our children, having clear limits, and modeling obedience for them.

Connect your family rules and rituals to the life of the Church. There are many ways to do this, such as making Sunday Liturgy mandatory because it is the day of the Lord and attending, as a family, the various services of the Church, because that is what we do as Christians. Try to set up the rules and expectations of the home according to the values and the virtues of the Kingdom of God. We teach patience, kindness, gentleness, forgiveness, and love because these are the guidelines we have received from God for how to thrive as families. Make your best effort to incorporate the fasting and feasting cycles of the Church into the home. Use the fasting periods of the Church as a time to fast and go to confession. In addition, use fasting periods to cut off technology, video games, media, and various forms of entertainment and replace them with the reading of Scripture and other spiritual readings, acts of charity, and prayer time. This is a challenge for families. If it seems to be too heavy a burden, try doing this for the first week of Great Lent or for Holy Week. At a minimum, parents can try to cut these things out of their lives so that their children will learn that adults follow the guidelines of the Church. Have your home blessed at Theophany. Cense your house on Saturday evenings in preparation for Sunday Liturgy. As children observe the parents living the sacramental life of the Church, they will internalize the life of the Church as real. If they experience this life as joyful, they internalize the joy of obedience.

Keep in mind, however, that if the external practices of the Church in the home are not accompanied by love, caring, and connection, children will develop a distaste for these practices. Prioritize peace, love, and repentance as you do your best to connect the Church to the home. Children will learn that material things are fleeting if during fasting periods they experience an increase in connection and intimacy as the family prays together and follows Christ together. Living a life in Christ is a struggle, but it should not make us miserable. We follow God as an act of love, not as a cold requirement.

CHAPTER 15

Nurture a Culture of Listening in the Home

Our children should feel that they can peacefully say anything:
questions, doubts, criticisms, points of view. They should feel
that we are genuinely interested in what they do and think.
— Sister Magdalen, *Children in the Church Today*

I RECOGNIZE THAT FOR MANY PARENTS the word *obedience*
seems like a harsh word. Plus, my children never respond
well when I talk about obedience. The Greek word for "obedience" has the same root as the word for "to listen." When we
are talking about obedience, we are talking about listening. To
listen to someone is not just to hear what they are saying, but
to do what they say. Listening is an act of obedience. Children
do best when they are inclined to listen to their parents. We
want our kids to recognize the fact that in order to succeed in
life and relationships, you need to know how to listen to others and listen to God.

✍ Use your parental authority to nurture a culture of listening in the home.

The most common complaint I hear from parents is, "My kids don't listen to me." The most common mistake I see parents make is that they do not listen to their children. If we want our children to listen to us, we need to model listening and nurture a culture of listening in our homes.

We model listening by listening to our spouses. When a mom reports to me that her children do not listen, I ask what examples of listening they see in the home. If Dad ignores what Mom says, he models for the children that they do not really need to listen either. If kids witness Mom and Dad listening and respecting each other, they learn that listening is not just what kids need to do but is the path of life for everyone.

Nurture a culture of listening between siblings. Encourage each person in the home to use his or her words, rather than act out when they're upset. Require each member of the household to respect the words of others. Prohibit interrupting people when they're speaking. Make a rule that only one person speaks at a time at the dinner table. Pay attention to the smallest or quietest voices in the family who are least likely to be heard. The larger the family, the more opportunities there are to teach patience as everyone practices listening to the one person speaking. It's a good goal to work toward.

Listening as an Act of Veneration

The best way to teach listening is to listen to our children. We venerate our children (and our spouses) as icons of Christ by listening to them. As persons, children deserve the same respect as adults. Listening to children, allowing for verbal give and take when making decisions or setting limits, communicates respect and is a powerful way of connecting.

Remember that children long to connect with us. Take more time listening to your child than talking to your child. Try to take a genuine interest in what your child is seeing, thinking, feeling, and learning. Taking time out for our kids regularly and making an effort to listen to them in the midst of daily life offers them positive avenues to connect with us. More than anything, our children desire to be known and loved by us. More than encouragement, affirmations, praise, or a new cell phone, they need to connect with us as persons. This requires that we make our children a priority by taking the time and making the effort to listen to them. The more connected they feel with us as parents, the more they will follow our guidance.

Listening is an act of love. Real listening requires that we resist the temptation to ignore, interrupt, give advice, criticize, or react. It requires selflessness and is an ascetic act of self-giving. When we listen to someone, we make ourselves present and attentive to what the person is saying. It is a type of self-denial and a real act of love. Listening communicates that we respect our child, care for her, and think that she is important. When we venerate our child by listening, our child internalizes the notion that she is an icon of Christ. Children develop a sense of themselves as someone respected, loved, and cared for as we listen to them, even as we are the ones setting limits and giving consequences.

✥ Few things communicate love more than simply listening.

Listening When Children Behave

The challenge of parenting is to listen to our children when they are behaving well as much as when they're behaving poorly. Parents are tempted to be so self-absorbed with our adult world and the "real problems" of adulthood, such as jobs, mortgages, marital struggles, and finances, that we disregard the world of children as childish and insignificant. If we dismiss their world and their problems, we are dismissing and disrespecting them and teaching our children to dismiss their inner world. We can only teach self-respect and respect for others by respecting our child's world, by listening to her and whatever experiences, struggles, or problems she considers serious. When we pay attention to the inner world of our child, her thoughts and feelings, we teach her how to pay attention to her inner world. Listening to children nurtures self-reflection, awareness, and critical thinking in ourselves and in our children. Beware of disrespecting your children by dismissing their real experiences as "just childish."

My last day of school was my oldest daughter Kyranna's first day of school. On the day I defended my PhD dissertation, she was going to her first day of school. Which one was more important? While I am the authority in my home, if I respect my daughter, I understand that her first day of school is as serious for her as my last day of school is for me, at least emotionally. I'm not going to miss my dissertation defense because of her first day of school, but if I want to nurture a culture of listening, I'll put my "real adult issues" aside and ask her all about her first day.

Listening When Children Misbehave

⤜ We listen to show we care, not just to get information or solve problems.

"But I already know what my child is struggling with!" a mother challenged me when I suggested that listening to her angry eight-year-old was an appropriate response.

Listening communicates that we are more interested in the

person of our child than in getting them to behave. It's impossible to know what our child is struggling with without checking in with them. It's impossible to teach our children how to think and make decisions without listening to how they're feeling and what they're thinking. Listening to our child's struggles is how we care for them and ease their burdens. Try to listen to your children at all times, particularly when they misbehave.

✥ Don't confuse listening with leniency.

Some parents might feel threatened by simply listening to their children. You are likely going to feel less in control when you listen to your child. However, listening does not undermine our authority as parents. It is an expression of our authority and the context for exercising our control. Sometimes, when parents do listen to their children, they are tempted to be lenient or give in. We've talked about how important it is to keep our limits firm. Listening does not mean giving in or doing what our children want. It simply means paying attention to what life is like for our children as they struggle. Listening to our children is an act of obedience on our part.

✥ Give children a voice, even when they don't have a choice.

Listen by Naming Their Struggles and Feelings

Listening to children when they are struggling is tough because we come face to face with their struggles, which we can't solve. Often, when parents listen to their kids, they hear things like "I don't want to go to bed" or "I want a cookie!"

"Then what do I do?" asked a mother of a five-year-old, feeling stuck and out of control as she imagined listening to her child.

"Keep the limit firm, and name his struggle. Name his feelings," I suggested.

"But that doesn't change his feelings," she replied.

"I know," I said. "We can't change his feelings, and we don't need to. That's not our goal. We can venerate him when he struggles and keep the limits firm." He'll have to struggle with your limit, and you can be on his side as he does.

✎ Listening to our children does not mean giving in to them. It means respecting them.

"What's going on? You're hitting each other?" I said as I stepped between my two daughters (nine and eleven) fighting in the kitchen. What kind of terrible kids do I have that they hit each other? Well, I have intelligent, caring pre-adolescent girls who get fed up with each other and are learning patience and conflict-resolution skills—that's what kind of girls I have. They are still icons of Christ. I don't expect my children to remember that, but our parenting intervention needs to reflect that fact. The only thing worse than two kids acting like kids is when an "adult" reacts like a child and escalates the situation.

» "She hit me first!"
» "She's making fun of me!"
» "She's just standing around not helping!"

The arguments and blaming comments flew through the air. Same story. Different day.

I separated my daughters and allowed a few moments for things to calm down. When things were calm, I gave them each a chance to explain not only what the other person did that was wrong, but what each one was struggling with and what choices each of them made. We brainstormed together the other choices each had when facing her particular struggle. After apologies, each one received a consequence for the bad choices she made, such as a loss of a privilege or an additional chore. I have found, however, that intervening in a way that invites remorse and repentance is far more effective in the long term than issuing consequences. We'll talk more about that in the next chapter. For now, it's important to know that listening first before issuing consequences nurtures respect and a culture of listening in the home. It is the best way to exercise our parental authority toward our long-term goals for our children.

❧ Listening before taking action models respect and the values and virtues we want our children to acquire.

In the end, there were plenty of opportunities for my daughters to take responsibility and apologize after they felt heard and supported in their struggle. Had I reacted and jumped in with commands and condemnations of their choices, nothing good would have happened.

Listening first with questions like, "What's going on? What happened? Tell me what you were thinking," or even, "Why did you hit your sister?" is respectful and invites children to reflect. Listening to children does not mean we don't set limits and give consequences. It means we check in with them before we do anything. That is our struggle: to model respect and teach them that they are icons of Christ by listening before we set limits or give consequences.

Be stricter in requiring yourself to listen than in requiring your children to listen to you. We have to set the rules, enforce the rules, and keep order (as much as this is possible). That's unavoidable. What's required to teach our long-term goals is that we listen to our children as we do these things. Listening first, before we set a limit or give a consequence, communicates respect for our child as a person no matter what they did. Parents are not police, and our job is not primarily to keep law and order but to love and teach love. Responding by listening first communicates this in the midst of all the things that need to get done. Children are persons to be loved, not problems to be solved.

❧ Take their feelings seriously, but not necessarily their words.

It's tough to focus on listening when we feel attacked by our children (or our spouses, but this is a parenting book). It is easier to condemn our child's misbehavior or rude talk than to focus on loving the child who is misbehaving.

» "You're mean."
» "You're a terrible mom!"
» "I hate you!"
» Or, my personal favorite: "This is the worst family on the planet!" My ten-year-old daughter exclaimed this as she faced the torturous task of cleaning her room.

———◆———

Connect with your child before your correct your child.

Laura Markman, *Peaceful Parents, Happy Kids*

———◆———

If our child's angry, childish reactions are met with angry, childish reactions from us, we end up escalating the conflict, and it is not clear who the adults are anymore. When we react, we lose our authority as parents. Children don't usually talk rudely because they think it is okay to talk like this. They're saying these things because they're overwhelmed by their feelings, and they're not thinking.

As we mentioned in Chapter 11, it is appropriate at times to remain silent and ignore these statements or offer a listening response:

» "Are you angry?"
» "Are you upset?"
» "What is wrong? Are you sad to end the day?"
» "Are you frustrated?"

Listening first, instead of reacting, is how we take their struggles seriously, even when we should not take their words seriously. If they do want to talk, I want to be ready to listen to whatever is upsetting them. Then I can empathize with their struggle and keep the limits firm.

Listening de-escalates situations and allows us to stay in control of ourselves, if not the situation or our child. Once a child has calmed down, been heard, and gotten back on task, it is appropriate to set limits to their talk and teach them how to ask for forgiveness. We'll talk more about that in the next chapter.

✎ **The power of our authority is greatest when we listen to the person before dealing with the misbehavior.**

Once our child is calm, with our authority intact, we can then follow up with clear guidelines for behavior even later in the day or at bedtime, as we discussed in Chapter 11.

» "We don't talk like that."
» "We don't use that word in this house."
» "We don't ever talk to your mother that way!"

The same statements that are ineffective when we react become very effective as responses, after we've attended to their feelings.

≪≫ Listen first, because children learn more from what we do than from what we say.

Frame Struggles in the Context of Listening

We spoke in Chapter 5 about how framing our child's struggles according to the values and the virtues of the Kingdom of God helps children to understand the nature of life's struggles. We can add listening to the ways we can frame their struggles. Learning to listen is an overarching goal of childhood and encompasses many of our long-term goals as parents. As we frame our kids' struggles as learning how to listen, we teach the joy of obedience as they come to understand how learning to listen is an essential part of growing up. Whether we are getting children out the door in the morning or back in the house at the end of the day, they are learning to follow a schedule or, rather, learning to listen to our instructions.

"Is it hard to listen when I say come in for dinner?" we can ask our child who did not come in the first time we called.

"Your sister said that she was using her sweater. You need to listen to her words," you might frame a sibling conflict over a sweater.

"I already called everyone in once. I need everyone to listen the first time I call," we might say, instead of repeating ourselves. Or, even better, as we discussed in Chapter 9, after we say things once, we can follow up with our actions. Go and get your child as you say, "I called once, and it is time to come in. You need to listen the first time I call."

I will never convince Alexios that baseball pants are not appropriate for weddings, but I don't need to. I need to allow him to struggle and can frame the struggle as a struggle to listen, rather than to learn how to dress at weddings. I can simply name his struggle and keep the limit firm.

"It's hard to listen when Dad says you have to wear pants to weddings," I could state. This is a good alternative to the classic "Because I said so" parenting response.

"When Dad says we wear pants to weddings, then we wear pants to weddings." Okay, this is the same thing as, "Because I said so." I can remind him of this fact, if necessary, but I don't need to get mad, and he does not need a consequence.

Talk about listening during quiet times when you are following up with your child. Bedtime is a good time to mention instances when you noticed your child listening and times when she struggled to listen. Without emotional intensity, it is very powerful to comment with statements like, "I noticed you had a hard time listening to your mom/sister/brother/dad today. What would happen if nobody listened to Mom/Dad in this family?"

This will not necessarily help our children listen the first time, but it will help them understand how listening is essential to a peaceful home and healthy relationships.

Reward First-Time Listening

If we want to help children understand the value of listening, recognize their efforts to listen and honor their successes. Remark on first-time listening when you see it, with a comment, a smile, and a connection. Avoid taking listening for granted or only commenting when your kids don't listen.

> » "I noticed that you came in the first time I called."
> » "Good job listening to your sister when she asked you to turn down the music."

Look for Opportunities to Explicitly Teach Listening

Mealtimes are essential to staying connected as a family and excellent opportunities to teach listening. Breaking bread together as a family is an act of communion in the home. Dinnertime is the practice field for learning the values and the virtues of the Kingdom of God and also for listening. We should expect learning more than peace.

Try to use mealtime as a time of listening to each other. Create rituals around mealtime for sharing and listening, maybe by going around and asking each person to share one highlight of their day. If children are learning at mealtime, we should be teaching. We teach listening by modeling it to our kids as they learn to listen to us and each other. There should be time for adults and children to speak and listen. If your children are struggling to sit still, it is far more effective to teach listening by checking in with each child in turn, giving each person an opportunity to speak and requiring everyone else at the table to listen, rather than expecting young kids to sit quietly and listen to adult conversations. If children struggle to learn, look first to connect with them before correcting them. Do not expect this to go smoothly, but try to use this opportunity to connect with each other as everyone learns to take turns, speak, and listen.

Notice that we use our God-given authority not to silence our children, but to set the expectation that the home is where we are all learning to listen. We should be strict about requiring listening but stricter about modeling listening and focusing on connecting with our children as they are learning.

If you child does not listen the first time you say something, it is appropriate to check in with them before repeating yourself. They might be distracted by what they're doing or have that intermittent deafness kids experience when they hear a parent's voice. It is more effective to get your child's attention with a gentle touch than to repeat yourself. When they finally do listen, you can suggest that they go back and try again to listen the first time you say something.

"It seems like you need a little practice listening the first time. Please go back upstairs, and I'll call again."

Beware, it is very difficult to teach listening if our children do not see or experience the adults in the home listening to them. As we nurture a culture of listening in the home, closely connected to the Church, we nurture a respect for listening and an understanding of how critical listening and obedience are in life. We don't need to force this issue with each parenting incident, but we do need to nurture a household in which everyone is learning to listen.

If you're like me when I wrote this book, you might be feeling very aware of how many things you do wrong with your children. I react too quickly and too often. I'm often forgetting to check in and connect with my kids until they are misbehaving. I use consequences the wrong way. I'm a bad listener a lot of the time. The list is endless of the mistakes I make with my children—and I'm the one writing the book! One of the most painful things I've experienced in life is realizing that my actions have hurt my children. How can I teach about parenting without being a hypocrite? The answer is repentance.

❧ PRINCIPLE VI ❧

Teach the Joy
of Repentance

CHAPTER 16

Repentance

Blessed are those whose transgressions are forgiven,
And whose sins are covered.

—Psalm 31:1 (LXX)

What saves and makes for good children is the life of the parents in the home. The parents need to devote themselves to the
love of God. They need to become saints in the relation to their
children. And the joy that will come to them, the holiness that
will visit them, will shower grace on their children.

—St. Porphyrios, *Wounded by Love*

THIS FINAL PRINCIPLE PROVIDES A CORRECTIVE for some
of the risks of reading a parenting book and in some ways
is the most important principle. It's easy, when we read about
parenting, to become so focused on parenting the "right" way
that we lose sight of the heart of parenting. Ultimately, children need to be loved. If we are more focused on parenting the
right way than loving our kids, that's not good for our kids.

If we're always second-guessing ourselves, we might be reacting more to the parenting manual than responding to our children.

———

And when we say "love," we don't mean the virtues that we will acquire, but the heart that is pervaded by love towards Christ and others.

St. Porphyrios, *Wounded by Love*

———

At the heart of parenting is our devotion to God and a recognition that God is working in us and our children in every parenting interaction. In order to direct our children's lives toward God, the way we parent our children needs to be an expression of our call to love the Lord our God with all our heart, soul, mind, and strength, and our neighbor as ourselves. If you're trying to love God as you learn to respond, not react, or set limits to behaviors while you listen to their feelings, your children will experience God's love in the home. They will understand that life is about learning how to love God and neighbor. If you're trying to "do it right" or be perfect, you will frustrate yourself and your children. Divine perfection is our heavenly goal, but perfectionism is a disease that we want to heal from rather than passing it along to our children. However, it's important to reflect on our parenting. We can improve our skills. It is not a choice between having parenting skills and living a life of faith; we learn parenting skills within our life of faith.

Another risk of reading a parenting book is that you will notice your parenting mistakes. Whenever I read or hear a talk about parenting, I become aware of all the things I'm doing wrong. Sometimes it seems like I do the exact opposite of what

I should do. This happens all the time, and sometimes I'm the one giving the parenting talk! When we reflect on our parenting, it's easy to feel the inner pain of having done things the "wrong way." Some parents give up trying to improve because of this.

At this point in the book it is appropriate to admit that only a saint could parent the way I've described in this book. Only a saint can be patient, respond and never react, know the best way to intervene each time, and put up with the constant struggles that come with raising children.

It is not only hard to parent, but it is impossible to be perfect parents. Fortunately, that's not our goal or even what our children need. Just as we should not expect our children to be perfect but to be learning and growing, we should not expect ourselves to be perfect. We should expect ourselves to be learning and growing. Mistakes are part of the process. We are going to make mistakes, and the only way to improve our parenting is to accept this fact. In fact, learning how to parent is not about trying to be the perfect parent, but being perfected as parents. Our call as parents is to become holy, to be sanctified and healed, in and through our parenting.

—◆—

[If we are parents] it is the sacred task of parenthood which will sanctify us as much as our fasting, private prayer and reading.
Sister Magdalen, *Children in the Church Today*

—◆—

Being Perfected as Parents

We become holy, or sanctified, by being filled with the Holy Spirit, who heals our diseases and fills us with love, joy, peace, longsuffering, kindness, goodness, faithfulness, gentleness, and self-control (Gal. 5:22–23), the very things we need as parents. It is important that we understand the role of the Holy Spirit in the Christian life and, by extension, in our parenting.

———

For the kingdom of God is not eating and drinking, but righteousness and peace and joy in the Holy Spirit. (Romans 14:17)

———

As Christians, we don't just believe in Christ, but in the Holy Spirit and God the Father. Christ Himself told His apostles that He would send the Holy Spirit, who would guide the Christian community to all truth. The Holy Spirit opens our minds and hearts and makes the Father and the Son known to us. The Holy Spirit fills our hearts and our homes with peace, love, and joy and transforms us in the image and likeness of Christ. We must walk in the Spirit in our daily lives and raise our children to experience the ongoing life in the Spirit.

The truth is, we don't have the patience, kindness, gentleness, wisdom, and self-control to be the types of parents we might want to be, but God helps us acquire these virtues as fruits of the Holy Spirit. If we focus on trying to do everything perfectly, we will fail. If we focus on acquiring the Holy Spirit, the values and virtues of the Kingdom of God will fill our hearts and our homes.

———

The true aim of our Christian life consists of the acquisition of the Holy Spirit of God. As for fasts, and vigils, and prayer, and almsgiving, and every good deed done for Christ's sake, these are only the

means of acquiring the Holy Spirit of God.
St. Seraphim of Sarov, *On the Acquisition of the Holy Spirit*

❧ **The goal of parenting is to acquire the Holy Spirit and raise our children to walk in the Spirit.**

All the tools and skills identified in this book find their place within our own journey of acquiring the Holy Spirit. As Orthodox Christians, we understand that we acquire the Holy Spirit through participation in the sacramental life of the Church. This is not a magic process of simply going to church, but that's a great start. This process began with our baptism and chrismation when we were united to Christ and received the Holy Spirit, and it continues as we connect daily life intimately to the sacramental life of the Church.

Grace has been given mystically to those who have been baptized into Christ; and it becomes active within them to the extent that they actively observe the commandments.
St. Mark the Ascetic, "On Those Who Think They Are Made Righteous by Works" in *The Philokalia*

The Orthodox spiritual life is a synergy between God and us. We play a critical yet unequal role with God in our own transformation. To be perfected in Christ through the Holy Spirit requires our ongoing assent, our ongoing participation in the work of the Holy Spirit by turning away from sin, and turning toward Christ when we're not in church. A life in Christ, a life in the Spirit, must be lived out in the home and in the daily struggles of family life. In the home is where we are all working out our salvation, struggling to turn toward God and away from sin in our daily reactions and interactions with each other.

No matter how skilled we are as parents, if our lives are not pointed toward Christ and His Kingdom, our children will not internalize this reality. However, if we fast, pray, and go to church regularly but do not know how to respect our children and their struggles, connect with them, and respond appropriately when they misbehave, all our religious activity will seem empty to our children.

———•✦•———

Now hope does not disappoint, because the love
of God has been poured out in our hearts by the
Holy Spirit who was given to us. (Romans 5:5)

———•✦•———

This is not a book on acquiring the Holy Spirit, but to reach our long-term goals as parents, acquiring the Spirit must be our focus. We acquire the Holy Spirit by ascetically and selflessly resisting the temptation to react to our child's misbehaviors and checking in with him before we respond; resisting the temptation to pick up a child up when she falls, and drawing close; denying ourselves and listening to our children's struggles as we walk them to bed at night; letting go of our desires for a quiet and spill-free meal and attending to our children's learning. The list is endless.

This is not a book on the spiritual life, but our own spiritual journey is a central aspect of raising children who internalize the values and virtues of the Kingdom of God. In addition to cooking, cleaning, laundry, and picking up Cheerios, all the tools and strategies in this book find their place in the ascetic self-offering of parents toward their children. This is what it means to love our children. Love does not indulge a child or make a child's life easy. Love is not about pointing out a child's faults or controlling our children's behavior. Love is expressed as the real asceticism to resist the temptation to give in or get angry, to endure our kids' learning, not just their misbehaviors, and to set clear, consistent limits as we take the side of their feelings. The ascetic self-denial required of parenting is an act of love directed at our children and, we believe, toward Christ. We, as parents, are invited by Christ in every parenting interaction to turn away from our own impulses and desires and draw close to Him.

———

The spirit of faith and piety in the parents should be regarded as the most powerful means for the preservation, upbringing, and strengthening of the life of Grace in children.

St. Theophan the Recluse, *Raising Them Right*

———

The more we recognize God's invitation in every parenting interaction to turn away from our desires and impulses and turn toward Him, the more we open our hearts to be filled with His unending patience, kindness, wisdom, strength, and love. As we respond to God's invitation, we teach our children how God is inviting them, in every interaction, to love.

≪≫ If we want our children to understand themselves as children of God, we ourselves need to live as children of God daily in the home.

287

If we are trying to love our children and grow in Christ, then our mistakes become just another opportunity to teach. Remember, our children will learn more from how we live than from what we say. Children learn how to handle their mistakes by watching how we handle our own. The way we handle our failures, then, needs to point our kids toward our long-term goals. To do that, we can't deny our mistakes or become overwhelmed by guilt. We need to teach our children the joy of repentance.

⸙ Children don't need perfect parents, just repentant parents.

A few years ago, we were celebrating my birthday with dinner as a family. Each person was invited to share one thing they were thankful for about their dad. When it came to Alexandra, age fourteen at the time, she thought about it for a moment and shared, "I am thankful for Daddy because he is always the one who says he is sorry when he makes a mistake."

Although I felt a twinge of shame when I heard her words, I quickly realized that she was remembering my repentance at least as much as my mistakes. I can't always control my mistakes, but I can always repent. She had watched me fall and get back up again many times. I make a lot of mistakes as a dad and can confess that I am not perfect at following the very guidelines I have written about in previous chapters. But I follow this chapter really well. Our children don't need us to be perfect to teach them the right way to live, but they do need us to admit when we've fallen off the path. The very act of admitting we made a mistake teaches our children that there is a right way, and we blew it. When we repent we show our children both the right path and how to get back on the path when we fall off.

—◆—

We must have the courage to be imperfect.
Rudolf Dreikurs, *Children: The Challenge*

—◆—

Repentance

Teaching the joy of repentance must be at the core of our parenting, because repentance is at the core of our spiritual life in Christ.

—◆—

St. John the Baptist and our Lord Jesus Christ both begin their preaching with exactly the same words: "Repent, for the Kingdom of Heaven is at hand" (Matthew 3:2; 4:17). Such is the starting point of the Good News—repentance. Without repentance there can be no new life, no salvation, no entry into the Kingdom.
Metropolitan Kallistos Ware, *The Inner Kingdom*

—◆—

Repentance is central to growing closer to God, because sin is a part of our fallen human condition, and sin separates us from God and others. We all make mistakes, and our selfish tendencies and reactions hurt our relationships with God and others. This is particularly true in our most intimate relationships in the home. If we leave these sins and mistakes unattended, resentment and hurt fill our hearts. Repentance and forgiveness protect us from the destructive power of sin and enable us to continue to grow closer to God and each other in the face of our fallenness.

The repentant person is the one who accepts the mir-
acle that God does indeed have the power to forgive
sins. . . . Divine forgiveness breaks the chain of cause
and effect, and unties the knots in our hearts which
by ourselves we are not able to loose.

Metropolitan Kallistos Ware, *The Inner Kingdom*

―――――

Repentance and the Bagel Bite

"Waaaaaaah!" Alexios (then seven) cried from the kitchen. I came in to find him in tears with Nikolia (thirteen), chewing a mouthful of his bagel, standing next to him.

"She took a bite out of my bagel! I just made myself a bagel!"

Nikolia, who had earlier made him his first bagel, felt entitled to a bite of his second, and he was upset.

"I just took a little bite," she said defensively.

"Well, you didn't ask!"

"I'll make you a whole other bagel."

"I don't want you to. I want mine!"

"If you want yours, then it has to have a bite in it," she reasoned unapologetically.

"Waaaaaaah!"

These types of unavoidable, unsolvable struggles happen all the time. If you are hoping that these daily little squabbles, skirmishes, and transgressions will stop, you will become frustrated and upset. Instead of aiming to eliminate them altogether, we want to figure out how to respond, quickly and effectively, toward our long-term goals. We can't take a lot of time for these exchanges because they happen so frequently.

There's not really a good consequence, except maybe having Nikolia make Alexios another sandwich.

"But I want that first one! And she can't just eat my food!"

Alexios argued. He had a point; she should have asked first. But at this point that was not an option. "You're mean!" he yelled at her.

"I just made you one. You can share," she argued. She had a point, too. He just sobbed.

"You have to make her stop!" Alexios demanded of me.

"Good luck," I thought to myself.

Getting upset at Nikolia for taking his food or at Alexios for crying would do nothing good. But these situations are very upsetting. I can't get his whole bagel back again, and he is hurt. Without any solution, we can feel stuck and over-whelmed as parents. However, when we incorporate repentance and forgiveness into our parenting, these unsolvable problems are opportunities for learning, which is at the heart of parenting and at the heart of the spiritual life.

❧ At the heart of raising resilient children is raising children who know how to be repentant, not perfect.

Our children need to learn that mistakes happen. They will hurt others and be hurt by others. We need to teach them what to do when they make mistakes and how to respond when others make mistakes.

"Alexi, did Nikolia bite your bagel?" I asked, drawing close to him in his struggle.

"I made that myself," he wailed as he came toward me for a hug. I couldn't solve the problem, but I could draw close to him.

"Nikolia, what do you say to Alexi for biting his bagel without asking?"

"But I just made him a bagel."

"I know. Good job, but we don't take people's food without asking."

"Forgive me, Alexi, for not asking first. I won't do that again," she said softly.

"Does Nikolia always help you when you need something?" I asked, to give him a little perspective.

"Yes, but she can't take a bite without asking," he maintained.

"What do you say to Nikolia?"

"I forgive you," he said quietly.

And that was it. He was still sad. Nikolia realized her mistake, although she still felt a bit slighted, because she does take care of him. I can't solve that, and I don't need to. Nikolia needs to learn to repent, and Alexios needs to learn to forgive. They will have these transgressions and conversations hundreds of time, and the roles will be reversed. My goal is to keep my peace, particularly when my children have lost theirs, join them in their struggles, and point them along the path of forgiveness and repentance. Ten minutes later, it was old news, and Alexios finished his incomplete bagel.

———

We learn the joy of being forgiven when we ourselves forgive others; we experience the blessing of being loved when we also love others; we learn to receive and accept the repentance of others when we ourselves repent sincerely and authentically.

Fr. Peter Chamberas,
The Sacrament of Repentance and Confession

———

When we embrace repentance and forgiveness, our mistakes and failures are no longer fatal. Repentance, confession, and forgiveness are the antidotes to sin, hurt, and our human failings. Sin and failures are a fact of our human condition and of family life. We do love each other as a family, but we fail to show it—often. We don't need to deny our failings, but recognize them and repent for them. In and through repentance and forgiveness, the mistakes and failures of daily life become a means of growing closer to each other and to God. We can either give our children a legacy of our sins or a legacy of repentance. We don't need to be perfect families, but if we want to grow, learn, and be perfected as families, we need to be repentant.

———

If we confess our sins, He is faithful and just to forgive us our sins and to cleanse us from all unrighteousness. (1 John 1:9)

———

It might seem that simply asking a child to repent is not really doing anything, because everyone knows this will happen again. Teaching forgiveness and repentance, in fact, is doing a powerful thing. We are teaching our children that when they make mistakes—not if—there is a path to restore relationships. Our mistakes are part of the process of growing in love when we walk the path of repentance.

Repentance is an appropriate follow-up to meltdowns once children calm themselves down.

» "What do you say for saying 'I hate you?'"
» "What do you say for yelling those horrible things when you were upset?"

As with everything else we've discussed in this book, if our goal is to get our children to stop making mistakes, forgiveness and repentance do not work. My kids will still yell when they're upset and eat each other's food without asking. We can either react to this misbehavior with anger, frustration, and lectures or respond by teaching the path of repentance and forgiveness. If our goal is to have our children internalize forgiveness and repentance as the path of life, each mistake and misbehavior is an opportunity to teach the joy of repentance.

CHAPTER 17

The Joy of Repentance

[Repentance] is an invitation to new life, an opening up of new horizons, the gaining of new vision.

—Dn. John Chryssavgis, *Repentance and Confession in the Orthodox Church*

LIKE OBEDIENCE, REPENTANCE IS NOT OFTEN ASSOCI-ATED with joy. However, repenting—taking responsibility for our bad decisions and mistakes—is about recognizing how much we actually do love each other and God and how we acted against that love. Our repentance is our response to God's unending love for us. His love is the context for our repentance. Within His eternal, unconditional love for us we are invited to see our mistakes and our need for healing, and to seek Him out and ask for forgiveness. His love is greater than our sins and brokenness. The more we focus on His love for us, the more we are able to recognize our deep need for healing.

It is in the divine nature of our merciful and loving
Father to accept us and to forgive us all when in true
repentance and contrite confession we return to His
loving embrace.

Fr. Peter Chamberas,
The Sacrament of Repentance and Confession

Consider the parable of the prodigal son. Beware—this is not a parable about parenting techniques or strategies. I do not recommend giving, and I would never give my child, what that son asked. This is a parable about God's love. The son did not get a consequence when he returned so that "he would never do that again," but he received a warm embrace and celebration that reflected his father's joy that he had returned. Repentance and confession are about returning to communion and fellowship with our loving Father and each other. It is a positive, although painful, act of "re-centering our life upon the Holy Trinity," writes Met. Kallistos. God does not seek to punish us but seeks to reconcile us to Himself. Repentance is an act of love and a confession of faith in a loving and merciful God.

A gracious God gives us the hope of forgiveness of
guilt, if we repent with contrition and set forth a firm
intention to flee past sins and not anger God by them.
This is the essence of repentance.

St. Theophan the Recluse,
The Spiritual Life and How to Be Attuned to It

As we understand the true nature of repentance and confession, we can see that it is more about love, joy, and freedom than sin, criticism, or blame. It only makes sense to learn to do this as often as possible.

Repentance is a healing response to an otherwise hopeless and painful experience. Recognizing our sins, our mistakes, our brokenness is painful and shameful. This is as true for our children as it is for us. Without repentance, confession, and forgiveness, we get trapped in that painful place or simply avoid it. Realizing our mistakes is the necessary first step in actually changing the way we live and behave. It we can't see that we made a bad choice, we hurt someone, or we're doing things the wrong way, we can't learn and grow. We should expect, if we want to improve our parenting, to face the uncomfortable or painful experience of seeing our failures. In this way we can understand that it is a gift from God each time we become aware of something we are doing wrong.

The sequence is not to repent first, and then to become aware of Christ; for it is only when the light of Christ has already in some measure entered our life that we begin to truly understand our sinfulness.
Metropolitan Kallistos Ware, *The Inner Kingdom*

Our children don't need us to be perfect, but they need us to be courageous in recognizing our mistakes and faithful in repenting. They do best when we are on the path of healing and growth. And that is the path of repentance and confession.

It is not enough for us just to feel bad or feel like we've failed. Repentance is different than remorse or guilt. It is about admitting our mistake, asking for forgiveness, and being committed to do things in a different way. Real repentance is more than feeling sorry for what I've done. It is a realization that I am going in the wrong direction and requires action to change my direction.

The joy of restored relationships is the fruit of repentance and confession. Our children need to feel the joy of intimacy with us and with each other that comes after they repent. The struggles and strife of family life happen, but with repentance and forgiveness, what remains are the relationships of love. The only way for our children to understand this is to experience joy in the home following repentance and forgiveness. Nikolia and Alexios played together the rest of the day. While they remembered the drama over the bagel, this was small in comparison to the positive connections they had throughout the day. They are learning how to navigate the inevitable transgressions. The sooner they take responsibility, repent, and forgive, the more their love and connection grow. After forgiveness and repentance, only intimacy, joy, and love remain.

In fact, the goal of parenting is to have children internalize the joy of repentance as one of the greatest gifts we have to thrive in marriage and in life. Children don't need consequences as much as they need repentance in their hearts. Even difficult days filled with struggles, mistakes, and frustrations can be beautiful and deeply connecting when they end with forgiveness and repentance, ready for another day. When our children experience the joy of reconciliation that follows the pain of sin and repenting, they learn that our sins are temporary, but God's love and mercy are eternal.

⋯•⋯

To repent, then, and to admit our brokenness before
God is to become free from the restrictions imposed by
sin, and to accept with joy the humility of our nature

and thereby be able to move forward, to recover our true nature before God.

Fr. Peter Chamberas,
The Sacrament of Repentance and Confession

—◆—

The joy of repentance protects us from the risks of perfectionism and heals the pain of realizing our mistakes. Repentance frees us from our own limitations and connects all our parenting to Christ and the grace of the Holy Spirit. We teach the joy of repentance, first and foremost, by modeling forgiveness and repentance as adults.

Modeling the Joy of Repentance

As with everything we teach our children, modeling repentance is the most effective way to teach. This is not a book on marriage, but we teach the joy of repentance to our children by modeling repentance in our marriage. Our children need to see us asking our spouse for forgiveness, particularly when they witness any conflict between us. While marital conflict is painful for children to witness, our decision to repent, ask for forgiveness, and improve our relationship is a gift we can give to our children. We can't always control ourselves, but we can always repent.

Learning to respond, not react, to our children is actually an opportunity to repent. We will react because it's hard to control ourselves. When we react, we need to repent and then respond in the right way. Because repentance is more than just realizing our mistakes but a commitment to do things differently, when we ask our children for forgiveness, it is important to let them know how we will respond next time.

» "Forgive me for getting upset. Next time I see the ball in the house, I will take it away."

» "Forgive me for interrupting you. What were you saying about school?"

» "Forgive me for getting distracted by my cell phone. What is it that you need?"

We don't need to apologize to our children for setting limits, giving consequences, or forcing them to clean up their rooms. We do need to apologize when we react and when we act in a way that does not reflect the values and the virtues that we want our children to learn.

We don't always need to ask our child for forgiveness, but we always need to repent. Children need us to change the way we respond, engage, set limits, and give consequences more than just hear that we are sorry. They do best when we learn from our mistakes rather than just feel bad about them. They need to see us admit our wrongs and change the way we respond. If we are learning from our mistakes, we are improving our parenting all the time.

When you realize you've made a mistake, before you ask your child for forgiveness, take some time to reflect on how you should have responded. If you don't know how you should have responded, you might consult with your spouse, your priest, other parents, or a professional, or read a parenting book. You're not supposed to know everything, but you are supposed to learn. Our children make the same mistakes all the time, which allows us plenty of opportunities to learn to respond effectively. Once you're clear about a better response, asking forgiveness is appropriate as you change your behavior.

❧ **Our children don't need perfect parents, just attentive parents.**

Parenting toward the Kingdom is an invitation to be watchful and attentive. We need to be attentive to our child's inner world to respond appropriately. We need to be attentive to our children's feelings as we set limits to their behaviors. We need to pay attention to their learning as we keep the rules firm and allow them to struggle. We need to pay attention to our children's abilities as we allow more privileges and responsibilities as they grow. We need to be attentive to our own inner world to raise children who are attentive to theirs.

———◆◆———

> *Watchfulness is a continual fixing and halting of thought at the entrance of the heart.*
> St. Hesychios the Priest, "On Watchfulness and Holiness" in *The Philokalia*

———◆◆———

Loving our children requires that we pay attention to our reactions and responses to our children. We can't expect our kids to pay attention to their behaviors if we are not paying attention to our own. Our children will push our buttons because they are wired to do that. We should expect it but not accept it. Our buttons that get pushed are buttons that need to be healed in us. When do you get upset? When do you feel overwhelmed? When do you get hurt, sad, anxious, or scared? Every reaction we have needs to be attended to, not acted upon. We can be thankful for these discoveries as we learn to repent and change the way we respond to our children. With repentance, as we attend to our reactions, we grow and become more attentive to our children's inner world and teach them to be attentive.

———◆◆———

The Lord's call to repentance does not mean that we are to be converted once only, nor that we should repent from time to time (though one ought to begin with that). It means that our whole life should be a conversion, a constant repentance.

Archimandrite Vasileios, *Hymn of Entry*

I am not writing a parenting book because I am a perfect parent. I make more mistakes than most parents and work hard to learn from them. Parents who embrace the joy of repentance raise up children who internalize the joy of repentance. I have witnessed how much my children learn about the values and virtues of the Kingdom of God as they see me learning the same things.

» "Forgive me for getting upset. What did you say your sister did to you?"

» "You're right, I did give in to your brother's whining. That was a mistake. Next time I need to be strong."

» "You're right, I'm not going to take your toys away for good. I should not have said that. You will lose them for an hour."

When our children see us making mistakes, taking responsibility, and learning from them, we communicate that the values and the virtues of the Kingdom of God are real, and we teach them how to acquire them. It's okay for your kids to see you make mistakes if you then ask forgiveness and do it better next time. It can be difficult for our kids to see that we are human. Our mistakes hurt and confuse them. But if they see that we are repentant humans, they learn that we really love them and that repentance is real. Consider how you want your children to respond when they misbehave, and model that for them when you misbehave. We want them to learn that admitting mistakes and changing the way we respond is the path of life. This is the beauty of God's mercy and love. Even in our failures—particularly in our failures—we can teach our children how to thrive in life.

———•———

> Say, "Lord Jesus Christ, Give Your light to my children. I entrust them to You. You gave them to me, but I am weak and unable to guide them, so please, illuminate them."
>
> St. Porphyrios, *Wounded by Love*

———•———

Learning to repent as parents reminds us that God is co-parenting with us. It is God, through His Holy Spirit, who nurtures and transforms our children's hearts. Recognizing God's role in raising our children, by repenting from our mistakes and living our home life closely connected to the Church, relieves us of the pressure of having to be perfect and teaches our children the central role God plays in all of life.

While modeling repentance is essential to teaching our children, for them to internalize the joy of repentance as real, we need to nurture repentance and confession in the home.

CHAPTER 18

Nurture Repentance and Confession in the Home

It is a good thing to dispose him ahead of time to repentance, so that without fear, with trust and with tears, he might come and say, "I did something wrong."
—St. Theophan the Recluse, *Raising Them Right*

WE NURTURE A CULTURE OF FORGIVENESS and repentance in the home by including forgiveness in our parenting interventions—not instead of limits and consequences, but along with them. We can teach our children each time they misbehave, hurt, interrupt, break something, back talk—the list is endless—to ask for forgiveness.

"What do you say to your sister?" the mother of three-year-old Ksenia asked.

"Forgive me for hitting you," she replied.

"If you want to play with Juliana (age one) you need to be gentle. Next time you hit her, you will need to play alone," her mother reminded her. If Juliana were old enough to speak, she could be instructed to say, "I forgive you." In fact, by the time she is old enough to speak, she will have learned all about forgiveness from her older sister.

We can't always set the right limits or know the best consequences, but asking for forgiveness is always appropriate. Specifically including explicit forgiveness as we attend to the misbehaviors keeps everyone focused on our journey of growing in love. Teaching children to ask for and grant forgiveness shifts the focus from misbehaviors and transgressions toward love, kindness, and respect.

Teaching children to ask for forgiveness allows us a pathway to address misbehaviors when there are no consequences or when consequences don't make sense. If we hand out consequences for every misdeed, family life becomes nothing but a series of consequences for mistakes. Rather, if we require our children to ask for forgiveness, family life becomes filled with constantly getting back on the right path. The more our homes are filled with forgiveness, the more our children learn that everyone makes mistakes, quite often, and everyone is on the path of growing and learning.

- » "What do you say for hitting/poking/hurting/laughing at your brother?"
- » "You need to ask your sister for forgiveness for taking her sweater/touching her stuff/being rude to her."
- » "What do you say for going outside without permission?"
- » "Go ask your mother for forgiveness for not listening when she asked you to [fill in the blank]."

The list is endless of the opportunities for forgiveness in family life.

Children don't always, or even very often, feel remorse when they ask for forgiveness, but when we include forgiveness in our parenting, they nurture the discipline of taking responsibility for their actions and learn the practice of asking for forgiveness. They don't necessarily need to feel it. Remember, it's destructive to try to control our kids' feelings but helpful to have expectations about their behaviors. Remorse will develop in our children, along with empathy, as they mature and watch adults ask for forgiveness. It is a gift to give our children the discipline of repentance and forgiveness even before they completely understand.

To teach repentance, reduce the consequence if your child repents.

"What do you say for hitting your brother, Markos?" I asked. (Markos was eight and George, six.)

"Forgive me, George," he said quietly.

"Because you apologized, you can keep playing together. If you cannot control yourself, Markos, you will need to come in the house."

If Markos is hitting because he's exhausted, bringing him in the house right away is probably a good idea. However, if I want him to learn the joy of repentance, giving him another chance after he's repented allows him to taste the fruit of taking responsibility and asking forgiveness. He will hit again, I'm pretty sure. And next time, without anger, threats, or leniency, he will need to come in. While George might protest, "You didn't do anything to him!" I will tell him that because Markos admitted his mistake and apologized, he got another chance. It is just as likely, though, that George will hit Markos, and the roles will be reversed. It's not okay to hit, but my long-term goal is to teach them self-control, forgiveness, and repentance. They'll learn to stop hitting as they grow.

Our love for our children must be for them an image of God's love for mankind. This means that if a child confesses a misdeed, or shows repentance, we should temper the reprimand or punishment accordingly, at least in our own psychological disposition. It does not mean that we condone the sin, or even seem to condone it; we encourage our children not to try and hide their wrongdoings or "contrive excuses for sin." We wish to give them a taste of the joy of the returning prodigal, for this is our own relationship with God. Deceit is a much more serious characteristic than any amount of naughtiness, and if there is deceit between the child and his parents, it will be difficult to maintain the relationships.

Sister Magdalen, *Children in the Church Today*

Forgive Early and Often

⋘ We nurture a culture of forgiveness by being quick to forgive our children when they misbehave.

When our children misbehave, we need to be quick to forgive them as we take the side of their feelings and set limits to their behaviors. Forgiving our children means letting go of our feelings of fear, hurt, shame, frustration, anger, or resentment when they misbehave. If our limits are firm and our expectations clear, forgiving our children is not leniency, just love. Forgiving our children is about healing our hearts as our children learn and grow. It is an inner disposition in our hearts that says, "I will not hold your misbehaviors against you. I love you no matter how long it takes you to learn how to behave. And you have to learn how to behave."

If we're lenient and change our limits and behavioral expectations, we remove the opportunity for learning. If we don't forgive our children for their misbehaviors, we become frustrated and impatient as they learn. Forgiveness protects us from our unrealistic expectations of our children and allows us to walk in love as they grow and learn.

When your child repeats the same mistake, don't up the ante and increase the consequences. Forgive and keep the limits and consequences in place. In a sense, we forget about how many times they've made the same mistake as we let the limits do the teaching. When we forgive our children, we don't forget their misbehaviors, but we remember them with love instead of criticism or judgment. We should remember their misbehaviors as we figure out how to respond or help them work through them. We don't remember in order to use their mistakes against them.

Instead of, "That's the fifth time you've bothered your sister today," we might say, at bedtime, no matter how frustrated or tired we are, "I noticed you had a hard time listening to your sister's words today."

Love suffers long and is kind. (1 Corinthians 13:4)

The more quickly we forgive our children after they misbehave, the more we can connect with them throughout the day. The longer it takes us to forgive them, the more anger and resentment fill our relationships with them. With forgiveness in our hearts, we can check in with a child before issuing another consequence. We can keep a limit firm no matter how hard a child struggles and connect with him as soon as he gets back on track. We can listen to him when he's defiant or whining or teach him how to use his words when he's upset. With forgiveness on our hearts, we can take his struggle seriously when he's tired, even as we ignore his words.

When we forgive our children we can give them the emotional space to be upset or melt down and the time to pull themselves back together. Every meltdown does not need a consequence, but every meltdown does need forgiveness, peace, love, and prayer. Only when we forgive our kids for being kids can we give them a path to regain lost privileges and get back on track. And once they pull themselves together, like the loving father of the prodigal, we're just happy to have them back. They need to know that we are more delighted that they have returned than upset about what they did. They don't need our anger and frustration, just clear limits and consequences, and a kind parent who welcomes them back.

We need repentance and forgiveness because parenting wears us down. Throughout this book, I've suggested that children are learning most when they struggle, but these struggles create tension and wear us down. It's hard to be constantly setting limits, resisting the pushback, and responding firmly and patiently when our children whine, misbehave, or melt down. And now I'm suggesting that we should smile and be happy when they return! Yet, this is the path of their growth and learning. We need to have mechanisms in place to heal from the battle scars of learning and growing with our children. Nurturing forgiveness in our hearts toward our children is critical to remaining peaceful in the struggles. Our peace in the tension and struggle is the most powerful force in shaping our children's internal identity in healthy ways and teaching them about the reality of God's values and virtues.

Our forgiveness teaches our children that, primarily, we

love and respect them no matter how they behave or how much they struggle with our limits and consequences.

We nurture forgiveness toward our children as we internalize the joy of repentance in our own hearts. The better we get at asking God and others for forgiveness, the more we are able, naturally, to forgive our children. And the more we forgive our children for being kids, the more we open our hearts to receive God's forgiveness when we act like children.

Practice Forgiveness Rituals

Confess your trespasses to one another, and pray for one another, that you may be healed. (James 5:16)

It's appropriate at the end of each day to ask each child for forgiveness and to teach your children to ask for forgiveness. While this can lead to long conversations about mistakes that happened throughout the day, children learn that bedtime is the time to forgive each other. If there isn't time to have long discussions, we can still teach that there is always time to ask for, and grant, forgiveness.

When asking each other for forgiveness, it's good to name your child's struggles, take the side of her feelings, and remind everyone of the ways we are called to act in the home. This is an appropriate way to end prayer time at the end of the day. We'll talk more about family prayer in a moment, but for now, ending prayer with forgiveness allows us to end the day in peace and love.

Weekly forgiveness rituals are important ways for families to prepare for church on Sundays. Most Orthodox Christians know that we don't eat anything before we take Communion on Sundays. What is even more important is that we ask each other for forgiveness before we take Communion. There is nothing we can do to be worthy to receive Communion, but we prepare to receive this free gift from God, in part, by asking each other for forgiveness. There are good ways for families to prepare Saturday evenings and Sunday mornings to receive Communion that I don't have room to detail here, but asking everyone for forgiveness before church on Sunday connects the life of the home and all the struggles of the week back to the Divine Liturgy.

When you are sincerely repentant and have a firm resolution to make amends, the Lord comes in His Holy Mysteries and enters you, and He will be with you and you will be with Him.

St. Theophan the Recluse,
The Spiritual Life and How to Be Attuned to It

Our goal, as parents, is to teach our children that God is at the center of family life. Children learn this as we connect the struggles of daily life back to the Church.

Connect the Struggles of Daily Life Back to the Church

All families sin, make mistakes, and hurt each other. All parents fail in some ways. Only with Christ in the center of the home can we restore the relationships damaged by sin. Christ in the center of our hearts and homes enables us to constantly restore our relationships in the face of our brokenness.

When we hurt each other, when we sin against each other, we also sin against God. We want to teach our children that with every mistake, every time we miss the mark and fail to act in love, we sin against God and His love. In addition to asking each other for forgiveness, we must turn to God and as His forgiveness as well by going to confession. In this way, children learn and experience the reality of God's presence in the center of our lives.

And as a sacrament of healing, Confession is not simply a painful necessity, a discipline imposed on us by the Church authority, but an action full of joy and saving grace.

Metropolitan Kallistos Ware, *The Inner Kingdom*

Going to confession is how we make things right with God when we've sinned. We are, in fact, confessing to Christ, with the priest as a witness. While it is important to repent in the privacy of our homes, the very difficulty of going before Christ, with someone standing next to you as a witness, speaks of the power and reality of the Sacrament of Confession. It was not enough for the prodigal son to come to his senses. He needed to return home with a broken and contrite heart.

We ask God for forgiveness in confession with the priest as a witness because what happens in our own private lives affects the whole Body of Christ. We are not individual Christians in isolated homes, but all are one in Christ. Our sins and mistakes affect the whole community. Going to confession is how we restore our communion with the whole Body of Christ.

If we confess our sins, He is faithful and just to forgive us our sins and to cleanse us from all unrighteousness. (1 John 1:9)

This is not a book on confession, and there are plenty of those that are great to read, but going to confession, as parents and as a family, is central to parenting toward the Kingdom. Our children need to connect the learning we're all doing in the home to God's healing grace in the life of the Church. What happens in our homes is intimately related to the reality of God's Kingdom, His Church. We want our children to learn that church is not something we go to, but who we are. We are not private Christians, each with our own individual relationship with God. We are, together, the Body of Christ, not just on Sundays when we gather but throughout the week. We can't impose faith or the values and virtues of the Kingdom of God on our children. What we can do is live that faith and those values and virtues in the home and connect our struggles in the home to our growth in Christ by practicing regular confession. It's easy to lose sight of the fact that the liturgical, sacramental life of the Church is very real and personal.

Every sacrament of the Church, every liturgical prayer of corporate worship and every prayer of private devotions, every sacred hymn, every holy icon, every liturgical practice and every authentic gesture of corporate and personal piety in Orthodox Christianity contains an element and a reminder of this all-embracing spiritual reality of Repentance and Confession.

Fr. Peter Chamberas,
The Sacrament of Repentance and Confession

As children witness authentic faith in their parents at home and experience the grace that flows in the home through parents who respect them, they internalize the reality of God in our hearts and our midst. When our children see that we are trying to live out the Gospel in our homes and going to regular confession as part of that journey, they make the connection between the Gospel they hear in church and the struggles and learning that happen in the home. In this way, our children learn that God and His Kingdom are real. Parenting is not about stopping misbehaviors but about shaping children's hearts and minds according to the Gospel and God's Kingdom.

⟨⟨⟩⟩

Along with mourning for one's sins and resolving
not to sin, it is necessary to add diligent prayer to the
Lord so that He will grant His help in opposing sin.

St. Theophan the Recluse,
The Spiritual Life and How to Be Attuned to It

⟨⟨⟩⟩

Nurture a Culture of Prayer in the Home

The religious education of children is mainly brought
about by example, and by the atmosphere of love
and prayer in the home. The child's heart is touched;
without explanation he acquires prayer as a natural
activity, and without needing logical proofs he knows
God's presence.

Sister Magdalen, *Children in the Church Today*

⟨⟨⟩⟩

This is not a book on prayer, but prayer is at the heart of parenting toward the Kingdom. Not only do we need prayer to sustain us as we parent, but we need prayer to invite God into our parenting. Our children are God's children also, and He cares for them more than we do. We are parenting with Him and need Him to be transforming our children's hearts. We invite God, the Source of Life, into our hearts, our homes, our parenting, and our children's lives through prayer.

⸙

Prayer is one wing, faith the other, that lifts us heavenward. With only one wing no one can fly: prayer without faith is as meaningless as faith without prayer.
Tito Colliander, The Way of the Ascetic

⤞ Prayer keeps our hearts centered on Christ and our minds focused on our long-term goals.

In the upbringing of children, a knowledge of child psychology, or even a fine intuition about one's own children, will not lead to eternal Being unless we also invite divine grace by prayer.
Sister Magdalen, Children in the Church Today

⸙

We should try to take a deep breath and say a prayer when we're tempted to react. We need to pray for our children, and our parenting responses need to be an expression of prayer. We need to learn how to retreat at regular times or at the end of the day in prayer to be healed, strengthened, and transformed in the daily struggles of parenting. It is not enough to pray regularly and then react to your child or pay no attention to their struggles. But it is a life of prayer in the home that sustains us as we develop our parenting skills and enables our children to experience God's grace deeply and personally.

We don't always know how to respond to our children, where to set the limits, and what the consequence should be, but we can always pray. As we learn to turn to Christ in prayer and to parent with prayer, we will discover the endless love of God, which enables us to parent in peace and raise our children in peace, joy, and love.

We must pray in the morning, in the evening, at any moment when we need to know God's will, and learn to discern the inspiration of God. By the practice of prayer we achieve our highest aim: to be saved, and to help our children reach eternal life.
Sister Magdalen, *Children in the Church Today*

☙ If you want to learn to pray, hang around people who pray.

Regular prayer as a family at meal times, in the evening, and, if possible, some sort of prayer in the morning are important routines to establish. The exact nature of your family prayer is best established by talking to a priest, spiritual father, and other families who pray together. The most important aspect of family prayer is not the length or the attentiveness of the children, but the inner attentiveness of the hearts of the parents. When we pray, we stop parenting, if only for a few moments, focus our hearts on prayer, and allow the Holy Spirit to take care of our children.

If we pray, and learn little by little to live in the spirit of prayer, we create an atmosphere in which children taste prayer and God's presence. If we dwell in this spirit, even without words, even before a child can speak, they acquire a natural taste for prayer, and the desire to know God.

Sister Magdalen, *Children in the Church Today*

❧ The goal of parenting is that when our children grow up and leave our home, they will carry Christ and His Church in their hearts.

When we connect with our children and respect them in the way we respond to their misbehaviors, they learn that we love them. Most parents love their children, and most parents can learn to improve their skills in responding to misbehaviors in ways that communicate God's love. When our children see that our learning is connected to Christ and His Church, they learn that God is the source of love and the Church is His living body. To parent toward the Kingdom requires us to improve the way we interact with our children in every situation and to connect our hearts and homes to Christ and His Church. In this way our children experience the love of God in the home and encounter Christ and His Church in the center of it. That doesn't solve their problems or make their lives easy, but it does allow them to internalize the reality of God and the values and the virtues of His Kingdom deep within their hearts. That way, when they leave our home, they carry within their hearts Christ and His Church to guide them toward the Kingdom.

For Further Reading

Works Cited

Titles listed in boldface type are especially recommended reading.

Akathist to the Mother of God, Nurturer of Children. **Safford, AZ: St. Paisius Orthodox Monastery, 2001.**

Barnes, Bridget A., and Steven M. York. *Common Sense Parenting of Toddlers and Preschoolers.* Boys Town, NE: Boys Town Press, 2001.

Bronson, Po, and Ashley Merryman. *NurtureShock: New Thinking about Children.* New York: Twelve, 2009.

Chamberas, Peter A. *The Mystery of Repentance and Confession in the Orthodox Church.* United States: Peter A. Chamberas, 2010.

Chrysostom, John, Catharine P. Roth, and David Anderson. *On Marriage and Family Life.* Crestwood, NY: St. Vladimir's Seminary Press, 1986.

Chryssavgis, John. *Repentance and Confession in the Orthodox Church.* Brookline, MA: Holy Cross Orthodox Press, 1990.

Clement of Alexandria. "Who Is the Rich Man That Shall Be Saved," in *The One Who Knows God.* Scroll Pub Co., 1990.

Climacus, John, Colm Luibheid, Norman Russell, and Kallistos Ware. *John Climacus: The Ladder of Divine Ascent.* London: SPCK, 1982.

Cline, Foster, and Jim Fay. *Parenting with Love and Logic: Teaching Children Responsibility.* Colorado Springs, CO: Piñon Press, 2006.

Colliander, Tito. *Way of the Ascetics.* San Francisco: Harper & Row, 1982.

Coniaris, Anthony M. *Making God Real in the Orthodox Christian Home.* Minneapolis: Light and Life Pub., 1977.

Dreikurs, Rudolf, and Vicki Soltz. *Children: The Challenge.* New York: Duell, Sloan & Pearce, 1964.

Easley, Jennifer, and Howard Glasser. *Transforming the Difficult Child: True Stories of Triumph.* Tucson, AZ: Howard Glasser, 2008.

Faber, Adele, and Elaine Mazlish. *How to Talk so Kids Will Listen & Listen so Kids Will Talk.* New York: Avon, 1982.

Fulghum, Robert. *All I Really Need to Know I Learned in Kindergarten: Uncommon Thoughts on Common Things.* New York: Villard Books, 1988.

Gibson, William. *The Miracle Worker; a Play for Television.* New York: Knopf, 1957.

Galinsky, Ellen. *Mind in the Making: The Seven Essential Life Skills Every Child Needs.* HarperCollins Publishers, 2010.

Gottman, John Mordechai., and Joan DeClaire. *The Heart of Parenting: How to Raise an Emotionally Intelligent Child.* New York: Simon & Schuster, 1997.

Greene, Ross W. *The Explosive Child: A New Approach for Understanding and Parenting Easily Frustrated, "Chronically Inflexible" Children*. New York: HarperCollins Publishers, 1998.

Hesychios the Priest. "On Watchfulness and Holiness," in *The Philokalia*, vol. 1, trans. Palmer, Sherrard, Ware (London: Faber and Faber, 1990)

Irenaeus. *On the Upbringing of Children*. Wildwood, CA: St. Xenia Skete, 1991.

Laistner, M. L. W., and John Chrysostom. *Christianity and Pagan Culture in the Later Roman Empire; Together with an English Translation of John Chrysostom's Address on Vainglory and the Right Way for Parents to Bring up Their Children*. Ithaca: Cornell University Press, 1951.

Magdalen. *Conversations with Children: Communicating Our Faith*. Maldon: Stavropegic Monastery of St. John the Baptist, 2001.

Magdalen. *Children in the Church Today: An Orthodox Perspective*. Crestwood, NY: St. Vladimir's Seminary Press, 1991.

Mark the Ascetic. "On the Spiritual Law: Two Hundred Texts," in *The Philokalia*, vol. 1, trans. Palmer, Sherrard, Ware (London: Faber and Faber, 1990)

Markham, Laura. *Peaceful Parent, Happy Kids: How to Stop Yelling and Start Connecting*. New York: Perigee Books, 2012.

Nelsen, Jane. *Positive Discipline*. New York: Ballantine Books, 1987.

Newmark, Gerald. *How to Raise Emotionally Healthy Children: Meeting the Five Critical Needs of Children . . . and Parents Too!* Tarzana, CA: NMI Publishers, 2008.

Porphyrios, Geron. *Wounded by Love: The Life and the Wisdom of Elder Porphyrios.* Limni, Evia, Greece: Denise Harvey, 2005.

Runkel, Hal Edward. *Screamfree Parenting: Raising Your Kids by Keeping Your Cool.* Duluth, GA: Oakmont Pub., 2005.

Runkel, Hal Edward. *Screamfree Parenting: The Revolutionary Approach to Raising Your Kids without Losing Your Cool.* New York: Broadway Books, 2007.

Seraphim of Sarov. *On the Acquisition of the Holy Spirit*

Siegel, Daniel J., and Mary Hartzell. *Parenting from the Inside Out: How a Deeper Self-understanding Can Help You Raise Children Who Thrive.* New York: J. P. Tarcher/Putnam, 2003.

Siegel, Daniel J., and Tina Payne Bryson. *The Whole-Brain Child: 12 Revolutionary Strategies to Nurture Your Child's Developing Mind.* New York: Delacorte Press, 2011.

Skenazy, Lenore. *Free-Range Kids: Giving Our Children the Freedom We Had without Going Nuts with Worry.* San Francisco: Jossey-Bass, 2009.

Theophan. *Raising Them Right: A Saint's Advice on Raising Children.* Mount Hermon, CA: Conciliar Press, 1989.

Theophan. *The Path to Salvation: A Manual of Spiritual Transformation.* Platina, CA: St. Herman of Alaska Brotherhood, 1996.

Theophan. *The Spiritual Life: And How to Be Attuned to It.* Platina, CA: St. Herman of Alaska Brotherhood, 1995.

Vasileios. *Hymn of Entry: Liturgy and Life in the Orthodox Church.* Crestwood, NY: St. Vladimir's Seminary Press, 1984.

Ware, Kallistos. *The Inner Kingdom.* Crestwood, NY: St. Vladimir's Seminary Press, 2001.

Additional Recommended Reading

Galinsky, Ellen. *Mind in the Making: The Seven Essential Life Skills Every Child Needs.* HarperCollins, 2010.

MacKenzie, Robert J. *Setting Limits with Your Strong-Willed Child: Eliminating Conflict by Establishing Clear, Firm, and Respectful Boundaries.* Roseville, CA: Prima, 2001.

Eliades, M. L. (Ed.). *Orthodox Christian Parenting: Cultivating God's Creation.* Dunlap, CA: Zoe Press 2015.

White, E. *Walking in Wonder: Nurturing Orthodox Christian Virtues in Your Children.* Conciliar Press, 2004.

About the Author

Dr. Philip Mamalakis, with his wife Georgia and seven children, lives in Boston, Massachusetts, where he is the Assistant Professor of Pastoral Care at Holy Cross Greek Orthodox School of Theology. Dr. Mamalakis directs the field education program and teaches classes on pastoral care, marriage and family, grief, death and dying, and topics related to pastoral counseling. He has a private practice in Newton, Massachusetts, where he works with individuals, couples, and families. Dr. Mamalakis has an M.Div. from Holy Cross and a Ph.D. from Purdue University in child development and family studies, specializing in marriage and family therapy. He has been offering parenting courses and writing on parenting for 21 years. He enjoys leading seminars and retreats on intimacy, relationships, marriage, parenting, and family life as well as on Orthodoxy and psychology.

Also from Ancient Faith Publishing

Blueprints for the Little Church
Creating an Orthodox Home

by Elissa Bjeletich & Caleb Shoemaker

How do we as Orthodox parents keep our children in the Church throughout their lives? It all begins with involving them in the life of the Church from birth onward—in the parish and also at home. *Blueprints for the Little Church* provides practical ideas and encouragement—without judgment—for incorporating the primary practices of Orthodox spirituality into your family life at every stage of its growth and throughout the church year.

Heaven Meets Earth
Celebrating Pascha and the Twelve Feasts

by John Kosmas Skinas

Enhance your family's celebration of the Great Feasts of the Orthodox Church with this beautifully designed book. Written for all ages and illustrated with icons and more, the book brings alive each of the Twelve Great Feasts (plus Pascha, the Feast of Feasts) with hymns, traditions, Old and New Testament scriptures, explanations of the festal icon, and quotes from the Fathers. A wonderful companion as we journey through the liturgical calendar year after year, deepening our faith one feast at a time.

Following a Sacred Path: Raising Godly Children

by Elizabeth White

Practical advice for parents (and educators) on raising children to understand and love their faith. Includes activities the family can share that encourage children to discover spiritual truths for themselves and own them for life.

Raising Them Right
A Saint's Advice on Raising Children

by St. Theophan the Recluse (from The Path to Salvation*)*

Saint Theophan, while from a different era and country, has an uncanny ability to communicate with modern Westerners. *Raising Them Right* provides both practical and spiritual insight into a variety of practical areas, such as baptism, the spiritual and psychological development of children through their teens, and preserving grace in a child's life.

All titles available at store.ancientfaith.com